Expose: The Reckoning by Channah Gambit

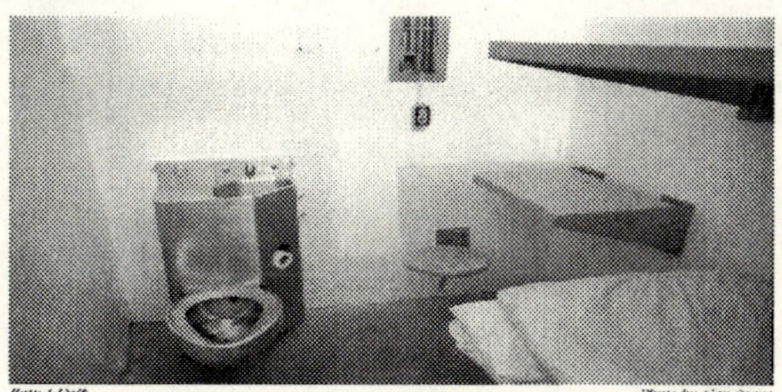

[illegible] Photo by Alan Pogue

Expose′:

THE RECKONING

Channah Gambit

***

Lulu.Com
North Carolina

Expose: The Reckoning by Channah Gambit

Library of Congress Cataloging-in-Publication Data

Gabler, Cheryl
Expose′: The Reckoning/Channah Gambit--2nd ed.
P. cm.
ISBN: 978-0-6152-1183-1
1. Memoir

First Edition: June, 2008

10 9 8 7 6 5 4 3 2 1

Dedication

To my beloved

Jaime Arielle and David Jacob

(Next year, in Jerusalem, my Children!)

Expose: The Reckoning by Channah Gambit

INTRODUCTION

This is the true story of Channah Gambit, from recent years a convicted felon, creator of grave offenses, including three misdemeanors.

Her chief enemy, if there was one, was Daddy Gambit, although her brother, the "notorious B.I.G." was worse. Somehow, a murderous and nasty mood bubbled up to the surface, sometime in late 2005, from the primordial ooze of family, and manifested in a domestic conflict of epic mendacity and ugliness. Everyone's true colors were seen, so to speak.

The family of Daddy Gambit was Jewish, and had been in the United States for three generations. A group of fortunate emigrants, they had come to Ellis Island, settled on the Lower East Side, and then gravitated to Kings, the Bronx, and Nassau Counties. Eastern Europe was vaguely recalled as a place to suffer poverty in, and all hoped for streets of gold in America. They had come with sacrifice, but there was an exception. One ancestor had had some White Russian bastard connection, and brought in some diamonds sewn into coat linings. That was all that was a legacy from a White Russian estate near Minsk. This Edith started a bank with a son, loaning funds from the moment she stepped off the boat, and it became the Irving Trust, and much of a success. Edith supported the entire clan with loans, right from the start. Her father, Charles, a former loyal subject of the tsar, spent the remainder of his life in a back bedroom of her tenement apartment, refusing to speak anything but Russian.

Another grandfather had studied to be a tailor in Italy, and came with his large, gentle wife to make his life as a pushcart peddler. He became the patriarch of six children, all strong and prosperous, among them a doctor, a doll factory owner, a records manufacturer, a writer, and a housewife.

There were many stories, from many countries they had visited prior to America. It was all a gossamer tin pastiche of lies, bragging, dreams, ambitions, and heartfelt needs. Their culture meant everything to these Jews, and they especially enjoyed eating gefilte fish, chopped liver, chicken they flecked themselves, and stuffed derma. They "had always had" some affiliation with synagogues and maintained one when they arrived. The first generation of emigrants were Orthodox, then the second loosened up and became Conservative, somewhat less strenuous. Some of the men still went to *shul* daily, in the early morning. There was a hearty share of relatives who were agnostic. But, as they were scared of the tailor, they showed up to listen politely to the patriarch say Hebrew prayers every weekend over the large communal *Shabbat* meals, hosted by his excellent cook of a wife, Sue. Most of the women in the clan were good cooks, trained by her, or by her daughters-in-law.

Then, along came the next, spoiled, and glib generation. They thought being Jewish was "cool", but they had no notion of G-D, and they didn't feel they needed to. They were opportunists, out to make a lot of money, simply ambitious, ready to make

Expose: The Reckoning by Channah Gambit

their mark on the world, despite the fact that they were in a minority. To be more exact, regarding their belief in Yahweh, they had a sentimental belief until they reached the age of sixteen. After that, it was girls, baseball, comedy, and the *gelt* you won at Passover for finding the missing *radiomen.* As this generation aged, they dated a lot of non-Jews, but chose Jewish mates for the most part, perhaps for comfort, security and pleasure.

There was a strong tendency in this family, especially displayed in Channah's choices, to drift away from Judaism and be an "oddball". There were the cousins exploring and teaching yoga, or marrying into Greek Orthodox, or relocating to Germany to be ardent Tibetan Buddhists. There was one cousin who followed J.D. Salinger's Franny in "Franny and Zoey" by muttering the eastern church Jesus prayer under his breath continuously for weeks.

There was the other, snobby branch of the family which did not readily recall a relationship to the East Side crew. The Paleys had been advisors to a president (all six of them), and chose the West Coast. There were the Kasifs, who clung to their East German roots of wealth and European snootiness. This drove a second cousin into research of the family tree as a point of pride. Well, he created one, filling in where he cared to, and produced a masterpiece after ten years. Aiding him in this endeavor were all the grandmothers, each one hoping for immortality, embroidering in stories and yarns from the old country. Seven generations ago, back in Minsk and Vilna, that Zalman character, the Rabbi known as the Vilna Gaon, had been an ancestor. His vast intellect, perfect memory, and child savant life story made every male in the family look good. This also got Grandma Sue the right to wear a *tallis*, a man's holy shawl, in temple. This was a radical feminist item which one points with the young women in the clan. The family tree got everyone very excited, made for better marriage encounters, and gave the religious an aura of pedigree.

There was a branch of the family down South which Channah had fervently prayed would adopt her for years, as it was chock-full of medical professionals. She had wanted to be a doctor for most of her adolescence, and they touted medical miracles when they visited, as if it was their own special brand of the Jewish faith. Even though Channah was chronically ill as a child, this aunt and uncle limited their love to packages of new medications mailed up North.

During his early married life, Daddy Gambit rose to leadership in the JWV. His friends were in it. Like Fred Flintstone, he had his "Order of the Imperial Poo-Bah" to enjoy. The youngsters only went to the Field Day Athletic Competitions the Jewish War Veterans ran each summer. Either that, or they played bingo down in the Hall on Wednesday nights, trying to win cash prizes they were ineligible for.

The clan had a lot of *Jewishkeit*, and quite a bit of the love and affection was genuine for most of Channah's childhood. As time passed, the great-aunts and uncles expired, the weekly meetings to *nosh* and talk grew infrequent, and the visits to one another's homes ceased. There was a newsletter, full of tidbits regarding births, deaths, and reunion barbeques, produced by that same second cousin who had built the family tree. The clan was actively collecting money at all times to bring over distant cousins from Russia.

More and more of the cousins moved to California. There was one charismatic cousin who had become an international celebrity. He made a career out of working the *shticks* and Jewish cultural stereotypes of the Gambit family into his stand up routines as well as a big Broadway hit he wrote. As this made a splash in New York, the love and affection of the family, always Daddy Chambit excessive and *schmaltzy*, began to wear thin and seem artificial to the young people.

As for Channah, she had become disillusioned with family long ago, as an apprentice hippy during the 1960's. Trying to get the old feeling back, she had made the mistake of visiting a big cousin up in Boston, who came from that old Southern medical branch.

One night in his home, he played a lacquer record for her, dating from 1947. It had been made *ad lib* during a convocation of Sue's six children in the living room, right after World War II. "Let's set up a real Jewish household" the brother, the surgeon said. "Let's try this out as an experiment!" and they all had agreed. Larry even gave Channah a copy to take home. After this revelation, she disregarded any expressed sincerities or sentiments expressed by any of her aunts and uncles. They hadn't been real Jews--they had been "scientists" or "socialists" trying on Jewish life as an experiment. What had they been before, for real? The story about the Vilna Gaon was fake, and the Gambit family was nothing but a group of actors, a *charade*. No one noticed her sea change except Channah. The instigator, her Boston cousin, was both a Socialist and adopted in, but she didn't analyze that. He didn't have strong family feelings to speak of, and didn't think anyone should bother to, either.

Channah was rather confused and disillusioned about her roots at the time of this memoir, but still had a certain strength and cultural identity. She had Jewish roots, she believed. Her family was a bit like the movie family in "It's a Wonderful Day".

The leap to the realization that Daddy Gambit and his family were capable of a great deal of deception, as well as criminal acts, did not enter anybody's mind in early 2005. But--that was the case. It was a bad family, pure and simple. Channah's position in the family, to be more exact, was like the girl Gloria in the Adam's Family television sit-com. She was normal, but the rest of the family members were monsters.

Whether the family changed, or had always been that way, was something that Channah needed to ascertain after 2005. Was it a weird "Clingon" family in a space ship with a "cloaking device" as in Star Trek, the television series? Or was it not a case of deception, but rather, that someone in the family had sent shock waves through it, causing all the personalities there to lose love, buckle and fold, and twist and turn?

That chiefly, is why the author, identity concealed in *the third person*, is writing this

Expose: The Reckoning by Channah Gambit
short memoir of what transpired. It is an effort to learn why beloved people suddenly were strangers, doing malevolent and harmfully destructive things to her: body, mind, and soul.

Expose: The Reckoning by Channah Gambit

Chapter 1: The Calm Years

This tale takes place in the a sleepy suburb of the resort town of Long Ditch, in Nassau County, New York and at the Sheriff's Correctional Center Holding Pen in Westapple.

The family Gambit had prospered over the forty years since arriving at Ellis Island. The matriarch, Julius' wife Sarah, had moved her brood out to Long Ditch. They had spread out into various residences down east, in short order. It was considered *the Jewish part of town.* All Gambits were comfortable there, although they rarely attended temple..

Daddy Gambit had a large ranch colonial situated in an expensive neighborhood, along the South Shore of Long Island, New York, on a barrier beach resort community stretch. The rear yard fronted on a public golf course, and the top porch afforded an unrestricted, 6-mile panoramic view of a channel and all the marshes and islands surrounding the city. It was the reason he bought the property, back in 1952. "I'm getting in on the ground floor!" he proclaimed to his best friend, Harvey. For after all, with the G.I. Bill, he had gotten it for a song, with modifications he requested. It was for his expanding brood, with his wife pregnant with her third.

The village was Beeritz, predominantly beachcomber and Jewish. Parts of it were bungalows dating back to the twenties. Streets were quiet, filled with bulrushes, frogs, mice, and sounds of dogs, cats, children, and the ever-sighing wind from the beach. The beach was surrounded by high dunes, well-maintained by the village of Beeritz Civic Community. They had been planted with weeds and ivy to prevent erosion. Even so, from heights above 25 feet in the 1950's, the dunes had dwindled and reduced down to a maximum height of 15 feet by the 1970's. The community worked on stone jetties, seeking to maintain the little island, and make it grow.

There was little to do in Beeritz, besides going to the beach or a cabana club, your choice of several, down the highway. There were only a few businesses there. The Italian pizza restaurant, Queens, across from the high school, had passed through several owner's hands. The realtor's door was always quiet. There had been a pharmacy for several decades, owned by Tugged, a German. That didn't prosper so he retired to Florida with his sons. The best attraction in Beeritz was the Marvel stand, a wonderful drive up, with classic 1940's cement decor. The attraction was the perfect carvel cone. During the summer, the crowds at night never lessened. The windows of the stand were papered in photographs of community residents eating carvel custard.

The greater city of Long Ditch had been restricted to mandatory Spanish Grandee style tiles and stucco during the 1930's. It had had quaint brick streets for decades, but since WWII was repaved in asphalt. It was dominated by a two mile boardwalk, a symbol of prosperity. The boardwalk had been built by elephants, and provided a perfect overview of the classic, white sand beach, which was Long Ditch's finest draw.

The city proper along the water contained a long stretch of assisted living homes, retirement cooperatives, and rich, upscale condominiums. There were many undeveloped sand lots, which had languished for decades with way too high price tags.

The center of town had a few apartment houses with Spanish architecture, a host of medical buildings and practices, and at least thirty restaurants, the majority of which were

Expose: The Reckoning by Channah Gambit
Chinese/Japanese in cuisine.
The town was flat, with a nice plaza in front of City Hall. It contained fountains, trees, and a mailbox to return old, used flags, maintained by the Veterans of Foreign Wars.

The west end of town was Irish and multiracial, with small crowded restored bungalows. The main street had a usual suburban assortment of stores and businesses, many long-standing. Further west, there were developments contained residences worth in excess of $1,000,000.

The east end of town was formerly Jewish, but now multiracial as well. Homes there were illegal two families, on quiet, landscaped streets filled with trees and cars. Businesses on the main street were the lifeblood of local residents, and they met there for morning coffee, gossip, and small shopping runs.

The north side of town was dominated by a water plant, a hospital, and a bridge.

The hospital was a source of pride to the community. Behind City Hall, was a black shanty town, segregated, which had gone through some HUD development, and featured a Martin Luther King Community Center. There was a lot of crime back there, and few people walked through after dusk.

Beeritz was the most desirable suburb, but could not sustain itself. To the east of it were later wealthy developments of big homes, several beach clubs, beaches run by the government, and a small village, eccentric and rich, rather like "Palm Beach North", with beachfront properties worth in excess of 2.5 million. Point Palm contained several realtors, a post office, a liquor store, and a grocery. At the west end was the ramp entry to the Ocean or Loop parkway, providing escape to the mainland and Joins Beach, a Robert Moshe extravaganza of scenic beaches, golf courses, a boardwalk and empty wind swept vistas.

The ebb and flow of residents gave Beeritz and Long Ditch an unusual year. The populace swelled to over 200,000 during summer months. Winters, with only 20,000 residents, were quiet and cold, with acceptable rentals, encouraging students, drifters and commuters to Manhattan to stay on.

It was in the temperate zone, with maple deciduous forests filled with some scrub pines and copper beaches. The town was too humid most months, and filled with a *sirocco* wind during the winter. The air had a salt tang to it, and weathered wood was everywhere, silvered in short order.

Regarding Daddy Gambit's home, he had lavished considerable expense to make it a comfortable ranch. Split level, girded in white aluminum siding, it had a brick front porch, cool windows of insulated glass, and a three car driveway. Gambit had landscaped in sod at the start, and installed an underground sprinkler system. His remodeling of the home, after his wife's death in 1992, had turned the downstairs into rental space. The back patio had served for a whole generation as a party place. The downstairs Florida room, a late addition, had contained a central, prominent, Jacuzzi hot tub, over ten feet wide.

Regarding decor, the home was decorated in distressed Colonial. Some pieces had been designed by the owner, and executed by his best friend Harvey, a master carpenter, right after the war. Floors were carpeted in worn, inexpensive broadloom. There was nothing distinguished or attractive about the home, but it was comfortable. The kitchen had full accoutrements, with all modern appliances.

A chief feature, and the owner's pride, was a series of acrylic, casein and oil paintings had done, reproductions of "famous moments in American History" or Audubon prints of birds. During a bankruptcy from 1964, to keep himself from going insane, Daddy Gambit had painted in marathons lasting days, churning out these huge canvases. He had some offers, especially for George Washington and the Boston Tea Party, but he refused to part with them. After the bad time, he had turned the large den downstairs, paneled in Cherry and dominated by a huge, state-of-the-art hi-fidelity system, into a printing business, with a sad, refurbished mimeo machine to start.

The children's bedrooms, downstairs and up, had been decorated in hand-me-down furniture from the rich cousins in east Long Ditch--entertainers, Hollywood bourgeoisie.

The family lived predominantly in the kitchen, television room, or in quiet bedroom spaces. The children inevitably chose to be elsewhere, or to visit friends, rather than have friends in.

The back yard, surrounded by a Fort Apache wood fence, had had a face lift with a dog run. There was a shower cabana, used summers for cleaning up after a beach visit, and other times for storage of chairs, chaise lounges, and umbrellas.

The downstairs, though well equipped during the 1960's to entertain, had never been used for that. Gambit was not a social man, not comfortable as the genial host.

The den found other uses. For many years, after the printing business moved into town, became a miniature Coney Island Aquarium, for Mr. Gambit's hobby in leisure moments was tropical fish, fresh water and community. He had a 100, 25 and 10 gallon tank, with a sofa parked in front for long relaxed evening watches. The built in cherry wood and Formica bar, with it's three bar stools in grilled iron, became a storage place for spun glass, Tetramin flakes, and sieve nets instead. The fish, expensive danios, discus, cichlids, angelfish, sharks and clown barbs, occasionally did kamikaze dives through the lid, ending up dead on the floor mornings. The room was stained and damaged by hobby equipment, moisture, and water leaks.

The house had central air conditioning, plenty of hot water at all times, and good heating. It went through prosperous and lean years, as did the occupants. The garage, holding one car, was the cliché wilderness of miss-storage, with a hodge-podge of family discards, tools, supplies, and an extra refrigerator.

It was the center of the Gambits' preoccupation, the house. Beach right property taxes ran the family $17,00 a year, but they hardly used it, the status symbol. A short walk away from a beach approaching the beauty of one in Monte Carlo--and they never saw it. A backyard vista of miles of south shore Long Island, particularly fine on July 4 the, but they never looked out the picture windows to appreciate it.

The Gambit house, originally purchased for around $125,000, with all its improvements and modifications, accrued in value until the end of Gambit's life, reaching the respectable assessed value of $1,000,000, in local listings. Not a bad piece of homestead, all things considered.

Down the road at the Point Pleasant Marina, Gambit had docked a 32-foot Bay liner for a year or two, another status symbol, rarely used.

Like an eagle's nest, the house stood in the center of lowland swamps, on a barrier

Expose: The Reckoning by Channah Gambit

beach, near all the comforts of a resort town, close to the biggest city in America, metropolitan New York. It was only 45 minutes from "the Big Apple", yet countrified. There were strip malls within 10 miles. Gambit could indulge his other hobby, bird watching, from a chair on the back porch, looking balefully down on the neighbors, the golf course, and his little kingdom.

Channah was a quiet, serious book worm throughout her early years attending Long Ditch Elementary School. In high school, she became an artist, winding up with the editorship of the senior literary magazine. She was well-respected by the bohemians and hippies in her Sophomore, junior, and senior classes during the late 1960's.

She was short for her age, due to the stunting from asthma, and rather ordinary in appearance, with thin straggly light brown hair she habitually brushed with a center part. Under thin eyebrows, her hazel green eyes peered out, with a questioning expression. Not big boned, Channah avoided phys-ed at every opportunity. This was no doubt due to the fact that Channah had been quite the invalid as a child, suffering from acute asthma. Later on, she had a bout of scoliosis, cured roughly with the aid of a back brace worn to school.

Walking down the hall one day in tenth grade, wearing the Milwaukee brace Mama Gambit had insisted on her wearing, she felt over the 140 pounds she weighed. She had a hunchback due to the metal plate forcing her shoulder blades forward, just like in *The Hunchback of Notre Dame*, by Victor Hugo. Channah was actually reading the book for comfort. Here she was, standing in front of the door to ALM Spanish 3, with Mr. Rubin, waiting for Sara. Vivacious Sara! Dark black curls, deep brown eyes and vivacious manner with all boys. Channah knew she was learning a lot from being best friends with her. Mr. Rubin was late. The students inside the room already were gossiping about it, mentioning that he was in the teacher's lounge.

Big florid faced Mr. Rubin was the only kind teacher, she thought, giving up on Sara, taking a seat in the back. "Now no one will stare at me!" she said to herself.

Mr. Rubin walked in and reached his desk in three purposeful strides. "He's so kind and gentle!" she thought. Sara walked in too, carrying a huge load of books, avoiding her gesture to sit at the seat saved for her, and averted her eyes.

"What? She's acting weird." Channah thought. Mr. Rubin's voice was droning on about the repetitive exercises they would commence with. He looked up from their textbook, wrote the page number on the board with a huge meaty hand, and said "Preguntas. Channah, como se tal?"

"Bien." she said, flushing.

"How are you feeling today?" he asked her in Spanish.

"A si, a si." Not bad, not bad, Mr. Rubin, she answered. He walked to the back of the room, telling the class to begin studying pagina ciento sesenta y cinco. His voice lowered to a whisper, as he spoke into her right ear. With the steel chin rest, she couldn't urn her head.

"When is this thing coming off, Gorgeous?" he said. She couldn't meet his gaze.

Rubin's hand shot out, and he threw a piece of chalk at the back of a head in the front row. "Roberto, you have something else to do: work!:" he yelled.

"How about a date?" he whispered. Channah flushed again. "Mr. Rubin, stop!"

Expose: The Reckoning by Channah Gambit

she begged, thinking that he must be well meaning. "That wouldn't be appropriate." Mr. Rubin had been looking up, but now straightened slightly, then returned to his desk at the front of the room, all business in attitude.

After class, although she waited for her to walk to their next class, Sara was gone. "She must have left at the bell." Channah thought, sighing.

She had borne the contraption gamely for the following eighteen months, although it did cost her her best friend Sara, who felt embarrassed by being required to gossip in public with her. Besides, she couldn't go out with boys! The only consolation was the sweet sympathy she collected as she wore the 18 pound steel and leather girdle under her clothes. Following this, there was a neurotic underpinning to her psyche, and low self esteem.

The Gambits had a print shop in town, where they sweated it out 24/7. As a result, over the years, they became friendly with every business owner in town. Berke Day Camp owed Mr. Gambit a big bill, so instead he forced them to hire Channah in 1966.

She was sixteen, and starting to wear brassieres. Elaine, the owner's daughter, liked her, and gave her a C.I.T. position by begging Mr. Berke to hire her.

"You're such a great babysitter!" Elaines said, steering Channah into the converted bungalow office. Mr. Berke, tall and jolly, was totally bald and weighed over 300 pounds. He liked to guffaw.

"Howdy, Channah. Welcome aboard! You've got the 10 year old girls." he said. "Elaine tells me you're so smart--how about Junior Counselor, not C.I.T.--do me a favor, see?" he said, his bright blue eyes staring into hers appealingly. His meaty hand held out a whistle on a lanyard, and he guided her out the door, down the ramp, and through the cement topped field to the place where sixteen ten year olds milled around, making a racket.

After surveying them, she agreed. "I have no choice," Channah thought, poking an errant bra strap that peaked out from her sleeveless t-shirt. "Sit on the ground, and cross your legs like an Indian." she said.

"Now, girls, here is your new camp counselor. Do whatever she says!" and her gave them a big smile, then Channah, his brow perspiring heavily. He wiped it with his forearm. "Good girl." Mr. Berke said, walking away, his arm around Elaine's shoulder.

There was a good summer, with Phillip, Channah;'s first boy friend, to hold a crush on. Every chance he got, Phillip would attack her physically, trying to stick his head under her gray sweatshirt! "What a pest!" Channah thought, "But, I like it!"

All went fine until early August, when Berke Camp held Field Day. Channah's "Wrens", were doing a team tournament for the White team, on the playground. Channah, busy talking to Diane, a new friend, forgot to watch the girls on the team. Yells, screams, and shouts went up from the campers who were seated on bleachers to the right of the play gym. "Oh, damn." Elaine swore, looking at Channah, her mouth full of hot dog. "It's one of yours!"

Channah gazed into the sun, blinked, then looked at the monkey bars, shaped into a geodesic dome about four feet high. Valerie, the oldest Wren, was writhing on the ground. She ran to her side.

"What's wrong?" Channah asked. "My arm! My arm!" Valerie cried. The parents, there for the day, began to trot across the field from the bleachers, while Mr. Berke walked calmly forward from the direction of the office.

"I'm doomed. I should have been watching. So Sorry, Sir." Channah said.

As it turned out, the arm was broken. That ended Channah's counselor career, and her friendship with Elaine. Mr. Berke paid Mr. Gambit and stopped asking after Channah when he popped in for a print job on weekdays. "It turned out to be a foretaste, an omen regarding my problems with keeping counselor jobs when I was older." Channah told Dr. Kulkiny many years later, on her couch. "But, it was prophetic."

As she grew, Channah became prettier, stronger, and healthier. Attending a local community college, she aced all subjects. Her parents had demanded she stay home, because they were concerned about her mental fragility, and she had always been treated as a convalescent, requiring protection, a little "TLC (tender loving care) and rather co-dependent with them both. The Gambits could only afford a small Pinto car for her. Channah was thrilled to own a Ford. Well, actually…it was in daddy's name, but she did have a key!

June was fat, round, and confident. Her memory was elephantine, like her appearance, and she was generous to friends. Although Channah lived in a much more upscale neighborhood of Long Ditch, Beeritz, she wasn't a snob. June knew Channah had a Regents Scholarship, with college all paid for.

"But I like the way you're not a snob about it." she would say often to her. "You can't hitchhike the Loop to school, Channah," she would say, maternally, "You come in my car." It was a total bomb: a banged up Dodge Dart convertible. Channah would stand on the south side of the boulevard in front of the ranch, June would pick her up at 8 a.m., and off they'd go, drinking coffee, smoking and happy.

"Did you hear about *Bill, Love Freak?"* June would say, or "*My cousin Robert scored some excellent dope, how 'bout a try?*" playing devil's advocate, winking and snorting, her jet black hair in two Indian braids. She had a ratty security blanket of a baby blue plaid poncho she wore both semesters, regardless of weather.

"I won't." Channah would say, laughing. "You're a fool."

"No, it's in the glove." June would say, flipping it open, revealing the pipe."

"It reeks!" Channah would say, lighting up and taking a toke. Later, they would enjoy hanging out in the cafeteria with Steve, Bill, and Elizabeth. With all this, Channah pulled in A's. June would be an English teacher.

"I don't have to study. I'm a *sponge*!" she would retort to Channah's: *get serious speech* about school.

One day, tragedy was narrowly avoided. June and Channah, sitting in her Dart out by the health office. June3, smoking some sort of bong, offered it to her friend.

"No, I have a test." Channah said.

"I'm pixilated. This is awesome." June said. "You are really cool to join me."

"I think I'm going to end this friendship if you keep ruining yourself like this."

June was unusually quiet, making her uneasy. She glanced at her friend, who had her eyes closed. "Jesus," June said, low voiced. "I can't see."

"We have to get to class." Channah stated, primly.

"Shit! I'm blind." June's voice rose slightly.

Expose: The Reckoning by Channah Gambit

"What--you're kidding?" Channah said. She turned, looking into her friend's face. The bright dark eyes were squeezed closed, then opened, then blinked rapidly. "Holy moses!" Channah reached over, taking the pipe out of June's hand, laying it into the ashtray. "You're mistaken."

"Na-ah!" June said, "It's all black and fuzzy. What was in this shit Mike gave me? I'll kill Elizabeth!" She started to wail.

"Calm down, it'll pass. We'll go into the health office."

"NO WAY!!" June yelled. '

"Quiet down."

"Now I can't drive."

After about forty minutes, the dark spell passed and June's sight was restored.

Channah heaved a sigh of relief. "Now, maybe, you'll listen to me, and stop destroying your excellent mind. Now, I'm late for class." She got out of the dart, slamming the shotgun side door shut, leaning in through the window.

"You're judgmental, and obnoxious. Find yourself a new ride." June said, turning the key in the ignition, flushed and non plus'ed.

That was the start of a long cool period for their friendship, lasting years. Much later, Judy tried to steal Channah's husband away, out of meanness, spite, and vanity.

Channah was overjoyed, a few weeks later, to retire from having to hitchhike permanently, for Daddy's birthday gift on her 19th birthday was to receive he very own Pinto, with title in her name. This was an untold luxury! She kissed him repeatedly on the cheeks. "My little girl isn't going to be in danger on the streets." Daddy Gambit said, flattered by the affection.

Those were his "happy days", with the printer acting quite the father, a kind, approachable workaholic. He was subdued because of the busy schedule he adhered to. Mrs. Gambit, chronically overworked as his front office manager, barely had time to stick a bobby pin in her head, wispy black strands escaping. Even more so, they had little time to medically interfere with Channah, or monitor her experimentation with sex or drugs or academics. That was true of the other two children in the family, Big. and Mellow. Big was obsessed with building with blocks and going out bowling

If you met Mellow and Channah, you'd say they were not sisters. Some friends of the family said that in comparing the two, Mellow had been blessed, while Channah *got the short end of the stick.* Mellow was a good two inches taller, approaching fashion model quality, and ironed her long straight brown hair, which Ben watched in astonishment. That was before he had become mendacious Big. Mellow had an hour glass figure, whereas Channah was without much of an indentation around her middle, most years. She also had that brown hair, but the back of her head had a natural cowlick, and turned up, and it was unruly and wavy in all weather days. Mellow was a party girl, and dressed in loud colors. She gravitated to the wild, *nouveau*-rich crowd down in Old Westapple; a heyday ago, site of flapper events and the Roaring Twenties. Homes had been mansions in Gatsby's era, but were subdivided into swinging time shares for spoiled college kids. A jetsetter in appearance only, Mellow suffered from a chronic lack of funds.

In high school, she hung out with a Gould, who gave her money. Winsome in her

Expose: The Reckoning by Channah Gambit

moccasins, hippy threads and colored beads, she drove Channah to distraction with her name dropping.

"I'm going out with Steven McCool tonight." she'd yell from the bathroom, while primping at the mirror.

Channah, in conservative ragged hippy jeans and a man's flannel shirt, propped in a second-hand blue Easy Boy in the den, would try to ignore Mellow's obvious attempts to make her jealous. "All too often, you make me jealous."

"Don't ask me for that black sweater ." Mellow retorted.

"I won't. Don't ask to borrow $20 from me either."

Mellow's head, covered in some paisley scarf, stuck itself in the doorway. "Don't have to. Got it this morning."

"Oh, don't tell me. You didn;'t--" Channah said.

"I did. Did the purse thing." Mellow was referring to their shared game of raiding their comatose parents wallet and purse in the master bedroom in the wee hours of the morning. The sibling joke was that, no matter how much was taken, the loss was never noticed or commented on."

"I'm going out too." Channah audibly sniffed.

"Allergies, again?" Mellow said, kindly.

"No." Channah said.

"Right." Mellow said, chuckling, as she picked up her hand clasp, threw the switch for the electric garage door, and vacated the premises, leaving a silent Channah in a chair, her hands folded over a book, gazing after her. This was a typical exchange. She picked herself and stalked to the side porch. Her sister, dressed in four primary colors, stuck her head out the window, having rolled it down.

"What..." she said.

"Let me come, please?" Channah asked. "It'll only take a moment.

"Oh, come on, we're five years younger than you." She looked into her sister's downcast face and pursed her full lips, slathered in bee balm ointment. "Oh, alright.:" she said.

"You won't be sorry. I won't drink too much, and I'll stay in the rear. Just let me grab a poncho." Channah rushed into the house. Mellow kept the car idling on the driveway, playing *Incredible String Band* and *Tom Rush* on the tape deck.

When Channah came out a half hour later, locking the front door, she looked at her and trumpeted audibly, in rage.

The bigger girl took up a seat *shotgun*. "Hey, what's that you have on?" she asked.

"What this?" Channah asked, grabbing the fringes of her fabulous soft, brown suede jacket in both hands, across her chest.

"It's mine, goddamn it." Mellow said.

"Let's not fight tonight." Channah said, "I'm not going to dirty it. You borrowed my polka dot suspenders last weekend!"

"No I didn't."

"Oh, sure you did! If found it behind your radiator when I was helping you look for Henry." Mellow looked blank. "You remember? When he got out of his cage?"

Expose: The Reckoning by Channah Gambit

Henry was Mellow's pet gerbil.

"Ahhh, yeah.:" Mellow fell silent, looking down at her hands. They had been warring for years. Several years ago, it had been physical. She had had her arms gouged, with a couple of moles clawed off by her sister's nails. She looked at her right arm, where the white faded full moon still shown palely in the fading afternoon light.

"Come on, then. I've burned up a quarter tank. You've got your nerve! Why can't you hang out with--"

"--my friends. I know." After a second, Channah lit a cigarette and blew the smoke out the window. For the rest of the night, they didn't speak to one another.

It was a lopsided, volatile relationship. Channah liked to influence her extrovert sister, and use her to gain an audience. Mellow, on her end, enjoyed teasing her older sister about her lack of "people" skills. This, in turn, led to dislike and competitiveness, a life long animosity, and a decidedly cool downstairs kid quarters area in the colonial ranch.

Mellow was the best dresser in Beeritz. She protected Channah from tauts during the two years Channah wore portable traction to school. "Family pride," she thought to herself. "They can't step on her feelings while I'm there."

The sisters were rarely that supportive to each other. But, one day, Channah paid Mellow back for her kindnesses. It was the fall of 1969, her Senior year. Channah saw that Mellow and Steve McGool had had a falling out. "It has been a bad business, a bad love affair--obvious to me from the start, Mellow." She spoke up one day, when they both were enjoying a new quart of ice cream in the kitchen after shopping. It was warm up there with a pot roast cooking in the oven. Mrs. Gambit was *stretching out* upstairs, as always, after a long day of work. "This is comfort food, sis." Channah said.

"Right. Steve didn't mean it." Mellow said, recalling how he had struck her during the height of their argument last night, on Gilgo Beach.

"What led you and him to split up is obvious--Julie! Forget him! He's not worth it." Channah said, sticking a tablespoon of *Ben & Gerrie's Rocky Road* in her mouth.

Mellow started sobbing, even while dishing some *Whip and Gell* into a saucer. "Now, I'm alone. Poor me."

"Aw, better off. Even though you dated for three years. He's not serious!" Their eyes met, the hazels demanding reality from the chestnut brown ones. Channah's eyes fell on the *National Geographic* lying there. Mr. Gambit was insanely obsessed with the conservation agency, lovingly reading each issue, then binding it in red leather for a collection spanning decades in the living room foyer bookcase. Channah thought about how he never actually wanted to travel. She did! The article on Maine caught her eye.

"Why don't we just travel up the East Coast on a trip in my new Pinto?" she said.

"What." Mellow said. There was a silence for a long time. "Yeah, they'd never miss us.

"Just the thing--to get away from these bad *vibrations* and camp."

"But how...?" Mellow asked, looking in surprise at her normally reticent

Expose: The Reckoning by Channah Gambit
older sister.

"I'll show you how to forget men!" Channah pushed away from the table and rose to her feet. . They loaded the Pinto with pillows and blankets in the back seat, some grill items, and changes of clothes. Traveling up the I-1 route, they entered state after state, oooing and ahhhing until they got as high as Portland, Maine.

The girls found a little K3O campsite near a pond. The trees, silence, and long stretches of highway without habitation or strip shopping malls had cowed them, along with their own audacity. They had very little money, and no credit.

"We'll sleep in the car here. Hey--I used to be a Girl Scout." Channah said, and Mellow laughed. They, stayed the night, freezing in thin jackets, and swore eternal friendship and sisterhood. Eating Kielbasa, hard cheddar cheese bought in Vermont, and other goodies such as Hershey's Kisses, they made their lingering way south once more. Arriving home in Beeritz, they discovered, as usual, that neither parent had noticed the absence, although they had been gone for four days. That was status quo for the Gambits.

At a later time, when Mellow's moment of need came, Channah would forget the "Portland moment" between them, much to her chagrin.

Expose: The Reckoning by Channah Gambit

Chapter 2: Caina & Abela

After the college, there had been involvement in Yoga and the Eastern religions at a local experimental college Channah could not afford tuition for. Between the sisters there was mostly a wall of silence.

"How do you manage to transfer so easily?" Peter walked by her side one day, seemingly out of no where, at the N.C.C. student center atrium. His tall, good looks, fresh complexion, and curly long black hair all reminded her of a favorite rock musician, Michael Heron of Glasgow. He was her boyfriend Stephen's most interesting *sidekick*, a man she could also have a relentless crush on, or eventually call husband, so she immediately came to attention, running her hand through her long brown hair. Peter didn't seem to notice. Instead, he invited her up to a *yoga camp* in the Poconos for the Summer, as part of the independent study she needed to do on American culture.

"As your guest?" she asked, looking up at him from under her lashes.

He colored a little. "No, sorry. I'll be living in a pup tent on the North 440--a field in the rear of the farm." he said.

He explained that the guru there would ask for only $1,500 of her tuition money from the Scholarship program.

"After all, you'll have a wonderful time!" Peter said. "And it'll seem that you're going to school. Get to take a spiritual *siesta*, and use some of the state money the right way!" His aqua eyes sparkled in a smile. She would get to live up in the Pocono mountains, at a real Hindu ashram, working as a staff member, "And," as Peter said, "Live as an ascetic, with an honest-to-goodness vegetarian lifestyle, and seek to know God."

"I'm a little dubious, Peter." Channah said, putting her book bag down on the roof of the blue Pinto, hot glary sun pouring down around both of them. Later that night, she called Stephen, and spoke to him. "What do you think about it?"

"Great opportunity!" he said, his warm, expressive voice ringing in her ears. "You won't be sorry."

"Will you drop in the same time I do?" she asked.

` "Oh, I'll be up around the same time with Joyce." Peter said, popping a Dorito into his mouth.

Channah's faculty advisor quickly okayed the yoga study proposal, and she took a Greyhound Bus from the Port Authority terminal one April day out to Stroudsburg, alone except for a couple of duffle bags. Far away from family problems, she began to change inside.

As for Mellow, she had been indecisive and confused for at least a year, after visits to Greece and Israel, as was well known to her sister. Arriving back on Long Island, venturing into Centerport to live on Long Island in a spiritual center, she had adopted Guru Maharajah, a swarthy mentor, along with his ever-present mommy, as her saviors.

Mellow chose to join her. "I'm really messed up," she told Channah on the phone, almost the same day she got home. "You remember the pact we made in Maine? I need you now, Channah. Let me come up there. Dad and Mom won't let me live home--we're fighting about all the money I spent traveling. They don't like Guru Maharajah, and neither do I. I'm confused". There was much more to the story. Mellow had been living with a couple of men recently, in San Jose, and a relationship hadn't worked out.

"You need a way to sort things out. Up here, you'll have some real spiritual guidance." Channah told her. "Let me talk to Swami and get her permission."

It didn't take long. Taking some long strides out to a hand-made gazebo on the front lawn, she pushed open the screen door. Seated on a chaise lounge was a short woman in a baggy pantsuit, smoking cigarettes next to a large ashtray. "Swami!" she said.

"Yes? Have I read your palm yet?"

"No." Channah was still getting used to her. Swami was ageless, in white and gray hair long on her shoulders. Her face was Slavic and cat like, with it's best feature: violet eyes. The voice was deep and soothing, especially when she chanted "OOMMM:" at night, in their meditation circle.

Swami asked "Are you left or right-handed,"

"Left." Channah said, proffering a hand. She gazed into the woman's eyes as she, in turn, studied the palm in front of her, intently. "You've had an illness, both physical and mental. If you had not come here, you would have had a breakdown." She said, then let the palm drop.

"My sister, Mellow, is also suffering an illness at present. It's bad karma. Please let her visit me for a while." Channah said. She provided more details, hurrying through it, while knowing that her sister had little money. To her relief, her Gurani, after a moment of speculative staring off into space, said yes.

All it was was a log cabin in Tannersville. During the summer, children of employees of the Indian Embassy visited, and a day camp was run. It was temporary, a place in flux, as Channah wrote in her student journal. The philosophy, from Sankara and the Bhagavad-Gita gripped her. "Who am I? What is my purpose?" the gurani asked each and every disciple, forcing them to face themselves. Inner experiences, brought on by spiritual practices would lead to "self realization" and the knowledge that "there is a higher reality; a *divine presence."* she liked to say.

As for staff, they were expected to take jobs in the community, and contribute all wages. Channah didn't have to, at first, because her tuition money covered that.

"Is it all these amazing high things, or is it a Socialist Hindu front run by a savvy furniture business owner, a Jew, and his former fashion designer wife." she asked Peter one day, while seated on the blanket spread in front of his green tent.

"Just a tax shelter to invest in, with a race horse in the barn, retired. A great place to look good and great, and get in shape too, with a lover or two" he said, laughing. Joyce came outside, sat down, and took his hand.

"Lucky Joyce!" Channah said.

Peter and Joyce both giggled, looking into each other's eyes. A summer wind blew though the nearby maple woods, into the tent flaps, shaking in the stream of air, and around the trio. "Yep, Lucky Joyce." Peter said. "Get yourself some…"

"Stephen is preoccupied in High Falls, with Herman." Channah said, adjusting her peach *sari*, sweater and pail filled with brown eggs. "He's not thinking about *Shanti*." She spoke the word proudly, the sign of an initiate. She was in!

Expose: The Reckoning by Channah Gambit

Hitching a ride in the camp van later that day, Channah picked her sister up at the Greyhound bus depot. Mellow looked twenty pounds heavier, out of sorts, and equipped for a stay with little more than a knapsack on her back. "I'll have to lend you a wardrobe." Channah said, glad to see family just the same.

It was 1970. She was 19, and Mellow was only 17. They were at the best time of their lives, and Channah knew it.

Mellow looked at Channah curiously. "You've changed so much!" she said.

"Here is why," Channah said, in the communal dining room late that afternoon. "There has been some magic Brewers Yeast that Swami has insisted I take in everything I've eaten for the past three months. So--I've lost 25 pounds! But, guess what: I'm doing hand stands, the advanced Scorpion *asana*, and waking up at 3 a.m." Mellow, sitting on a stool, looked suitably impressed. There was something in the Yeast which made her feel sicker, delusional, and fatigued to the point of fainting early mornings. Perhaps that led to her resistance to *Lord Krishna*, and the blind devotion required there by *Swami*, which was becoming an increasing bone of contention in spiritual conferences each week. Channah couldn't bring herself to complain to Peter, or her faculty advisor, John, about it.

It was attractive, the dining room of the ashram. The log cabin's largest room, it was dominated by a huge, old, black cast-iron stove. The large windows were made of hand blown turquoise blue Beacon glass from Boston, complete with embedded bubbles. The huge round tables, surrounded by stools upholstered by *brahmacharis* doing selfless service chores in the barn held over twenty people for meals.

Channah looked around at the other yoga disciples, as Mellow began to eat some whole wheat *chappati* and squash. There was Jerry, the banker's son, proud, gentle, and good. Initiated last week as *Jay*, he had recently become a Sanskrit scholar, and a mainspring of the *Living Temple*, as Swami called the place.

Then, she noticed that Swami's hand rested possessively on his knee, and that they had eyes only for each other. She sighed.

Over in the corner, Jnana attacked his mango dessert. *Jnana,* as guests called him since his moment of self realization, he wrote, played violin, and wrote press releases and news letters to build the membership of visitors from Manhattan. He was tall, thin, and sported a beard. Maybe she could transfer her affections to him.

"I'm celibate, right." Channah said to Mellow, out on the porch after chores. "I'm watching my *gurani* act out with the chief disciple."

"He's beautiful, and it's obvious he's taken." Mellow said. She was holding onto the railing, with the moon light flooding the porch, the construction palings around the cabin rising up to a new fourth floor. Her gaze went up there. Channah snorted. "It's hypocrisy. She said she's been celibate for over ten years."

"Well, she's not. What about it?"

"I'm going crazy with the pretense." Channah said.

"So we'll leave." Mellow was quietly staring up at *Bhakta*, one of the burly bearded aspirants who had arrived this summer alone, with a knapsack.

'He's a warm, kind-hearted man." Channah thought she understood her sister.

"Jnana's free, if Stephen isn't. And he's tall." Mellow said.

Expose: The Reckoning by Channah Gambit

For four months, the sisters rose as staff at 4 a.m., worked hours at cleaning the place, and refraining from driving, making phone calls, writing, reading, or eating meat.

Daddy and Fay Gambit, finally noticing that the girls had vanished, drove up in July, 1971 to see what was going on.

"It's a good thing you came," Channah said, after the parents had driven the girls into town to take them out to a restaurant: the Stroudsburg IHOP. "Our clothes are in tatters."

The nervous parents followed up dinner with a shopping spree at the local female apparel retail store on Main Street.

Despite, or due to the loss of weight, both girls looked amazingly well. Their skin was clear, their eyes keen and bright, and they had the energy, as well as appetites, of panthers. Dressed in all orange garments sewed by their yoga leader, both had much news.

Bhakta had definitely taken a liking to Mellow. Their affair had progressed to trysts on the roof during the day, with him hauling up stones for the façade work, and her bringing up thermos' of lemonade, to catch a kiss behind the chimney.

Channah had seduced Jnana during a trip to the goat farm for milk.

"I'm going to propose," Jnana said. Chiding him, Channah would blush behind her vacuum cleaner.

The parents, replenishing their pocket money, stayed over at the local Hampton Inn, then left, reluctantly, on a fine summer morning, leaving the girls behind. They had refused to return to Long Island, rejecting their mother and father.

"I know I'm hurting them, but they are so possessive!" Channah said. Called into the office, she fetched her sister.

"I'm sorry to tell both of you we are not doing so well, here, financially," The guru said. The fire in the stone fireplace burned brightly. Perched in a rocking chair,Channah followed her finger, pointing to some white uniforms resting on top of a wooden trunk.

"If you two want to stay here, you'll have to go to work." Jay walked in. Her eyes met his, she smiled broadly and rose, wrapping a sheet around her ample shoulders. Now, we're going to my house for the weekend. Look through the classifieds." She placed a newspaper next to Mellow, then walked out briskly, Jay shutting the door behind them

"The honeymoon is over." Channah said, and Mellow laughed.

In the month after, Mellow waitresses at the Pocono Diner. Channah procrastinated, arguing that she had donated a large sum to the ashram. Her own *sadhana,* or spiritual practice, was constantly on her mind. Love affair on the back burner, she spend hours daily in silent meditation.

"I want you to marry me," Jnana said, one morning, getting down on one knee, much to her astonishment.

"Oh, don't do that," Channah stammered. "We're from different backgrounds-- I'm Jewish."

"I'm Protestant. But, I know my father will love you as his own daughter," Jnana said earnestly.

"I'm not ready to marriage. I'm sorry," she said. "I have to go soon." Channah

Expose: The Reckoning by Channah Gambit

didn't want to sleep with him. It had happened already twice: an ecstatic, impromptu, passionate coupling on a couch in her parent's home, when they returned for a brother's *bar mitzvah.* "Some chaperone you turned out to be.:" She told Jnana in August, when they had become accustomed to being viewed by the staff as "a couple".

"My *sadhana* is messed up!: Channah thought, walking past the seasoned pine door jambs into the office to confront Jay.

"Your sister has to go." He said, briskly. "I know it's hard to face, but all of this romantic encounter is chasing guests away,"

"Yes, well--tell her." she said.

"I'm surprised at you, Channah, What will happen to her if Bhakta breaks it off"

"I guess she'll get upset." Channah said, sitting on the stone hearth and watching the laborers through a window.

"Well, okay. Have you noticed? She's been acting a little funny lately," Jay said,

`"How so."

"Well, she's been talking to herself." Channah was stunned. It was true that Mellow had cut her hair shorter, that she had lost twenty-five pounds since July, and that her complexion was marred by acne. "Maybe there's something I should know?"

"Yes, you ought to talk to her first. Swami is telling her she has to go tonight,." Jay said, ending the session and dismissing her, as chief disciple in the ashram.

She walked out as he indicated, closing the door. "How dare he treat me this way, the whore!" she thought. Her teeth, clenched together, bit her tongue.

That night, Channah walked down the hall, hearing a large argument behind the office door. Shortly afterward, the door slammed, and the sound of quick flip-flops climbing up to the communal attic bedroom was heard. Mellow had been thrown out, she surmised.

Heading down the six flights of stairs into the mudroom, Mellow turned and called up the bare staircase to her sister. "Channah…" she pleaded. Channah, looking out a guest room window, saw the guru's station wagon pulled up, Bhakta at the wheel, the engine making a staccato sound through the countryside silence.

She didn't answer. She felt like she had Gorilla Glue on her feet. "Why did she have to come up in the first place! She ruins everything! Such problems!" she said to herself, clutching her meditation mohair shawl closer to the side.

After what felt like fifteen minutes, the front storm door slammed, and she watched Mellow get into the car, which disappeared down the gravel road. Channah was in disgrace.

Mellow made it to town. Bhakta paid for the ticket himself.. The Greyhound bus she had been on could not contain her, however. According to the Stroudsburg policeman's report, "She appeared incoherent, was mumbling, and was no doubt, drugged by someone with a psychotropic. She got off on the I-80 shoulder near Stroudsburg and headed into traffic."

"Am I my sister's keeper or Sister Caina?" thought Channah, recalling how Mellow had said goodbye from the stair well below, her voice filled with fear and anxiety. It just hadn't registered in time. "Perhaps I should have left too. I can't believe what I'm witnessing here. School is over…" she thought.

Expose: The Reckoning by Channah Gambit

The phone call which followed, came from Stroudsburg hospital, from Rupi. Jnana drove Channah into town, where she waited long hours for her parents to arrive. They refused her the right to see her sister, who was in restraint in the locked behavioral health ward. Channah rejected being Shanti utterly. Home was the only thing she wante to know now. She was well aware that both her sister and herself had been hurt by a viscious woman.

She went back for her things. "Ive crossed a line in my heart." she said, weeping bitterly in the office. In the presence of the swami and her lover, she lambasted them condemning "…the whole cult and your foul brainwashing," she screamed. "You are a total hypocrite. You claim to be celibate, but you screw Jay on weekends when your husband is away in the city, at his business."

"You're out of here." Jay said, sternly.

"Don't ever come back, Channah." Swami warned.

A taxi took her back to the hospital During the two hour ride home, caravanning with a rented ambulance carrying Mellow, Channah repeated a mantra to herself. "Blood is thicker than water. Blood is thicker than water." It was inane, but she couldn't control it.

Three weeks later, Mellow was permitted to be outpatient in a day program at North Shore Medical Center.

"You weren't there for me." she said, the first afternoon they were alone in the kitchen.

"Come on," Channah said.

"You heard me call to you, and you didn't come. I hate you." Mellow said. Channah walked out the rear kitchen door, "Come outside with me, please, Mellow." she said.

"You promised. You got me into such a bad way. That damn diner job! It was awful, I was sweating like a pig, working my ass off, and you, "Divine Holiness", didn't have to work--I did. You didn't care." She began to sob loudly.

"We had a deal. We agreed to be there for each other. Now, you don't have a sister no more."

Abruptly, turning from the view of the golf course and her sister, she ran in, down to her bedroom, slamming the screen door behind her. Channah gripped the railing hard, trying to stop the migraine which was already beginning behind her temples, willing herself not to cry tears.

After months of recuperation, both women returned to an uneasy life under the parent Gambit's roof. The peace of Beeritz offset the several breakdowns and upheavals which followed that debacle in Pennsylvania. Worse yet, there was a permanent rift between the sisters, Caina and Abela--for the betrayal of the elder sister in abandoning her Mellow to her own devices. It had nearly cost her her life. The false quiet in the split colonial ranch was deafening for weeks.

Expose: The Reckoning by Channah Gambit

Chapter 3: To School; To Teach

. Beeritz: a desk, computer, use of a library, and accoutrements--it was in this quiet habitat, this wind-swept oasis of peace and bored tranquility, that Channah Gambit's ordeal began, early in the Spring of 2005. She had been working for Leander Woodrow, the principal of a new magnet school in Brooklyn, the Tertiary School for Legal Change in America.

Channah spent two eventful terms as a new special educator, and was coming close to the point where she might win tenure. It was a particularly unfavorable fall semester, politically for her. She had plotted doggedly through week after week of hard obstacles, few teaching materials, and lack of curriculum, like hundreds of other eager young beavers, drafted by the Chancellor..

"Hey, I don't have to listen to you! I'm going to be a teacher, too!" said a short, stout and dark woman, seated in her classroom the second week of her first semester. Sporting a bonnet of bright color fabric in a bun, horn-rimmed glasses, and several bangle bracelets, she looked like a wrinkled prune. Paraprofessional, Decorah, an African-American about the same age as Channah, was simply an aging out product of the system, well-versed in procrastination, and sassy and demanding as all get-go. Decorah (an apt name), insisted on arriving when she chose to, spent gym and lunch periods away from the charges she was supposed to help control, and did everything in her power to thwart Ms. Gambit.

"I wouldn't do it that way! I won't take it from that child--such disrespect!" Devorah would say.

"But he's emotionally disturbed. He's can't help himself. You left them alone in the gym yesterday!" Channah would say.

Devorah's loud alto, cussing and arguing with Ms. Gambit, could be heard many afternoons after school, emanating from behind the closed door of room 214. They spent hours weekly at *pow-wows,* discussing ways to manage the kids better, a group of know-it-all sixth graders that ran the gamut of all characteristics, from learning disabled to mixed autism spectrum. The kids were the best part about the job. Ms. Gambit was spending as much time managing to make her assistant agreeable.

"Why am I having to appease her, Lorna?" she asked, during the first month. "Why do I have to force her to photocopy, or be an assistant to me?"

"Now, now," Loran Peaches chided her, gently. "She has wanted to be a teacher for years, and she's just a bit frustrated, that's all. Why, Mz. Jackson has been here longer than I am. John Jay Israel--this building--is over a 100 years old. Her family has been employed here that whole time."

"Oh." Her own voice made a hollow ring in Channah's ears, as she sat in the Assistant Principals, office. It was a converted library room, with walls covered with shelves. Peaces was seen daily, riding her bicycle up the front entrance ramp, bringing up in the elevator. Parked in her room, it shared space with a few book carts, a microwave, a couch and comforter, hat rack, and piles of collateral office material, newly purchased.

Channah's supervisor, "Miz Peaches", or Lorna Peaches, to be exact, had given her a generous budget for purchasing teaching tools, so she quieted down quickly. The woman looked like an Army drill sergeant, with brown frizzy hair, a nose which looked like a dried apple, and the after effects of injuries suffered in a car accident affecting her walk. The left leg dragged slightly, but no cane was in sight. Lorna preferred to spend long hours after school in her room. "We're very proud to have you, Channah." she said, the first week of school. "You've got all those credits from a fine teacher's college. No doubt, you've done your homework." Her blue eyes appeared magnified by the lenses of her tortoise shell glasses. "We hope you stay a good long time. There's nothing we can't do, if we work as a team. You'll get used to Decorah. Just let her do her thing."

Channah stood up, holding her lesson planner tightly against her chest. "I'll do my best to manage her."

"Good, and shut the door as you leave." Peaches said briskly, turning away.

On a return run to the classroom Channah discovered that a new friend, Berta Hones, the art teacher, had donated a wooden swivel chair to her. Ginger, the office secretary, donated a file cabinet later that afternoon, and had it sent up.. With the budget allowance given her, Channah purchased over $300 in games, manipulative, maps, activity books, and art tools from a supply catalog, borrowed from Ginger Jones..

The whole term as a new teacher, launching her second career, was buoyant, but not without rough moments.

Take Mahogany Silver, the personification of trouble. Entering the room with an arrogance, this *diva* from the Projects near Bedford Stuy was already over five foot five and every inch over-developed for her age. Discussing her the first week during phys-ed, Channah told Devorah "She's confident, but is learning disabled, emotionally disturbed mixed, according to her I.E.P." Decorah took the time to say, simply, "That girl is trouble, and if she don't respect me, she's in for it. She has already lost her virginity, so I hear. Humm--mumm."

That afternoon in early September, 2005, during the second week of Miss Gambit's career launch as a professional teacher, Mahogany decked her. The young woman had gotten into a tussle with Carlos Rodriguez, over a silver CD player hidden under his sweatshirt. Grappling with him, as twelve other students chortled, egging them on, Mahogany and Carlos ricocheted off desks, threw the teacher's chair over on its side, and bounced off a window wall. Channah flew into the fray, aghast at the ferocity of their violence. Decorah, was, as usual, no where to be found when you needed her. It was right after lunch, and juice boxes, lunch boxes, and books were clattering to the ground. Trying to separate the two students, Channah took hold of Mahogany's left arm near the bulletin board. Pulling with all her might, she could not believe at the strength of the child. Carlos' left eye was already sporting a huge pink scratch mark under it. It looked like he'd be leaving on a stretcher, Channah reflected.

All of a sudden, Mahogany's arm went flying back in preparation for landing a punch. Unexpected, this threw Channah off balance, she went flying backward, landed on her back, and slid across the room over thirty feet, landing with a smack at the front door, her head making a smack as it hit it.

Everyone stopped what they were doing, stunned. The combatants immediately separated, shocked. A huge chorus of laughter and shouts immediately descended on the disheveled teacher, and all around the happy screams and cat calls continued, making a racket. Channah rose to her feet, in what she felt was a dignified fashion, her eyes boring into the eyes of Mahogany and Carlos. "Get to your seats, NOW!!" she yelled. But, the laughter did not subside. "Oh, god, I've lost control of the class." she said into the intercom, having called down to the front entrance security guard. "Send someone up to Room 213 now!" As she stood there, she felt a glue ball hit her left shoulder blade.

She turned, to see that Decorah had reentered from lunch, and was standing there with hands on her hips, lips shaped into an *oh my goodness.*

Channah felt her head gingerly. A lump the size of a golf ball already was starting to swell. Mahogany and Carlos, acting like angels, were seated at their desks. Mahogany was painting her nails with *White Out*, a specifically forbidden item. Carlos was placing the headphones on his head. A security guard, tall and glowering, peered around the lockers, staring intently at the children. There was suddenly dead silence.

The children were averaging seven physical fights a day, but they were marvels, and such a mixed bag of blessings, she told herself. Several were socially defiant. She had a mildly retarded, placid boy named Tony. There were four learning disabled-autistic spectrum. Should she remain in teaching?

Mahogany, who came to class decked out in $250 designer jean coordinates *because mommy loved her ooh so much*, came to school the next day with a note of apology, requested by the teacher. Mrs. Jones was strong on discipline, if you phoned home, Decorah told her. "But you haven't done your homework sheet, Mahogany!" Channah said, exasperated. After an ice pack, she decided to try to last the full term.

"I admire your spunk and dedication." Lorna said frequently, that difficult first year.

"It takes three years to become a teacher." Woodrow encouraged her, at *weekly Wednesdays* faculty meetings in his office. Channah's four observations during the term went well, and she aced a satisfactory on her annual 2003 evaluation. Reward came from Peaches and the principal

Woodrow. Obviously liked her. He was a stiff, stodgy, *educator's educator,* and always tried to discuss education theory and practices with everyone. Ginger, his secretary, zealously guarded his door like a bull terrier, but adored him. She told Channah that she was truly liked by administration early that Winter, making her glow.

"I know my stuff. I am worth it. It seems that I am finally a success in something." she said to a friend during her first Summer break, spent at the beach or biking on the boardwalk. She rested, and dated a little.

Her second term promised to be more of the same. She was assigned the same *beloved* students, with just one or two exceptions, and they advanced. It was Life Science, not Astronomy now. The curriculum was at the third grade level, although they were seventh graders. Emotion heated up the tiny classroom daily, but, with an expensive store with good behavior prizes, she and Miss Jones averaged only two fights per week. Ms. Peaches purred her approval and praise on several occasions. Channah basked in all that attention.

There was cheer in her heart, as she left home each morning at 4 a.m. to hit the Belt Parkway, pass Kenney Airport, and swing up South Conduit Avenue into Atlantic

Expose: The Reckoning by Channah Gambit

Avenue territory, with it's shuttered grilled store fronts, stray cats, and discarded garbage. She would spend almost two hours each day on the commute, but had her places along the way to stop. Her cheer was infectious, and she readily made friends. She managed to breeze through the first administrative review with flying colors.

The kids knew what to expect when fall term, 2004 began. Catching a glance of her when entering the door, Carlos let out an exaggerated groan. Antony, whose mother had lavished chocolate Peter Rabbits and presents last year, was back again, grinning.

Her math coach Eugenia Lakes was back to supervise. Something new in the wind, though, she thought to herself, gazing at Woodrow's expressionless greeting.

Fall and winter went off without a hitch. Glenn, the astronomy teacher, asked Channah to come to his Astronomy Club, and view the Pleides shower from the roof of his brownstone.

Friendships grew with all special ed faculty. Milton Rosenberg, there for decades, dropped in between classes. His curly black hair reminded her of her old friend Peter's. His black eyes, with deep circles under them, followed every move the kids made in his classroom, when she came in to observe. Heidi, the Muslim woman who assisted him, liked her too, and shared management tactics.

These good moments added to a golden time, and she was able to devote herself to patiently working on the kids' weaknesses in reading, computing, or memorizing. Up and down they went, twice a week, to the speech therapist, Patricia, to read *Captain Underpants,* and master phonics. Down in 213, they played Channah devised for them. Shooting consonant blends with water guns, or aiming bean bags at *Dolce* sight words were great fun. With yardsticks borrowed from the supply room, her class trudged down to the basement, measuring a staircase for a wheelchair ramp design--part of lessons in geometry.

Channah loved every moment of planning curriculum. Her weekends were all work, spent devising games, challenges, or creative dramas for them to enact in four subjects. She went to the local office supply store, photocopying in pastel paper to motivate them, buying self-stickers of fantastic Ninjas or hot wheels, or baking up little treats for token rewards.

Woodrow said she had hidden talents as a diagnostician. She ran running records of all of them, as they read out loud. With Decorah's help, *who was interested in spite of herself in Channah's methodology,* they set up a clock and learning center for Fridays, having the kids rotate through ten different classwork stations, with moves triggered by a cow bell. It was all fun and progress. Occasionally, Channah slowed the class down enough to watch a movie, something like "Batman Revisited", as a reward. Their reading and writing levels, aided by a Pen pal program in the computer lab with a sister class in England, jumped forward by almost a year.

Nona Gubel, thumbing through the D.O.L. reports per student, said "Job well done!" to Channah one January afternoon. A half Hindu wild woman with wavy jet-black hair, originally from the Bronx, seemed to belong in a sari, but instead chose sharp business suits of red and black. Her flashing dark eyes, and rapid speech, made Channah dizzy. As instructional specialist, she dropped in once a week, but had little need to tweak the program, as she examined the teacher's curriculum planner, chock full of entries. Channah, standing by the window, said "Thank you so much, Nona, for helping me learn my craft. After two years in Graduate School, and all the work I've had lately, it feels great to hear a compliment."

Nona looked quizzical. "Well, you don't know? I've had to return to Graduate School, to keep my N.Y.C. teaching license." Channah said.

"You mean, your masters degree in deaf studies wasn't enough?" Nona said. She stood up from the teacher's chair, allowing her to return to it.

"No, since last Summer, I've been enrolled in Special Ed: Inclusionary Settings, a new Masters program."

"I respect you highly for your dedication." Nona sorted through some handouts. "Oh, here's a test to give your kids, to see what kind of learners they are. It'll really help you design lessons." she smiled brightly, her eyes affectionate.

"Really don't have a choice," Channah said, preoccupied, "I had to enter a new Masters program to qualify for those loans." She played with a cord from a busted shade.

"Well, your reward will be more success in the long run." Nona said, picking up her leather valise and squeezing Channah's arm as she prepared to go.

"I've never felt so *behind the eight ball*, Nona."

"I'm not sure what that American expression means, Channah. I'm Indian."

"Oh, it's Americanese for "in debt". Channah said, waving goodbye to her friend, standing in the doorway. February, 2005 continued in a smooth, productive track.

Then something started to develop which, at first, puzzled, then confused Channah. Watching Lorna Peaches day in, day out, she decided that her supervisor must be going through menopause. Every time you turned around, quarreling was emanating from the Dean's room. Channah, walking by and sticking a head in, would hear Peaches say, "Nope, sorry. Can't spare any time for you now." and would return to a phone call.

"I stopped in the other day, to have lunch there." she told Berta Hones one day, tearfully, "And she shooed us all out. What is going on?"

Eating in her own room, she was accosted by Mz. Peaches one day. "Hi, I'm coming in later to do an "unofficial" observe." she said. Channah noticed that stray gray hairs were escaping from her bun, and she looked rushed.

"Fine." she said. She knew she had nothing ready to show.

The lesson on homonyms was without a plan, handouts, or manipulative. As mentioned, Peaches came in at the start of fifth period, taking a seat in the rear. Interrupting halfway through, she walked to the front of the classroom, beginning to instruct the class herself.

"I know they all adore her." Channah told Decorah after that. "She keeps a *huge* jar of candies in her office, and they all get reinforced when they come for a visit."

"Don't worry about it." Decorah said, sympathetically. "It was a good lesson."

"Why did she take over? That's not an *observe*!" Channah said. As the supervisor left, after the period bell rang, she said, "Channah, stop by my office after school."

In a short conference there, after gesturing Channah to a stool, she came right to the point: Channah's lessons were too hard for the class. They had to be *chunked* more. After all, she was still a new teacher. After Christmas, there had been some remark by another observer. Channah must be prepared properly to teach there. She would have to see Ms. Gubel for remediation. She must go through reevaluation, at a later times. Channah's face grew warmer as she listened to this.

"Yes, Mz. Peaches," she said, over and over again.

"You will have to prepare a second lesson for submission for your next *observation*," Mz. Peaches said, standing up and removing a sheaf of papers from a binder. "These are, once again, way over their heads, Ms. Gambit." She handed back the proposal, and Channah's nerveless hand took it, thrusting it somewhere in her handbag.

Jon Milltown met her in the hallway, as he headed toward the library for a faculty meeting. "Are you coming? Hey, Channah, you look like you've lost your best friend."

"Can't talk right now," she said. He looked at her closely, and glanced at Peaches' closed door.

"Is she Peaches?" Channah said.

"Yes, as far as I know. I see--she said something *out of character*."

"May I talk to you sometime about what's happening, Jon?"

"Sure, he said. But, not now!" he said.

"Well, okay," she went home, feeling numb to the bone.

A few short weeks passed, with events in her classroom progressing much as before, except for the sporadic intrusions of Gubel, who was awkward and embarrassed about having to treat her like a junior teacher.

"I'm trying to remain humble," Channah told Berta one day, as they shared lunch in the faculty lounge.

"Sure, just eat crow. It must have been something you said. You've got to try to work with her on this."

Channah screwed her brown bag into a ball. "I just feel so upset."

"Try to visit a gym--work out. Maybe you should get a therapist. I have one." Berta's long fingernails fidgeted at her book bag.

"Yes, you're right. I will." Channah said, pushing back and rising to her feet. The dank, chalky white walls muffled student sounds, but everything they said to one another echoed enough through the room to make other teachers and aides eating or reading there eavesdrop. She felt like she was broadcasting too loud. "See ya later," she said, leaving.

Preparing a lesson offering for the second evaluation with Nona, she was forced to revise it once before acceptance, by Peaches. There was another nasty conference in the Assistant Principal's office during the week.

Puppets aided the class, in a cheery presentation of a famous picture book "The Mouse and the Candle". The kids behaved, as they had been bribed with chocolate chip cookies in the cafeteria tomorrow, "Five each!" Channah was shameless. Afterward, when Peaches had left, she stuck out her tongue to her receding back and said to Jones, "It went off without a hitch!"

"You were great!" Decorah said, complimenting her for the first time in their relationship. Channah's eyes began to tear, as she looked at her in wonder.

After a week, she found the evaluation from the Assistant Principal in her mailbox, early one Tuesday morning. Tearing the envelope open near the punch clock at 6 a.m. she began to read.

"Are you okay?" Mavis asked her, noting how her face had changed. "Your face is

Expose: The Reckoning by Channah Gambit
as white as a sheet!"

"I'll be fine." Channah said, crumpling the papers and taking refuge in the women's lounge. The review of the demonstration lesson before the class this time, though kindly, was borderline satisfactory, with much negative criticism.

"What's got into her?" she thought, as she stood there. Her hand was shaking as she applied fresh red lipstick. "What's happening? Channah was beside herself, and the relationship between them became more distant, immediately.

"I haven't done anything different!" She wailed to her favorite Teacher's Union representative, Jon.Miltown, within a couple of hours.

"No, honey, you have." he said. "You have approached the time of tenure. It's simply political." Jon explained that region 9 only gave out so many *sats* or satisfactory a year. In fact, they were obligated to give out only a certain figure. This was to induce teacher effort, and diligent improvement, and fits of over-exertion mentally at the continuing education workshops after school every other week.

Then, again, there was the impossibility of getting an *ice skater's Triple* flip. A teacher with three annual reviews of satisfactory rating automatically was given tenure. Tenure was the state of matrimony with the Chancellor, as well as the Board of the Department of Education, City of New York , which granted a teacher automatic and permanent full time employment, barring injury or extreme gaffe. Channah's goal and main preoccupation was that. This was something Mr. Chancellor Joe Kline did not like to do at all. This was, according to Jon, the real reason behind "Our Mize Bitchez" change of tune. It would continue the rest of the term. Nothing could be done to change her tactic. The Assistant Dean was instructed to eliminate the new teacher from the roster of permanent faculty.

A second political reason was the fact that Miss Gambit was already in her late forties. If given tenure, she would be retiring out in less than twenty years. In fact, she'd be encouraged to do so. Woodrow preferred to give tenure to ripe, young, twenty year olds with a lot of staying power.

This was irrefutable logic. The result was, however, that a previously blissful job, as hard as it had been to pull off, became a new source of anxiety and stress. After the review of her second evaluation was a borderline *satisfactory*, as predicted, Channah was told *not good enough,* and made a total subordinate of Nona Gubel's. She was now the new supervisor.

With Mz. Peaches' express orders, she was put in total control of Channah Gambit's classroom. She began to change many things about the classroom, much to Channah's chagrin. The new teacher was powerless, and stopped planning curriculum. Slowly, bit by bit, where the class was given up to the instructional specialist instead. At the end of the Spring, a new lesson plan, hardly her original concept, passed muster immediately. The lesson, coached heavily by the Hindu, brought an instant satisfactory from Peaches. Channah's confidence as a teacher, however, was shaken, and had reached an all-time low.

Meeting with Woodrow in his office, for the annual end of term summing up, she was criticized yet again, but given a satisfactory rating for the second term. Woodrow paced back and forth, his hands clasped behind him, in a trim gray pinstripe suit which

Expose: The Reckoning by Channah Gambit

showed up his lean athletic build, setting off his youthful shock of graying hair.

"The trouble with you, Ms. Gambit, is that you are *too damn intelligent* to be teaching special ed." he told her. "Milton Rosenberg talks well of you, so I'm keeping you are." She looked at him, gratefully, astonishment making her blink her eyes lately. "So, I've come to a compromise. I'm going to try to place you in some other situation, where you can grow with us."

"Am I getting my *kids* back for a third year?" she asked.

"No, I'm afraid not. They would benefit from exposure to someone new. That was unusual; it was brought to our attention." He went into a long digression regarding a Stephen Trubell, an administrator in Region 9 who had some criticism of her, but had decided to not put her on probation. "Yes, he encouraged me to think outside the box, stop fighting the flow, and put you in charge of a ninth grade self-contained class."

"Oh Leander, I am so grateful. I know I'm gushing, but you won't be sorry, I assure you." She stood up, brushing her suit jacket down, her eyes glassy with earnestness.

After some pleasantries, Woodrow let her go.

Afterward, she rushed right up to Jon's classroom. "Let's conference at the Greek diner." he said. "I'm teaching right now." She had poked her head in without thinking.

They met and she told him everything. "I'm back next year."

"I have to tell you, you're not back. You see, dear, you have won a battle but lost the war." Jon was a history teacher, and often spoke in such terms and metaphors.

"I don't understand." Channah said.

"Go on, drink your tea." he said, sourly. "The truth is, your direct supervisor is Mz. Lorna Peaches, not Leander Woodrow. And, honey…" he dropped his voice to a conciliatory whisper, "She doesn't want you. That is obvious. She doesn't like you."

"I feel that. It's nothing I did." she said.

"No, it may just be she's been told to do it. But, you see, Channah, if you don't have your direct supervisor behind you, you can remain at a job, but she will just make it impossible. You should expect many unpleasant moments, and a lot of tension, in the future. And Woodrow knows it too. It's going to be rough, at best, next year, until she gets what she wants--you leaving." Jon said. He said "I know I'm being unkind here, but you need to face the truth. It's a political beast. I never liked her." He folded his newspaper up, rose, and left.

The term ended a few days after that, the kids dispersing happily to their tenement homes to spend a sweltering summer of love, open hydrants, and no homework. The summer was one of anxiety, a series of interviews up and down the East Coast, and printed copies of resumes mailed out to plush Long Island districts, to no avail

As predicted, by the Fall of 2005, the Assistant Principal began to use scare tactics and other maneuvers to deprive Channah of students. One example, whereas Mr. Woodrow had informed her the prior June that she would teach ninth graders, a better fit, none materialized after September 14th in 2005. Nevertheless, Region 9 took the guesswork out of where the students would go--it *had* assigned over 25 new ninth graders to her school. The Assistant Principal, holding fast to an agenda of termination, asked a good friend and colleague, who just happened to be the senior honcho in special education upstairs, to take the students upstairs two floors, to her room instead. They vanished.

Channah, sure of her credentials, but bewildered, spent two weeks preparing a huge empty classroom. Peaches lips curved in scorn. Woodrow remained completely in the dark. \

Pressed by a teacher frantic at the prospect of late reassignment, Woodrow, assigned her a couple of eighth graders, dipping into Mr. Samuel's over-abundance in Room 117.. Channah spent two weeks teaching 2 students, her voice echoing from in front of a sea of empty desks.

Peaches wasn't finished yet.

She had already hired a replacement, a seasoned professional from Connecticut with over twenty years under her belt.

"I'm not a special ed teacher." Gail said gaily, "But I'm willing to help out." One bright Monday, Channah was informed indirectly, that Mrs. Peaches had taken two subjects of self-contained work away, placing both math and science into Gail's competent hands instead.

Channah was fit to be tied. "Have you ever done special ed?" she asked, too brightly.

"No, dear," our Ms. Brooke said patronizingly. "But, if you want to assist, stay in that period."

Ms. Gambit walked slowly down to the Assistant Principal's office.

"Now, Channah, you know you have three periods a day to teach, with one preparation." she said.

"I know, but I need five a day to qualify as a full-time teacher under contract." Channah said.

"Well, I'm going to come in soon to do an impromptu, unofficial observation of your English class. You had a few problems last year, if you recall." Peaches said.

"Yes, mostly *you."* Gambit thought.

"....and I want to see if you retained what you learned." Mrs. Peaches added.

Channah walked slowly back, fuming. She knew that the odds against her having come this close to tenure were sheer astronomical. She did not care for the administrator's scare tactics. The deprivation of a promised student roster struck her as odd. And then, she found them upstairs, in Roses' room. Fuming, she took what she expected to her Union friend, Jon.

"It is to be expected," Jon said, "...that you will be forced out." He was sitting on the corner edge of his desk, in his large social studies room, where she had surprised him sorting textbooks. Channah thought he resembled a miniature *Charlie Rose*, with his natty wool plaid suit, pastel tie, and disheveled and overly long light brown hair.

"Why's that?" she said, noticing how his long expressive fingers were clasped over his right knee. A pipe and small leather tobacco pouch peeked out of his right top drawer.

"Well, look at it from the school board's point of view. With tenure, it is too expensive for the district to keep you at your presently-high salary level. Now--don't get me wrong!" he said quickly, noticing how the anger flared up in her eyes. "You deserve to have that. You're a very educated lady!"

"Yes, I've spent two years in graduate school to get a Masters, and then I had to

Expose: The Reckoning by Channah Gambit

go back--at the Chancellor's insistence, by the way!" she said, hazel eyes flashing, choking a little on the words. "To take another Master's program, with over 21 credit hours spent, *out of my pocket*, to keep the special educator license I need to teach here!"

"Yes, I know all that. You have numerous graduate level study credits in excess of the "plus 36" category allotment." Jon said, sympathetically, closing the drawer on his right. "But, Channah, decide to grow up.!"

"Get this! I heard a rumor yesterday, to the effect that my ninth grade students are upstairs, temporarily housed by someone named Rosy."

"Really, that's very interesting." Jon said, rising to his feet, coming close, and aimlessly walking between desks toward the back.

"No, this is interesting: the rumor is that it was done by Peaches, because she thinks I am considered bad risk, and an untrustworthy teacher. Can you believe that?"

He turned, walking to her side and staring her squarely in the face. His gray eyes probed her's deeply for a moment, then he resumed his seat at the desk. "After thirty odd years in this system, I'd believe anything. Why don't you take the hint. Leave! You have a clear sign from administration."

"No, I won't. It cost me too much to get this far." Channah thanked him for his time and walked out.

The next day, Peaches showed up in Room 114, a pencil and legal pad in her hands. She sat in the back, took furious notes while Channah taught, then left. They were typed up in less than four hours. Presented to Channah as she left for the day as an "off the record *observe*", they included a memo requesting she report to Peaches office the next morning, for a related discussion.

Sitting in her white Hyundai at the side of the six story building, she speed read the contents of the observe. It was harshly critical, parsing and nit-picking every little thing real and imagined, and even fabricating what had been a part of her lesson. "Outrageous!' she snorted, glancing up to Jon's window upstairs. Then she relaxed. He was already gone for the day.

Channah walked out of the car, instead, entered a C.V.S. Drugs on the corner, bought a pack of Rolaids, and swallowed three.

Trudging in to school at 5 a.m. on Wednesday, the day after, she climbed four flights because the elevator was out of order, and walked to Jon's history classroom. He was working on textbooks in the back of the room, counting and making notes.

"Hi " he listlessly lifted his right hand in greeting as she pushed in through the door. He listened attentively to her story.

"It was hard last year, retaining a satisfactory annual review after one or two 'unsats', John." she said. "But--I followed that grievance process, you helped me, and I got through. Even so, I spent last Summer frantically seeking new employment, more local. I foresaw this personality clash with Peaches a long time ago! I am not liked enough, and there have been clear signs that I am going to be shown the door for political reasons. That's what you explained to me last year. Yes, I am too old. Remember what you said, Jon? *Take it as a clear indication that you'd be doing better if you had less of a commute trip, less trouble like this to deal with. Why not flow like water?* you said. Well, this Summer proved to be an endless ribbon of open-ended mailings, and it led to some productive interviews, but no hire." She stopped to catch her breath, winded.

She looked around the dirty, bare, room with it's ancient walls, streaked windows, and broken curtains askew. Channah draped a tan overcoat over a student seat, then sitting down.

"Well, sweetie, that's what I was trying to tell you. Don't take Peaches' actions personally. She's been given the job of axing you. Woodrow probably didn't like your grievance last year, and the fact that you resisted having your nose whacked with a newspaper. That's the type of subordinate he likes!" Jon said, looking at her kindly from under his craggy brows. "Start looking elsewhere. Or--just put up with retraining for a while. But--there are lots of other schools, Channah!" and he resumed his work, indicating that the discussion was over.

Thinking to herself, she returned to her classroom. This Fall, still testing the waters, administrators and their rearrangements of the grade structure had led, no doubt, to that inadequate assignment, contrary to projections by the Principal. That was all it was! She just couldn't fathom what her supervisor was capable of.

Channah was seriously angry. She was dealing with a two-hour commute, leaving home at four in the morning. There seemed a collusion of the construction agenda there to stymie her, as it deprived the surrounding blocks of at least 20 parking spaces.

She had already spent several unpleasant weeks negotiating terrain. Rising earlier and earlier each weekday, she was paying exorbitant sums at distant parking garages, then busing to work..

Trying another expensive strategy, Channah tried using the Long Island Railroad, but it made her late twice, and she was reprimanded sharply by Lorna Peaches, in the clock room.

After this final conference with Jon, and an unpleasant one with Peaches, one of her precious students named Erika, was "too old" to be there, and was reassigned to the Ross' high school group, leaving one. Reassignment seemed imminent.

The following day, Channah had a surprise real first semester *observation.* Creases appeared on her forehead as she read it the next day. It was a negative, for the first time in her career. The mistakes, and carelessly spoken language which it mentioned she had displayed while teaching one pupil were dim in her anxious memory, if non-existent, in her consciousness.

She read the handwriting on the wall, and was close to despair. One gray, foggy morning in October, Channah walked up to the Principal, handed him a resignation letter, and walked out. She passed the African-American security guard in the front lobby quietly, like a ghost. She left behind a cadre of energetic, street-smart, but slightly damaged adolescents she had known and grown to love over two years.

But, best move yet, as she told herself, Channah landed a new suburban job. In doing so, she made it easier on herself, as she rationalized it. The new St. Joaquin post replaced five hours of commuting with a sweet twenty-minute ride. She'd be working for an agency with the developmentally disabled.

"Yay!" she chortled in the empty car. Gambit was soon working with eight heavily retarded, emotionally disturbed, and medicated male adolescents with keepers. "To me, this job is easier." she told Mellow, one morning, while micro waving dinner. Mellow had come over for a visit, out of concern, and was a dinner guest at the apartment.

The week before she started, Channah went back to Brooklyn, to visit Mavis the bookkeeper, to roll over her pension. Mavis was only too happy to help her. Theirs was a cordial relationship, or so she thought. After the paperwork was finished, she provided her with a forwarding address, for any unfinished business. Mavis Morir wished her well. It was true, however, that Mavis had made a slight mistake on her payroll, shorting her over $3,000. This would be discovered almost three years in the future, after desperate Channah Gambit was let out of jail and found herself in extreme poverty, without friends, and homeless.

Mavis was informed of the mistake by the Regional bookkeeping department in the spring of 2006. But, somehow, she could not locate a current address for Ms. Gambit, as requested. The paycheck, held for thirty days, was sent back and redeposited in the main fund, indefinitely. The region seemed to be anti-Semitic, or perhaps it was just Mavis. Channah would reapply to the employer sometime in 2006, and be informed of that windfall. To her credit, Mavis never so much as blushed when recontacted by the former employee afterward.

"I'll need some sort of forwarding address to mail the check to." Mavis said.

"Here it is," Channah handed her a business card, printed with it Somehow, the bookkeeper lost a piece of information, although she had been most conscientious for over thirty years, and was valued, admired, and tenured.

Channah was in therapy now, a result of Mz. Peaches' political maneuverings. She had lost several new Brooklyn colleague chums, a lot of her confidence, strength, and about fifteen pounds, out of anxiety. Jack Peralt, a new talk counselor, suggested almost immediately, that she resign. It was like icing on cake. She could take no more.

By October, 2005, she had bowed to the inevitable.

Expose: The Reckoning by Channah Gambit

Chapter 4: The Downward Mystery Spiral

By January of 2003, Channah had been softened up by happenstances, as she liked to call them, around her apartment in the parental palace. Since the year 2000, someone had been damaging or stealing property, vandalizing, and doing malicious mischief. Scissors, knives and other housewares vanished. Plants, such as a huge aloe, melted after being dosed with vinegar. Likewise, the pet fish in the community tank perished after someone added salt one day, no doubt, while she was out for grocery shopping. A leather coat she had bought for a song at a thrift shop suddenly had a cut off semi-circle on the right elbow, and was now missed a leather button, difficult to replace. That kind of thing kept occurring day by day.

The poisons added to her refrigerated beverages were the worst. Why did she call them that? It was because they produced deep migraines after only fifteen minutes--something unusual in a liter of Sprite opened just the previous evening. "Maybe someone came in last night while I ran to the A & P for milk." she would think. It made her uneasy, and a bit paranoid. She noticed how her son only ate what he brought in, from the deli job or take out. She looked up at this disheveled giant, his brown eyes hard and probing. "I don't like what you buy." he'd say.

After he had been permitted to move in by his Dad, she had been besides herself with joy. Channah was willing to cater to him completely. "Just give me a list." she said. "I'll buy all your favorite foods." He would not allow her to.

"Why are you paranoid, Mom?" He said. "What in the drinks is making you sick? It's your imagination!" He'd wrap his huge hand around a shoulder and squeeze reassuringly. How could she tell him?

Were the additives harmful? Not fatally so. They only made her squeamish, but the effects added up over time, and she was nervous when she ate, inevitably alone.

Mellow made it a point to drop in on her once a month or so. She had thinned down by dieting, and dyed her hair to a streaky mixture of brown and auburn. "I have my own problems," she said at the kitchen table, drinking a Chamomile tea. "I do not care to share them with you." There had been no sisterly chats, not for years, since the ashram disaster. "Michael was very mean to me, and that's why we divorced." She was fond of saying. "He couldn't deal with my becoming an invalid emotionally!" Mel stayed on her recuperative course, distracted by bouts of multiple sclerosis, developed in the late 1980's seemingly out of nowhere..

Competing with Channah's academic success, as she did habitually in every area of life, she embarked on an ambitious *return to college* of her own, financing a certificate program in Animation and Web Master computer programming. Greg, her son, had left home, to pursue video games programming. Her gorgeous daughter Marie was entering the field of Marketing at C.W. Post "There is a lot of happiness on my plate." Mellow was fond of saying. Unfortunately, Mellow's multiple sclerosis *plaques* were too much for her sense of well-being, even after the diseasse had gone into remission. "It's those immune serum injections I gave myself." she said, proudly.

Another piece of bad luck was the car accident in 1999, which totaled the car, producing some permanent injury: now 47, she walked with a limp. Chronically furious,

Expose: The Reckoning by Channah Gambit

incapacitated by a flare up of multiple sclerosis, she was forced to drop a demanding college attendance schedule. Her energy and fury were channeled into being jealous of Channah. instead.

It started in early August, with Mellow bringing over organic foods from her kitchen. Once, in the third week of the month, she appeared at the glass front door, a casserole in hand. "Let me in, it's hot." she said, smiling.

Channah was disconcerted by the smile. "How are you? Won't you come in and sit down?" she said. The refrigerator was not fully stocked. She waved Mellow to the table.

Her sister was dressed in a turquoise sweatsuit outfit, and chose to remain standing. "So, what have you been up to? When do you start that job in Fresh Meadow?"

"Tomorrow." Channah said, taking the casserole from her outstretched hands, and putting it into the oven to warm. "It's a bit unusual that you would take an interest in my plans."

"Well, Dad did let you move down here, and you do have to pay $1200 rent, you know." Mellow said, her voice rasping. In nervous fashion, one hand moved up and down the other arm, smoothing out the spandex. "Dad depends on your "gifts" to survive."

"I know. I know. Where are you coming from?"

"I was just over at the Lucida family. You remember my friend Lucille, don't you?" Mellow said, rising to her feet, pacing around, then sitting down on the sofa.

"What kind of casserole is it?" she asked, cracking open the oven door. "It smells great."

"Sausage and linguine. Lucille made it. I can't eat it--that is, I'm not hungry. I brought it over instead." Mellow rose to her feet again, walking through the den to the Florida room, to look out at her car, parked on the driveway. "Look, I have to go now. I have to get back. Sam is waiting for me."They exchanged pleasantries for a few minutes more, and she departed. "Enjoy it for me!" she said.

It was the first week that Channah was staying downstairs, on her own. She sat down at the table, realized she was starved, and ate most of the casserole. Washing the glass pan, she set it aside in the drain rack and watched some television.

At about nine o'clock, she rose to visit the bathroom. Much to her amazement, a few hours later--well after Mellow left, she found herself unable to urinate. What was this? It would have seemed inconsequential, except for the fact that so many other food producing illness incidents had preceded it.. She had already been suffering from a bad cold she just couldn't shake for weeks. Ignoring the precautions on the label, she took multi-symptom cold remedy tablets, day after day. "Oh, my god! My urinary sphincter has shut down.. OUCH! I can't urinate! How odd--I'd better not drink." That is how she spent that first night.

In the seven weeks ahead, with ten separate incidents of catheterization, including four at the Emergency Room at the hospital, she was brought to the brink of despair.

"I'm being punished!" she thought. "I'm being taken advantage of, for having the audacity to move in down here, not pay rent. I realize this is not logical thinking."

Her mind traveled back to a time when she had moved back in--for the first time

Expose: The Reckoning by Channah Gambit

since her marriage to Stephen Randell. What a shock that had been!

In January, 2000, Channah gave up a typing pool position with a small Holtsville firm and accepted Daddy Gambit's invite to live with him, attend Graduate School, and become a professional teacher.

Residing with him was going to be uncomfortable , she realized. There was no spare living room. Together, the old man and his daughter half-dragged the dining room table into the living room. No spare bedroom was to be had. The downstairs apartment was rented to an Italian couple: the Pomerantz's.

Instead, a small mattress on the linoleum dining room tiles would have to suffice. Clothing went into the front foyer closet, and coats were pushed upstairs. "I should be grateful; I am grateful." she told Jamo, her daughter, by phone, the first night. She imagined that blonde head, the big cheeks and light blue eyes, and all her Amazon qualities as her daughter congratulated her on passing the GMATs. "It's impossible, but grandpa is making it all happen for me, with his generosity. It's out of character." she said.

"Mom, don't question it. He is your surviving parent. He just wants to help us." Jamo said. Channah imagined her seated behind her desk up in the large suite of rooms Jamo shared with four other coeds. "Show your gratitude. You had nothing!"

"Yes, I will. " she answered her, "But it's totally out of character for him." she thought to herself, hanging up..

"Just as it is out of character for Mellow to give me anything free." she said to herself now, back in 2003, while clutching her stomach. "Could this have been caused by a drug, somehow?" When she visited the urologist that morning, he had said, "Cut out the Contact. That caused it." Channah was not so sure. She was gritting her teeth and making at least two pit stops while commuting to school, all without "productive success" as she put it. "Dry as Dry Gultch." she would say, coming out of the stall with a huge swollen belly.

Nevertheless, she suffered through the first two weeks of classes at Abern University that way. Tormented, she wrote down her notes, shopped for textbooks, and signed up for student health insurance, all just in time.

"Perhaps emotion in my family is semblances." she told herself, a month later, finally recuperated. She dialed her sister's telephone number, hearing the distant voice answer. "Hi, Mellow. I have this casserole to return. Would you please drop by for cheese cake?"

"How are you doing." Mellow asked.

"Not good. Why not come and see for yourself." She looked out at the winter scape, the backyard through the double storm doors, it's patio chairs covered in plastic, all furniture stacked in a corner, out of the wind.

"I'll be there eventually." Mellow said, after a few moments. She hung up the phone. Watching Lawrence Welk was amusing. It was so dated. She shut it off, going through her school folders. Missing too many classes had dropped her by a grade in one course. Mellow walked in through the front door, having used her key.

Channah wailed. "I'm clinging to this work assignments and term paper schedule with my fingernails." she said. "What a cliff hanger this illness has been! No one in the family is sympathetic." Mellow took off her coat, and grabbed a captain's chair. They were upstairs in the big warm kitchen. She listened to her sister. "Everyone takes it for granted that I'll master the work. I've had to adjust to the new *bus stop* bedroom. I've tried to acclimate to the needs of a demanding father, terribly insecure regarding his health." she finished, holding out a cup of coffee with one hand.

"Yes, well, you can't live with me. I have a boyfriend, no room--and we don't get along." Mellow stated quickly.

"Whose fault is that?" Channah said crossly.

"Yours. But let's not talk about good times." Mellow's sarcasm was biting. The two women heard Daddy Gambit stand up and turn off the set in the television room on the top floor. He was shuffling about, and would soon come downstairs.

"I'm going to go. When you're in a mood like this, we always fight." Mellow said, removing the cups and plates from the table, standing at the sink, and washing them up.

"Tell me--did you make that casserole or Lucille?" Channah asked, angrily.

Mellow looked at her, no expression on her face. "What has that got to do with anything?" She dried her hands with a towel, then took a closer look at Channah, seeing that she was serious. "I told you: Lucille made it from a pack of sausages I gave her. Why, did you get sick?"

"What! Are you blind! Do you have any idea what I have been going through, the last seven weeks?" Channah's voice rose to a crescendo, and was full of feeling.

"Yes, I heard from Dad." Mellow said, picking up the glass pan. "You had a touch of stomach virus."

"No, it wasn't a virus, Mellow." Channah said. "It was something much more serious. If not for the health insurance--and the bills from the hospital have been over $1,700. I'm poor. I can't pay for what happened. Have you ever been cathetered, or worn a portable catheter to work?" Her voice had an icy quality, to her own ears. Daddy Gambit was now in his bedroom, and they both heard him lie down to take a nap.

"Listen, this is ridiculous. I have to go." Mellow said, picking her sweater up off the chair and putting it on. She looked at Channah, her eyes flashing.

"It wasn't the casserole. You must have taken too much of that flu medication."

"Right. Honey, I don't believe it. I saw the commercial this week for Detrol."

"What does that do." Mellow said, starting to walk toward the front door. "Oh, don't be ridiculous!" she said, carrying a paper bag with handles, the pan inside.

"I think you put Detrol in that recipe. Or Lucille did."

"Why would I try to hurt you? Mellow said, fright in her eyes. "You're paranoid."

"What can I say? If it wasn't you, it was Lucille, then." Channah said to a slammed door. She sighed.

Over the weeks ahead, her hunch about Detrol faded. School took her full attention . She was well enough to do the work, and would return home, parking the small used car given to her by Dad on the side driveway.

She'd come in, hang up her coat, and listen for the blaring set, on volume ten, coming from the kitchen. Daddy would be up, bustling at the pantry, getting out his

Expose: The Reckoning by Channah Gambit

Green Giant from the freezer, or preparing the fish on a grill pan with foil or Chef Pierre Prudhomme seasoning.

He was a big man, built wide and short, with a lot of extra paunch from watching television over sixteen hours a day. His face was wrinkled and pale from being inside. Fingers like pale tallow with nails discolored with fungi would perform the tasks in robot-like motions. It was the same routine every night. His forehead, lined with worry lines from years of difficulty, would crease, he'd turn and frown, then--seeing her--brighten up in the dark eyes, a smile coming on.

Every night, like clockwork, at 6:30 p.m., Daddy Gambit would demand his daughter's presence in the kitchen, for dinner, to *keep him company.*

"You must have something with me. Is this how you show your gratitude? I'm alone all day!" he would berate her. Guilt would make her sit, eating nothing.

"I can't talk to you, Dad." she would say, "Because, Dad, the television is just too loud. Turn it down!" He would, sometimes.

Then, they'd have some semblance of conversation. "How was your day?" he'd say. "Ben called."

"That's nice. My day was okay, Dad. How was yours?" she'd say.

"Same as always. *R and R,* as your Mom, *may she rest in peace,* would say."

On the table, space was in high demand. To his right, a huge shoebox of bills and tax statements sat. On top of the set, an extra glass case was kept. The captain's chair to his right held an old brown valise, too heavy for her to lift, filled with months and months of paid bills. He liked to do the bills at the table, for hours at a time.

She remarked to herself, "He's getting a little senile. This is hard to see." In his prime, Daddy Gambit had been a powerful, dynamic man with an explosive temper. Now, to Channah, he was an aged old dancing bear. She looked distastefully at his draggy slacks and the carefully dry cleaned Oxford shirt with short sleeves he favored. When she had dated, and brought young Stephen Randell to the house, she had been ashamed of Dad's appearance.

His words brought her out of her reverie. "You should be grateful, you know." he said, placing the plate heaped with food down in front of his seat, on a brown vinyl placemat. "Your mother wouldn't have let you stay, for free."

She would sigh, knowing what was coming. There would follow a twenty minute lecture on how much he had done for his children in his life.

She now did what she normally did when Dad talked to her. She thought about something else while nodding her head. The doctors told her, no doubt, the inability to urinate was due to the flu remedy and *nerves* from the upheaval in her personal life. It couldn't be strange incidents which were happening, even now: the clothes deliberately torn or stolen; the missing class papers; erased documents on the PC--she hadn't brought herself to tell Daddy Gambit, knowing he wouldn't believe her. "What about the unpleasant headache and nausea caused by drinking the 2-liter bottle of soda kept just for her in his refrigerator? "Of course--it's all nothing!" Doctor Harry said. "Nerves!"

Not *Detrol*, a new prescription drug which came on the market barely two months later, helping women with weak bladders gain control. "It's time to see a therapist." Channah's doctor told her.

Expose: The Reckoning by Channah Gambit

Her mind traveled back to a nightmare she had had, just the other night. She was on the Lido-Point Lookout bus, heading for the East End, an important local resident, Dr. Joseph Kimble, drunk, commuting from his law firm in Manhattan. He gave her some free legal advice. "If you think someone is trying to poison you, go visit the Complaint Bureau in Mineola." he said. "I used to be a drug salesman, you know, and I know how easy it is to get hold of prescription drugs--over the counter samples!" He looked German, Joe, and he wore a classic brown wool suit. In her dream, he resembled *Snidely Whiplash, nemesis of Dudley Do Right, the Canadian Mountie.* Joe said, "Yes, it's true. I give them away: to druggists, doctors, nurses, and offices. I get them from free!" His wicked eyes bore into her's. "There's always a malpractice suit. But how are you going to prove it?" The bus driver, who looked into his rearview mirror, said as she left, "The family is out to get you."

As she walked down the dark street, quickening her pace, a whisper followed her: "Put into the Ragu Sauce, three quick stirs! Don't heat it too high, or the properties burn off." in Joe's voice. "Horrible!" she said, waking at two in the morning, her brow covered in perspiration.

If it wasn't for the fascination she had with being in Graduate School and beginning studies of the Deaf, she would have lost control of herself completely. Luckily, graduate school was a distraction. She got well, and the nightmares stopped.
After weeks of search, she found three part time jobs, and plunged into the lifestyle of a happy workaholic.

Channah maintained an aloofness and coolness toward her sister, her brother, and her father, unmistakable to her son, when he called

"Mom, you've got to remember what he's doing for you. He's making sacrifices." He'd say, in his baritone, from work or Dad's house.

She gritted her teeth and bore it, each night she arrived home. "I'm giving you a last chance, so don't screw it up!" Daddy Gambit said, mixing his favorite orange juice and cranberry cocktail. "These are sacrifices I'm making, so that you can enter a respectable profession. I will be gone soon," he said in that melodramatic way of his. "You haven't found a new husband. Who will support you? At least, as a teacher, you will be able to support yourself. I won't have to worry when I'm in the grave."

"Oh, Pop, stop it!" she answered, automatically, washing the dishes.

A terrible, unknown poisoner-*enemy* was forced into the background by trips to the Recreation Center to swim, or daily reading assignments. After two years, when she had at last graduated, he forced out the tenants with demands for an outrageous rent, and moved her down there.

"I want you to live down there, for two reasons." Daddy Gambit said in December, 2002, right after Hanukah. "It's my present to you instead of *gelt*," and he patted Channah's right cheek with his rough paw. "And, besides, I need family down there, in case, God forbid, I get a heart attack." She looked at him with amazed eyes. "You'll be home, and can call an ambulance real fast."

"Oh, Dad, nothing's going to happen." she said.

"Of course, you have to pay rent. I don't want it to show up as rent, though. You know why?" He was seated in the blue busted Lazy Boy in his t.v., room, Merv Griffith blaring on the huge, 24 inch screen. "I'd have to pay more taxes. No lease, no checks--just give me a gift of cash every month: $1100. That's because you're my daughter." he said, proudly. "With a new job, you'll be able to afford it."

"Dad, I haven't started one yet." she said, as she had been saying for days.

"Don't worry, *Cookie*, you will." he said, grabbing her, pulling her face down to his level, and bestowing a big sloppy kiss on her cheek.

"I know, Dad, I know what you're going to say next." He was alert tonight, and his cloudy eyes tracked her, reading her lips, as she spoke, his hand on the remote, with *mute* on. "You'd like me to stay for free, as I've been." He shook his head in agreement. "But, you just can't do that--because I am now your only source of income."

"Right! My big, educated lady! You're so smart, and I'm so proud of you: All those A's." Channah thought to herself, as she smiled, that these moments with Daddy were almost becoming *pleasant*. When he understood you, and you could speak to him, it was almost like a happy family relationship!

Big, dressed in construction clothes, stopping by every few weeks, had nothing but good things to say to her. Still, sometimes she fought with him or Mellow. When this happened, Daddy Gambit would grow taciturn and morose. "Why can't my family ever be happy together!" he exclaimed, in a tantrum.

On a freezing January afternoon in 2003, it took only two hours to move everything down, to the large unfurnished lower apartment..

As weeks with income began in April, Channah amused herself by decorating in new Scandinavian furniture. "I've always been a *tomboy."* she told a colleague. With tools from the unheated workbench in the garage, she built most of the *IKEA* pieces herself. Her son and his best friend, Mike, built two bookcases one weekend, for twenty dollars and 2 pizza pies.

As time passed, life downstairs was pleasant enough, with it's privacy. Theft incidents kept happening regularly, however: of household objects like scissors. "We have a poltergeist!" she told Davey, on the phone. Impotent, she occasionally found herself seething with rage. When she sat down and figured it all out on paper, it seemed that there were eight key holders to her front door. These included her brother Big, his best friend Wally, the next-door-neighbor Len, Mellow, Karen, Big's wife, Duvey, Jamo and herself. "It's camping out at a bus stop!" she thought. She was forced to endure daily coming and going of upstairs tenants, tracking mud through her duplex apartment, from the inside garage door, and back again. They fought about it, her and Dad, her and Big, her and Mellow.

"Can't lock the door." Daddy Gambit yelled. "Godforbid I have a heart attack, they have to get in, the Volunteer Fireman, or Helga next door. You'll have to put up with it."

"But, Dad--I have things disappearing out of here!" She yelled.

"Tough!" he roared, slamming the door between them, and bolting it on his side.

By 2003, she had managed to achieve most personal goals, in spite of daunting odds. Channah got her Masters degree, gaining certifications.

She spoke to Jamo on the phone, who listened maternally. "Over $75,000 in debt, dear." Channah would say. "But, it's so worthwhile."

Expose: The Reckoning by Channah Gambit

"Yes, mom. I knew you could do that." Jamo said.

"I've stopped the payments for 3 years, on hardship deferment. You should learn from this. I want you to go to graduate school."

"I'm going to Berkeley." Jamo said, hanging up..Channah had a lot to be thankful for, she told herself one day, sitting on the futon in front of the cablevision program "Iron Chef".

Take her daughter, for example. Jamo was a big girl, a huge success as a student, and had a huge number of friends, in all sorts of places. She had traveled the world, went to Baruch College on a 4-year scholarship, and was very talented. It was true that she had suffered emotionally from Channah's crack up with Randell. Forced to play the mother role to her kid brother, she had worked at babysitting since age 14, and had her share of hard knocks at college, managing the book store. Musical, wonderful Jamo, Channah thought. In recent years, Jamo had started to drink a little too much at night, and there had been sharp words of criticism from Mom.

"We're so proud of you, Mom." Jamo told her, calling up from the college. "Now, Aunt Mellow will have to respect you."

"Hi, Super Girl. How is it going? We had another attack on the apartment, yesterday."

"What, this time?" Jamo asked.

"Someone left a dead baby bird on the floor of the Florida room. It didn't even have feathers yet."

"Mom, maybe you should ask your therapist for some heavy medication. I'm sure you're imagining things. Dad says--"

"What your Dad says is the opposite of the truth, I've told you that before!" Channah said.

"We are proud of you, honey." Big told her, even though he had not brought his wife or come to her Commencement exercises in April, 2003. They were seated in the living room upstairs, where he had come to sit after fixing a closet door upstairs. She stared into his brown eyes. Big was taller than her, overweight, and strong, as he spent a lot of times at construction sites, walking around. His work boots were still on, attesting to the fact that he had come straight from Long Branch, the site of a new school the firm was building. Big was patronizing, but a compliment was nice to hear.

"I didn't think you'd ever finish something you started, but you did!" Daddy Gambit stated, one night at the dinner table, louder than the sound from the small television blaring there. He was dressed in a tattered black button-down sweater, his favorite, she noted. "I respect and admire you. This was a big step to take! God willing, soon you will have a job. See ! That's why I helped you do this--so that you would have a real profession you could fall back on. I'm not going to be here forever, to support you." He said, looking up at the ceiling as if he was communing with Jehovah.

Channah Gambit, fair-haired girl. she said to herself, one night, in the mirror, in a cold December, 2003, applying some pink lipstick. An exhaustive search for a job, lasting over six months, had led to the biggest salary in her life. She had a warm, comfortable and even luxurious lifestyle here, in the childhood habitat. For the first time in years, she was on good terms with others, family and friends.

Expose: The Reckoning by Channah Gambit

But--there was still no social life. No privacy. Someone kept chipping away at her happiness, destroying, damaging, stealing, breaking, hiding and then restoring items. A sinister, unknown figure kept putting unknown additives a into her foods or drinks--causing clear-cut symptoms which were unusual, sudden fevers, flushes, or quick colds. She was occasionally wracked with anxiety.

"I need to have Duvey living here." she told Stephen, in late December, 2001.

"Yeah, you can have him. I'll give you the tax deduction this year. For that reason, let's start it in January." He was very casual.

"You never let me win the custody battle. Let me have him now."

"Only too happy to." he drawled into the receiver, "The reason I didn't let you do it before was because you were mentally ill." He hung up before she could retort..

"My greatest triumph of all time!" she chortled to herself, throwing herself back on her bed and kicking up her heels. "I've won! I've got my son!" Duvey looked in on her, perplexed. He had a nice bedroom across the hall, decorated in black furniture. Dark red walls reverberated to rock music each night. Duvey was happier.

He had been easy to convince regarding the move. Channah was proud of the "quality times" they now shared--painting it together, building the IKEA furniture he had picked out himself. He loved gambling on the Internet, seated long hours at his computer.

"I'm so proud of myself. My little heart is swelling so big in my chest, it's going to explode." she thought. But....they say *hubris* is not just an ancient Greek malady. "Pride goeth before a Fall."

Channah was *on a roll,* to use a gambling term. Things would work out with her jobs too, even though she had left the Tertiary School for Legal Change in America. She had found the St. Joaquin Learning Center. She had given up her solid pension, real salary, and security in Brooklyn to enter a risky venture, a new school just set up by a large Christian agency.

After an entire lifetime of butterfly employment, new health benefits and prestige had been tossed aside. Channah had been challenged severely, and now took a hefty cut in pay. The original position she had sworn to do her best at proved to involve a group of students who were just too violent to control, even with medication. After the fifth *take-down* of the week, where a student had been forcefully brought to the floor by 6 teachers called in by walkie-talkie, Mrs. Dauphin, the Principal, pulled Channah out of the classroom, whispered "this is not a good fit", and put her on status as a fully-paid observer in another classroom downstairs. She was replaced by a large, maternal, heavy-set woman who was uncertified, and merely an aid. What an insult!

It was apparent to anyone who cared to observe, that her new job was doomed to failure after six weeks. She had jumped too soon, out of desperation, to get away from Miz Peaches, and taken a gamble.

Now, as she observed for two weeks, she began to view violations of disabled student care right and left. Outside storm doors were open, with retarded wanderers sometimes traipsing off the premises and going to pounce on cars and bank their roofs. She had taken a course to reduce tension in her life, but now it was on the increase.

One night, Daddy Gambit phoned down to ask her to come upstairs.

Expose: The Reckoning by Channah Gambit

"What's up, Dad?" she asked.

"I wanted to tell you how happy I am that you don't have to take a long commute anymore." he said, seated and drinking decaffeinated coffee for dessert. "It will be harder to support us on a smaller salary, but Duvey can help out." She looked at his disheveled blue sweater, with the torn elbows.

"You know, Dad, you really ought to get a new sweater." she said.

He looked vague. "Mellow will get me one." He favored her, and she catered better to his needs.

"Dad, things are going a little haywire at school." she said.

He blew up. "What are you saying, Channah. Talk slower, I can't hear you. You know my deaf ear." He beckoned to her to sit down across from him, at the table. She took a chair.

"Ahh, Duvey is giving me $200 a month toward the rent."

"Now, it's not rent--don't call it that." he said testily.

"The gift I'm giving, I mean. But, Dad, the job--" Channah said. She didn't have the heart to tell him.

She stood, leaving him staring off the space at the table. She called Big up, instead, and his wife, Karen, put him on the telephone immediately.

"Maybe it's time we dismantled the house, Channah." Big said, curtly. "Put him into assited living."

"But, you know, he told me he wants to live on his own." Channah said.

"I know, but its getting to the point where he can't manage to take care of himself."

"How are the kids?" She imagined Justin and Jill, his eight and ten year olds, playing at the coffee table at his home. He had a comfortable three bedroom in Queens.

"Don't you change the subject!" Big yelled. "Something's wrong. Let's have it!"

"Nothing is wrong." she said. "You must be psychic!" she told herself, saying goodbye.

Gramps appeased him somewhat later, by visiting a local law firm, Rusky and Associates. Big and Karen had finally talked him into something, along with Mellow's help. He said "I'm going to get a life trust set up, and a living estate. But, I'm staying here until I die."

"Yes, Pop." Channah told him, glaring at her siblings. "You don't need a nursing home."

"Going to die with my boots on." Mr. Gambit said, glowering at all of them from under his shaggy eyebrows, his brow deeply furrowed. "You'll get your money after I go!"

"You're not going anywhere." Big told him, pleased all the same.

Two weeks after that, St. Joaquin reduced Channah's job to observing other, more successful teachers. She made the mistake of coming home, dialing Big, and telling him the truth. She then went upstairs, accosted Daddy Gambit in the television room.

"Shut off the set, Dad. We have to talk." She said. He looked at her, doing it, almost immediately. "What's going on?"

"I just resigned from my new job." she said. "Actually, it wasn't a job at all."

Expose: The Reckoning by Channah Gambit

"I'm not being supported by an uppity gal who has just quit two jobs in a row--a butterfly!" he said.

"I didn't quit, Pop." Channah found herself whining. "I still get paid. I'm just observing. But I offered them a letter of resignation today."

Big knocked heavily on the front door. "Oh, the bell is busted." Channah walked down the carpeted stairs, through the foyer lit by Tiffany lamps, and let him in.

Ignoring her, he stalked upstairs, leaving his jacket draped over the hall bookcase. She busied with some sodas downstairs, placing them on a serving tray. The explosive argument started almost immediately.

"Observing? She already observed, doing student teaching. What is this horse manure?" Daddy Gambit said, to Big "This is not a real job! She gave up a perfectly good job in Brooklyn." The argument went on for over twenty minutes, back and forth yelling. She dreaded facing them, and stalled.

"I'm forced to agree." Big said, "I'll visit *your daughter* downstairs *and make my point*." There was the sound of his clumping boots on the front porch, and Channah let him sit down.

"Hey, I'm not a robot, okay." she said.

"I resigned from the Brooklyn school for many reasons!" she defended herself.

"It was due to a head injury, Big. There were no parking spaces, and betrayal by my supervisor." He nodded his head, drinking the soda, but was having none of it.

"You know, he could have a tenant down here, a stranger, and be collecting over $600 more a month than you are paying." Big ended the argument with that. "Also, you are not going to be able to pay rent now. You should move out. We're forcing him into assisted living, the children. Why did you have let him have his way to begin with?"

She wanted to mention the petty larcenies and the damages that had been happening on premises for several years, but stopped herself. He would not care.

She forced the issues. "Hey, Big, for the past few years, by way of persuasion, someone had been damaging or stealing property in my apartment, without signs of forced entry. Scissors have disappeared, as have knives, on a regular basis. Aloe plants have melted mysteriously, smelling of vinegar during an afternoon."

He folded his arms across his chest, in Indian fashion, almost making her laugh. He used to do that when he was a kid! "I didn't want to concern you about it, but, for the past 2 years, mysterious liquids have appeared in my refrigerator, labeled *Coca-Cola* or *Milk*, with new additives which made deep migraines or mysterious stomach aches instead.

"What do you want me to do about it?" Big said.

"That's all you've got to say!" Channah said.

"You're changing the subject, Channah!" he said. "You're supposed to *produce.*"

"How can I, living with such conditions? That all was your doing, Ben, wasn't it?" she demanded.

"Don't be ridiculous!" he said. "Of course, not.", then he laughed nastily, slamming the front storm door behind him. "You're going to have to move out if you don't find a new job!"

Regarding the malicious mischief and petty larcenies, they had not stopped after

Expose: The Reckoning by Channah Gambit

Duvey moved in with her. Now, they loomed big in her mind as a problem. She had finally had enough abuse, especially after the resignation from St. Joaquin. "I've decided to speak to a friend at the District Attorney's Criminal Complaint Bureau." she told a colleague, Terry, on the phone, in September.

The visit was short, but to the point. Warren Felgood advised her to protect herself, put all the malicious mischief incidents into writing, and file a complaint. "And, he's your landlord, so your dad will have to be the chief defendant."

"Fine with me. He's the one who passed out six keys to my front door to the neighbors and family members, from here to Oshkosh. It's a f-ing bus stop! OOPS! Excuse my language." she said.

"Yes." Warren said, after reading her submittal. "You go down to Family Court now. You have grounds for an Order of Protection against the Landlord."

She went quite readily, not considering the consequences, and appeared with her petition, before Judge Skinner. She vented and expressed indignation, citing from her complaint to the District Attorney's Bureau. It was granted, as a *Do Not Disturb* Order of Protection. It was to be served later that evening, to an astonished Daddy, who trumpeted with rage.

Daddy Gambit, failing to see that he had been selected only because he was the legal landlord, reacted with unbelievable savagery. His son contested with a protection order of his own, filled with innuendo and slander.

At every opportunity, Daddy Gambit expressed, his shock, humiliation, and anger at the unspeakable things she had put into writing. There were now altercations every morning in the garage, each of them taking a side of the vehicle, as he would prepare to go out for his breakfast and paper. He would be delayed in getting to C & P Coffee Shop by the degree of tolerance she displayed in listening to his tirades. Things began to get out of perspective.

The Order of Protection was granted to the landlord on the basis of lies, and put into effect. Increasingly malnourished, with an inattentive son concentrating on school alone, Channah avoided the problem, and spent one afternoon at the kitchen table, deciding about her fruitless job search. She could not avoid the fact that her pension was being delayed, as promised by the previous employer. Finally, it was. She deposited in Commerce bank Going to the vault, she placed all her most important legal documents there. Instead of spending money on a new apartment, she began to use the money for motel stays after arguments, or pointless trips in the cold to other towns to seek hire. Although the car was bound to be foreclosed, and insurance had lapsed, she sometimes drove it illegally. Still, she had notified Toyota it was ready to be picked up.

There was busy work to do, but no interviews, even after walking around downtown Long Ditch all day. This was a repeat of so many days prior. No one would give her a part time try out. She walked around in the freezing cold, or brought a bicycle in. Where were the kindnesses? The charitable souls? Who owned this god-awful town of theirs? It wasn't her town anymore, not an iota of it, not at all. She knew that her work history was spotty and had too many employers. She still thought she might get a chance with a retail outlet. Nobody would offer a teacher, with so much qualification in a professional field, a step down job. On top of that, business was bad, and little reason to hire existed in that town this winter. Businesses were losing money daily.

More and more, her son refused to visit, or to bring home groceries. He passed her ten or twenty dollars once a week, and urged her to see doctors. He didn't comprehend that Mom had no health insurance at all, and little means to pay out of pocket. She began to develop chronic headaches from the cold, and some of the tainted suspect food. She was getting a little crazy and fearful with each new theft while she was away. Her son, Duvey, was capitalizing it, and relishing calling his mother *paranoid.*

After all, here was a fifty-three year old woman driving around on a ten-speed--in December. When relatives came to visit upstairs, no one stopped in with a kind word, a bag of groceries, or even to fight. Her weight continued to drop, and she had a chronic sniffle. What bothered her most was the way the women in her family were ignoring her. This went on from early December well into late January.

She was able, however, in January, to begin to buy small amounts of food with the pension money. She settled some problems with creditors. Also, she used church food pantries to stretch her budget. Part of her guilt was in turning to Christians for charity, because her background was Jewish. This was a Big bone of contention, at least in playacting, between herself and the Gambit family.

Mr. Gambit's credit was getting used up to pay his utility bills and partial tax payments. He blew his top at night regularly, when Big would stop by, to visit and console him. His savings were being eaten up, because he had "…trusted, relied, and counted on my crazy daughter for support. I should have had my head examined!"

When she was released by Officer Barney, (or Detective--there is a bit of confusion to this day), she came back to a situation which was untenable. For one thing, someone in the family was still determined to evict her. Though knowing that she was down to few pennies, without a job, without savings…her own nearest kin did not so much as allow her a can of soup. They were oblivious upstairs, spending their time watching television from morning to night. When they weren't doing that, they were opening doors to her apartment, and shouting at her regarding small things like using the washer/drier incorrectly.

Then, one day, prior to the foreclosure, she decided to take apart the apartment, *in preparation for what might happen.* Before doing this, she broke out her Instamatic 35 mm camera and took a full set of photos of her apartment. Then, she wept prodigiously for over ten minutes, feeling sorry for herself. Munching on popcorn, the best she could do for lunch, she found some places to start, and began to sort papers out in the garage, formerly from college studies. The garage door, with its electric eye, began to open, indicating the automatic door opener eye had been beeped in Daddy Gambit's car, still a block away. Running into the apartment through the inside entrance, she slammed the deadbolt home. He later accused her in a new Order of Protection, of stealing his stored possessions.

In fact, what had occurred, was that she had removed some mementoes of his printing business years, so as to recall her father in future years to come, as she anticipated she would be leaving the Gambits forever shortly. The items included a scrapbook of some of his early design work, a few mechanicals he had made as a commercial artist, and an invoice from the print shop. They were rubbish, about to be

Expose: The Reckoning by Channah Gambit
picked up by a garbage truck.

It was a very nice apartment, as she surveyed it nervously, mentally saying *adios* inside. Split level, with the upstairs suite of two bedrooms, with a central bathroom containing a real tub. Soft carpeting in the rooms, and large sliding double door closets, a pair of them, in hers. Duvey's room done in red, painted fraternally by both of them the week before he moved in. She chuckled, remembering how he had hummed Sixties songs the whole time, how the taped edging on the ceiling had been only partly successful, how it had been freezing cold as he was moving in in January. *Angelic* Stephen Randell, her ex-spouse, insisted on a date like that in order to permit her a year to claim him as a tax exemption. Kindness was not his strong suit. There had been many fine days, with shopping for furniture together at Ikea, having Duvey's friend Mike Mornan over to put the two bookcases together with over 40 nuts and bolts. She, springing for a pizza and soda for the crew, and a $25 tip in Mornan's pocket for aiding his chubby, inept chum get it all done. Afterward, there had been the black entertainment center's acquisition, the purchase by Duvey of a kit computer, refurbished, out of the Midwest.

Expose: The Reckoning by Channah Gambit

Chapter 5: Duvey Gets Whacked?

She had some time, once, late in the month of January, 2006, to recall that strange incident with the break out from the bathroom in late last April, which she shuddered to think about right now. It had been so inexplicable, so unsettling--after that, his personality changed, and Duvey became more distant and moody. If he ate at all, it had to be take out. The galley kitchen, with it's well stocked refrigerator, no longer interested him, except as a place to throw his dirty dishes, or leave started bottles of soda in the cold fridge for later. At least they were not beer bottles!

"You seem to be losing weight." she would say, and he'd absent-mindedly nod.

Her mind wandering, Channah thought back to another, happier time when they were together:

It was one of those timeless, boring Passover sedars at Gambits' house. The kids were half sleepy from feasting. The women of the family had pulled together, since the matriarch, a real *balabusta* was deceased, and cooked various dishes, served buffet.

Daddy Gambit spent half the night watching television, keeping to his invariable routine, as if nothing was happening. He was overwhelmed with the hubbub in his home. All nieces and nephews were sharing stories, laughing, and *noshing* the remains of the hor durves on the couches. The television in the living room, set to Nickelodeon, was entertaining the younger ones, who had kicked off their shoes and lay sprawled on the broadloom in front of the set. The older cousins were in earnest conversation on the couches, talking college and boyfriends, girlfriends and the weather. Mellow was entertaining her new boyfriend, Ralph, with stories about the good old days, when the clan met over at Julius Gambit's small home on East Penn street, where hundreds of greedy eaters devoured Susie's matzo balls and chopped liver. Mellow was in her element, in a new skirt, with a little too much rouge on her face, according to Jamo, who did not care for her aunt. She thought she was loud-mouthed, and brassy, cheap, and a pain in the neck for treating Channah, her mom, so badly most of the time. Channah was busy in the kitchen, working on the tray of *kugel* to be served. She had Duvey busy, carving the turkey, since he was deli trained. Duvey, delighted, had his sleeves rolled up, and was digging into the endeavor, in earnest, his cousin Greg seated there, telling him about some new video game.

The kitchen was heated up from cooking, the windows perspiring, and both boys red faced, talking animatedly. "I'm up the level three," Greg said. "I'm going to win a prize for this program design."

"Oh yeah?" Duvey said, his mouth stuffed with a piece of meat, "Here, have some." He gave Greg a small piece. "So, you really like Florida?"

"I sure do. I'm not coming back."

"Well, I'd like you to design a poker game for me--on the Internet--Texas Stick'em."

"Never heard of that."

Channah pushed some hair out of her eyes, groping for a placemat. She had literally used up every available pot of her mother's in the kitchen. Thoroughly enjoying herself, she stacked laden platters on the kitchen table, utilizing every available space for a server. "Come on boys! Almost time!"

Running to the head of the stairs, Mellow called out "Dad!" and set some empty wine glasses down in the kitchen. All were now seated, except for the children. It was a long, drawn-out five course dinner. They did not do the seder for more than a half hour. Then, they put the *haggadahs* to the side and attacked the gefilte fish.

Afterward, while the women cleared the table, the boys went back to the carpet, sprawling on the floor and wrestling.

"Aunt Melodee, you'd better take some action photographs!" Justin said, tussling with his cousin Greg. Aunt Karen, Big's wife, came in, and started to grab Duvey around the butt, squeezing him until he collapsed into gales of helpless merriment, laughter causing his eyes to tear.

Channah came in, hearing the roar, and started to laugh at the sight.

"I'm giving you a wedgie," Aunt Karen was saying, embarrassing him even more with her rough horseplay. "Stop--. Stop--I can't breathe!" Duvey said, trying to turn over.

Mellow came over with a camera, and took some shots. "These will be great blackmail pictures for you, when you get married!" She said.

Greg stood up and watched. Justin and his sister, looking in amusement at each other, cracked up laughing--pointing at their mother. Karen stood up, "Whew!' she said. "What a holiday. That's enough boys! Why don't you do something to help--I know, why don't you take out the garbage!"

They hurriedly complied. The whole upper level of the split ranch was full of steam, smoke, and the smell of roasted foods. Daddy Gambit, not having eaten much at all, watched from a rocking chair as motion moved all around him.

The women began to clean up, and make coffee for dessert. Mellow and Channah, friendly for a while, busily split the leftover food into "Care Packages" as Channah put it.

The men, seated around the dining room table, talked.

"So you think the Giants will win this year?"

"I don't know. I don't care. I'm a Jets fan." Ralphie said. "Your wife better not try to give ME a *wedgie*, Big."

Big looked at him with total amusement, his eyes narrowed into little slits of brown enjoyment. Rubbing his stomach with one hand, he said "You don't want to marry into this family, unless you want a pot belly."

All the women served dessert together. Everyone sat around, totally satiated. There was a pause of movement, and the family moment hung suspended in time, forever. In the middle of the noise and hub-bub, Channah looked at her tall, handsome son, blushing for him, at the embarrassment he had experienced, getting *wedgied.*

Karen is just a little vulgar, just a little too coarse for me to stand. she thought to herself. *She better keep her hands to herself.* She recalled how Karen's brother Doug, a hospital employee, was in the habit of emailing his sister raunchy, off-color jokes every morning. She had to admit the woman was a perfect match for her down-to-earth, no-frills sibling.

She brought the present into focus and looked around, quite alone. Channah shuddered slightly, with the silence.

The sharp cherry wood paneled downstairs kitchen and living room, with her computer office corner, adjacent to the foyer entry of the Florida room, all glass: how proud to recall it when looking at photographs months later! The soft futon, white and virginal, never used--pine and solid, anticipated gift to her daughter up in Boston sooner or later had been a symbol of achievement when she bought it. "The world has simply gone mad", she told a therapist. As she surveyed her world, built cheap to provide comfort, it seemed precariously posed on a cliff.

Why had Duvey grown so distant? It was just one disquieting reason for dismay. "Are you in love?" she asked him.

"No, Mom." he said. "I've just found a guy to help me do my computer homework. He lives in Forest Hills. Got to go there now. I'll be home tomorrow."

"You have to sleep there?" she said, hearing the sound of the garage door opening.

On another occasion, she caught his sleeve and said "You know, I'm trying to understand you?"

"Yes, Mom. I know, but--why don't you find a job instead." he said, closing his bedroom door in her face.

This is how he had been since last Spring, she told herself. She remembered back to that day. Driving up the driveway, she had entered the apartment, only to find a large amount of splintered wood all over the upstairs foyer. The bathroom door was in smithereens. "Duvey? Where are you?" she called.

Duvey was not around for an explanation. "Hello, Steve? Is Duvey there?" she asked, having phoned his job. "You're okay!' she said, when he answered, but flinched as he stammered and swore once or twice on the phone. "I'll explain when I get home, Mom." he said, hanging up.

That night, he did not return before ten o'clock. She was waiting for him to get there, seated at the kitchen table, reading the newspaper. "What ever happened?" she said.

"Pretty stupid of me," he said, his face red and flushed. "I find that peculiar! You're anything but stupid."

"I took a shower, and when I went to leave the bathroom, there was no way--the knob had gotten loosened--probably by YOU!" he pointed a finger at her. "And it just kept turning and turning around. I didn't have any clothing to put on. There I was like a jerk wearing just a towel! So I started yelling and screaming for Grandpa upstairs to come down and open the door."

"Yes, go on." she said.

Gaining confidence, her son continued. "But, you know how he's deaf, so no matter how hard I yelled, he didn't come down." He looked sheepish. "Finally, after an hour or so, I got fed up. I was getting cold. So I just *ka-chunged* the door, around the knob a few times."

"You are kidding me." she said.

Duvey laughed awkwardly. "I got a few good kicks in too, and thank god it's hollow, it gave way, and I got out, finally." He flushed again, perspiring.

Expose: The Reckoning by Channah Gambit

"I don't know what to do about it." she said.

"Oh, don't worry about it. I'll pay for it and all." he said. "My friend Mornan will fix it. He knows how to build things. He's an electrician." he said, inanely. Then he did something stranger: he did an about face, and left the room.

She stared after him, then swiveled around to face her own front room, with the entry way into the apartment, choosing to think about other things, like the impending move elsewhere. Her mind cast back to a moment, long ago, when her other child had had a mishap, and she had become frightened. They were so frightening, and you were not always the reason for what took place, but felt guilty, as a parent, just the same.

Duvey was delicate, with a large head and eyes, when young. They were always open in a questioning, perplexed expression. He watched the world in wonder. She liked to give him a nap in the afternoon, and watch his sweet, slow breaths go in and out, in and out, the little chest rise and fall. Such a miracle, that this little being was made from the fabric of her and him, the Other. She'd put him in the rocker seat, soft cushioned, on the floor, as she worked on quilted curtains for the living room.

There were only two rooms there, with a half kitchen, deep below the earth, in the dank basement apartment. To come down to the storm door was eight steps, but the light shown in for at least four hours daily, so she thought it wasn't so bad. Rent was outrageous, at $850 a month. Stephen wasn't working as hard as he might have. At least he had a job.

The sassy seat, at the edge of the kitchen table, contained the other tousle head, fair-haired, sweet, with those soft blue orbs which seemed to contain so much light when baby Jamo looked and watched or blinked. There had been a nasty scare this week, and the little head had a bandage on the side. The sassy seat had been stable. Momo had put it, for some reason, on top of the kitchen table, to watch her daughter better, as she cooked *chapattis* for the Indian-style dinner with curry they'd be having, just the two of them, when he got home from his day job, and the two little ones were in the crib and in the little bed, put to sleep after bathing.

But silly, delicate Jamo, for some reason, while there, had suddenly leaned her body into a curl, and rolled a somersault, head over heels, out of the sassy seat, cracking her nape on the edge of the hard wood veneer pine circular edge, and then cascading in an eternal moment, so frustratingly out of reach from mother's grasping fingertips, head over heels, until she landed on the floor in a heap. Then, the inevitable wail and hysterics, phone calls to Brass, the pediatrician. The father away at his job was no help. Channah had to call a neighbor, to watch Duvey, while the taxi bore them both away to the doctor's office.

Miraculously enough, Jamo's reflexes were intact, and she was "just fine", as Dr. Brass pronounced. How could that be? It was, though, so Channah quickly paid the $80 cash she had for emergencies. Dr. Brass, was nice, but she hadn't been able to escape from his prying, disapproving eyes. "Do not put a sassy seat on top of furniture. Keep her on the floor, Mrs. Randall, for goodness sakes!" he had said, peering over his glasses like a copy of Ben Franklin, pursing his lips and saying "tsk, tsk, tsk" to her retreating back.

When she had returned home, and thanked Tom and Agatha Smith next door, for

Expose: The Reckoning by Channah Gambit

returning her other baby, she had sighed, and put them to bed--noticing the cold food on the server. Then giving the sassy seat a viscious little kick. She then cursed, and took a beer out of the refrigerator, even though it was *his.* When Steve got home later, she didn't mention it. They embraced, he held her head, with its bright brown hair, against his right shoulder, "peace, togetherness, serenity" messages emanating in the touch, tender and so meaningful.

The pregnancy had been *high risk*, for Jamo, and Duvey as well--so their lovemaking had stopped for quite a bit of the past three years. But now--that was behind them, and, who knew, they might, once again, entertain, socialize, see the *machatenesters*.

The night lay ahead, with the mandatory nursing she alone could provide.

The night was cold, damp and windy behind the screens there. They left most of the lights burning, hating the dismal place. They spoke about moving, while making love on the bed. Afterward, he cradled her head, they both listened to the sweet sounds coming from the crib and cot against the wall, and fell asleep.

The *Florida room*, totally made of glass windows was too cold now for use. It contained storage items, like her art supplies, basket collection, and the air conditioners, huge ugly metal monsters, their pipes covered with a purple tarp in a corner, squeezing out all the space. She decided to get busy, to take her mind off other things.

The sounds of her seven parakeets in their huge gold bird hotel, usually cheering to her ears and heart, reminded her that they couldn't stand a move.

Getting on the phone, she called *Parrots of the Century*.

"Hey, Paul?" she said. "I have some foster kids in need of a new home."

"Hi, when are you going to hold another political night at your place." Paul Alcatrez said, laughing into the receiver. "You sure tried to get Dean elected."

"Not anytime soon." She wanted to see him again. He was tan, agile, and fit--but taken.

"Sure, I'll find them a new home--all seven." he said. Channah kept herself busy to avoid worrying about Duvey for two more hours, then fixed some dinner. The bird hotel and snake plant were auctioned off on Ebay, and grassroots Craig's List, listed some furniture and textiles. She was only discarding inessential things, still believing that she would, in the future, salvage and move them to some new apartment. But, she would not be able to rely on her son to drive the truck!

Reverie #2--losing the sewing machine- levittown

` "When that other pension check comes in on April 15th, as promise--we're going to find a new place together!" she told Duvey honestly, but he avoided her eyes. Later, she'd discover that the traitor had already called his father, asking to return home

The antics of next door neighbors, Efram and Rivet Kopf, which occurred in January, produced a partial breakdown. "That's what you get for being a *Peeping Nelly*." she'd later to Dr. Kilkiny in therapy. Efram was a diamond merchant, living in common law with a beautiful Brazilian brokerage portfolio manager for Merrill Lynch. They had bought the split-level ranch on the right the previous Spring, and appeared to be charming, wealthy, Jewish people, who entertained frequently. Channah noticed a Jaguar

Expose: The Reckoning by Channah Gambit

in the driveway. She invited them over, during the Summer,for cheese and crackers. They responded with a bottle of white Zinfandel. Although there was some interesting conversation, no friendship developed. "They're way out of my league." she thought. "I don't have a million dollar portfolio to manage." and laughed.

.One night that January, she observed a party taking place in their living room, through the front bay window. A loud argument was going on between Efram and a guest, some tall, youthful man in his twenties with an unruly mop of long, frizzy auburn hair, who caught her attention. Much later, she watched the guests leave, through her own bedroom window. Following that, her interest was piqued by the arrival of a doctor, clearly apparent from the vanity plate. He entered their home, stayed for about an hour, then left.

A fitful sleep took hold of her around midnight, and she did not wake until about 630 a.m.. She had slept in her clothes. A pale gray light illuminated pine trees, she noticed, as she gazed out her window. Over on his side, Efram, was doing something difficult on his driveway. He was taking something from the garage, something heavy, in a plastic bag, shaped rather like a basketball, and placing it in a plastic trash can on a dolly. Then Efram, red faced from exertion, wheeled the thing all the way down to the sidewalk, then traveled down the block to the home, six doors away. He waited there, then unloaded the can on the curb. A, a garbage truck, bright yellow, with many blinking orange lights all over it, drove up to him, after a few minutes. Two men got out, loaded a bag into the rear, and drove away. Efram slowly trundled the empty dolly back to his garage, went in, then closed the electric door.

She did not recollect all this, until later that morning. Stepping out to the garbage can herself, an hour later, she noted the arrival of the regular truck. How should she explain the *special pickup* of two hours earlier? She began to make wild conclusions. Her puzzlement increased as she watched the neighbors drive off to work, sometime later. "No one is sick there, so--why was there a doctor's visit? Doctors don't make house calls anymore." she thought. "Maybe what I witnessed was a crime!" This was not good for morale. "Thank goodness, I didn't become a friend."

There was a discovery later that week in January which drove her berserk. In Duvey's disheveled, dirty and slovenly room, warren with dirty clothing, cans of spent soda, and match books, she had discovered a strange key on the carpet, while *straightening up*. It had a hole through the top: obviously a back door key. Really curious, she had tried every door in her own home, and then, because of something else she had once witnessed, walked over to Efram's house, quickly, while he was away at work. On the back steps leading to his rear door, there were large footprints permanently stained there. Someone mounting had stepped on wet creosote. The size of the shoe was enormous, like her son's size 16 feet. "Oh, my God!" she thought, finding that the key turned the lock in Efram's back door. This had occurred in October. Returning downstairs, she had decided that he had had a brief affair the previous summer with Efram's Cindy, daughter from a previous marriage, who had been visiting next door. The girl was a vivacious, beautiful brunette. Duvey had probably met her in town, and things had *blossomed*..

Now, with the trundling of the *ball* to the pick up, some concealment seemed to be going on. She thought, *Perhaps the ball is actually a body part, like a head. He's disposing of a body. I know I am not quite normal today, but I'm going to call somebody in authority. No, better, yet, I'll write it up and mail it to the Attorney General, Elliot Spitzer. Let him investigate.* So she did. Along with the complaint, or eyewitness account, she included the key from her son's room.

She was scared for her son. His aloofness and concealment of a *secret relationship* made him a figure of speculation day to day. She went ahead, and sent a duplicate of the letter to Spitzer to the F.B.I. Down at the Long Branch Post Office, clerk Peter Lorry took the last $18 she had.

Why was her life so chaotic, so out of control? She thought about it, visiting the mirror in the upstairs hall, to stare into her misty, distracted hazel eyes. *You're an educated lady--you practically have a Master's degree. You know the score; you've studied psychology and run a business and yet...something is happening that's criminal, someone's trying to hurt you--and the only suspect you can come up with is a family member?* She put on a sweater, looking at her checkbook ledger, down to the last fifty dollars. She had a premonition something worse was in store for her. As if on cue, there was a knock, and two beefy sheriff's officers said hello at her front door. "I've still got a scar under the eye from walking into a fire door at The Tertiary School." she was thinking. "I'll nurse it with a chamomile tea bag on the sofa. How do I pay for therapy?" She opened the door. Adding to pressures, and much to her dismay, she was served with Daddy Gambit's Temporary Order of Protection. . Oh, my gosh, I'm having an anxiety attack. I'm reading this first-rate *purple prose* about my mental illness written in superlatives into this Petition" Her face turned purple, she thought she would faint, "This is the big *get even.*" It was the non-harassment kind, and claimed she stole printing items from the garage recently.

Duvey wasn't in the mood to talk when he returned from a poker night at Mornan's house. Just the same, Channah confronted him in the kitchen. "Here, have some bread."

"Don't want any now, Mom. It's too late. Let me go to bed."

"Duvey, what's going to be with us?" she asked, hands placed on her hips in a cliché manner of spunk.

'What? I can't give you any money, Mom. I give you rent."

"Yes, you do. It's not money." Channah said.

"Then what do you want, Mom?" he said, not meeting her eyes.

"Look, I found something in your room. I need it explained."

"What, you were in my room, again?" he said, his eyes darkening. "I told you to keep out! I close the door, it stays closed. I can't take this anymore!" he said.

"I am sorry--but you don't clean."

"I will, I will." he said.

"No you won't. The clothes on the floor start to smell, then we get roaches." Before she knew it, they had gotten into a familiar argument. It went on, continuing as he walked upstairs. But this time, he did something unexpected.

"And what about the key?"

"They key? The key? What the hell are you talking about?" he said, picking up a knapsack. He began picking up jeans and black tees from the bookcase, stuffing them in.

"What are you doing?"

"I've had enough. I'm leaving." he said.

"Just like that? Now? You can't." she said.

"Oh, I have to. Yes, I can. I can't help you anymore." Duvey said, throwing in some belts, some books, notebooks, and his lighter.

"Look, this is a bad time."

"It's your own fault. You are crazy, and you are making me too. I can't work anymore, I can't be the one to support you."

"I know." she said.

"No, you don't. You don't know how crazy you've been acting. I came here to get away from craziness. It's just as bad here." Duvey stopped for a moment, looking down at his hands. He was a big, petulant teenager, strong, intelligent, and helpless with the waves of emotion flowing over him. "I spoke to Dad, and he told me you're sick. I have to admit--you have been acting crazy lately."

"What are you talking about? Why now, huh? Why do you have to hurt me now?"

I" don't know. It's just now, that's all. I can't help it. You told me last week that you thought somebody is actually putting shit in your soda? You're f-king *paranoid*." he said, his voice rising an octave from the usual baritone.

"I am not *paranoid.*" she yelled, mimicking his tone of voice exactly. "It's true."

"I don't have time for this. I can't--no, I *won't* deal with it anymore. You want to know about a key? I don't have to tell you anything!" He started to move to the stairs. Channah realized she was blocking his way, and stepped aside.

It felt like a divorce. She had relied on him so completely. Until the moment when he actually opened the front door, letting in a stream of frigid winter air, she wasn't a believer. "Where's your coat? I bought two of them for you. Don't leave without a coat!" she told him.

"You see how you've got me? I don't even remember to put on a jacket. Look, Mom, I just am going to have to stay with a friend for a while. I can't take Dad, I can't stand you when you're like this--"

"But how will I reach you? Don't leave, Duvey!" she screamed at him, tears welling up in her eyes, starting to cry at the understanding he had planned this.

"I'm sorry. You can call me at work. Here's some money." He threw a twenty dollar bill on the floor. She stood at the glass paned front door, watching him walk toward his black Camero, the day sack slung over his right shoulder. *He's already on the damned cell phone calling Mike. That's all he cares about. I've lost the last one, forever.* she thought helplessly, slowly closing the door and locking it.

Sitting on the couch for several hours, she tried to work out a plan. "I am intelligent, educated, a college graduate, for god's sake. There must be something I can do now! Let's see, I have the second installment of my IRA coming in, a bit of credit--finding some small room shouldn't be impossible." she told herself. "Maybe I'll travel down to Bethesda with the Accent before it's repossessed. Cousin Bill will take me in."

Expose: The Reckoning by Channah Gambit

She opened the refrigerator, removing a *Miller Lite* Duvey had left behind, and twisted off the cap savagely, taking a swig. "The Sheriff's injunction is to avoid family members. I'm fed up, and more than ready to go."

"Duvey, oh Duvey--why did you leave?" Sitting on the futon, she cradled the beer bottle in her hands. The pending eviction was two weeks away. Channah needed more time, to put her property into self-storage. Her forehead puckered in concentration. Rising to her feet after an hour, she found the medicine cabinet, and swallowed Ibuprofen gel-tabs.

She fell into a daydream. The Manor Haven apartment below ground, the weekly band practices, evasions, and long weekend jobs away had made her suspicious regarding his fidelity. Then, it had come: the denouement. She had discovered a receipt from Gurney's Inn in Montauk: an overnight slip for two. There were also a few inexplicable charges itemized on the Verizon bill--one, in particular, on the night Duvey had been born. While she had stayed at the hospital, he had apparently phoned an outside call, charged to their number, *from a local motel. It's painfully obvious.* she thought to herself. *It's so horribly cliché. The only thing he hasn't done is left a blond hair on his lapel. But then, he was never one for business suits, anyway.*

Home daily with the two babies, she had not returned to the workforce. Now, she frantically decided to leave him, aghast at his betrayal. She woke baby Duvey, dressed him in a layette item, and placed him in the small stroller. Jamo, she had all ready, strapped to her back in the saucy carrier. God, she was heavy--almost twenty-five pounds at age four. She took the children, some bottles, diaper supplies, put on a straw hat, and slowly left him. Up the stairs, make a left at the end of the walkway, onto the sidewalk, and "Away we go!" she told herself. He had been gone for long hours. Plenty of money, perhaps a motel--at least they could make it to Manhedren, the next town over.

I simply have to walk. I can't believe what he had done to us. She walked slowly, pushing the stroller. It was a warm Summer day, and over a month since she had been released from North Shore University Hospital, after suffering post-partum depression. Still taking medication, she was numb, and feeling no pain.

Jamo was happy, gurgling in her ear, simpering and prattling. Not worried about her, Channah kept walking. Four miles, five, and even though Duvey was napping comfortably, Jamo had gotten fussy. It was late in the day, after three. They had passed the many businesses along the Shore road. The Pearson Publishing Group, where she had worked as an editor prior to the pregnancy had fallen far behind. The shopping center with its traffic on the left had been a diversion. She had no need to stop, and wasn't really thinking about what to do next. Aimlessly wandering, they followed over a little bridge, pausing to sit on a bench to watch the ducks. Jamo was happy, reaching out to them, eager to explore, but Channah didn't allow it. She felt the loss of her man, deeply. She was totally alone, solo again--with responsibilities. How could she leave him, with the two babies? She just had to! She walked on, starting to tire.

At the Manhaven road, she turned right, passing Anchor Park. At a loss, she began to wonder how she would ever get back. Jamo, walking now beside her, was beginning to tire and pull on her hand. At the park, she turned right, spying a little dock.

I'm acting crazy. I have to stop doing this. I can't run away from my problems,

Expose: The Reckoning by Channah Gambit

the marriage, or him. she told herself, sitting the children and herself on a little bench, to watch the boats for a while. They stayed for three hours. She fed Duvey his bottle, and gave Jamo a banana. *Maybe if I go back, he'll never know what I did. I can retrieve that good bye note I left on the kitchen table. I'll just have to pretend for a while.*

She walked the children slowly and carefully up to an insurance office, and opened the door.

"Hi, I'm sorry to bother you." she said to the young woman, a brunette receptionist at the desk. "May I please use your phone to call a cab? My cell phone battery just died." The woman glanced at Jamo in her pretty red dress and smiled. "Sure," she said, offering Channah a seat and the receiver. After about fifteen minutes, the taxi came, they were driven home, and she put the two of them to bed, placating them because they were fussing and fretting. *Whew, close call.* She tore up the note, sitting down in the rocking chair, exhausted.

I didn't leave him until a year after that--but that is actually the day I left Stephen, that day, she thought now.

After a pointless trip to the Department of Health and Human Services, she decided to call some relatives once more. Mrs. Rodriguez had been very supportive, but withheld funds.

"It's not quite morning yet, Channah." she said. "You were working. It's not clear you resigned with justifiable cause, so unemployment is unavailable. And---you have that large pension check arriving in January. What can I do? You have no money now? I can give you a little food stamp allowance, once, okay?"

"Sigh." Channah managed.

Channah phoned Joseph Bee again, and left a message on his answering machine. "I'm totally destitute. My car is being repossessed by Toyota Finance. Credit card debts have doubling penalties--they're growing monstrous in size--Mr. Bee, what should be done?"

He phoned the next day. "Sorry, I can't be of much help. You haven't retained me. You have 30 days legally to stay there. Yes, use the car if you must--technically speaking, you're breaking the law." *Click.*

Channah thought of another attorney who might advise her: Antony Packins of Hempstead, who specialized in school law. His subsequent mistreatment during her imprisonment would mimic Bee's. Although he had been provided with documents which could work as an alibi, he did not respond to phone calls from the jail, for months. He had not been retained. Period. Now, he did not respond to a voice mail message. "Class acts, Mr. Bee and Mr. Packins." she told herself, packing a suitcase.

The next morning, Joseph Bee did, giving her an appointment. "Now of course, things will get better, even if I'm evicted."

Channah walked into town on a day, with the wind chill factor, of 21 degrees. He answered the door almost immediately. She gazed at Mr. Bee half-attentively, as he told her his background. He was tall, ram-rod thin, and quite attractive, with auburn hair cut into a crew cut, and a smooth, aquiline, clean-shaven appearance. He dressed professionally, even on days off, she was certain. Pausing for a moment, she considered his appearance, sans wardrobe. Alas, he was wearing a wedding ring, and her gaze shifted. "How long has your family been in Long Ditch?" she asked.

"I have Law Enforcement in my family--in my blood, so to speak! It's quite an asset to my practice." he said. He listened well to his new client, and heard her story out, without speaking for a long time. She could see that this was the type of attorney who had his own practice, *sans* secretary, and kept total confidentiality. He seemed most trustworthy. If only she could afford him!

His aid, however, was only determined by how much cash was placed in his palm. A lot of local attorneys, including Legal Aid lawyers, were like this, she'd discover in future months.

As a former assistant District Attorney, Bee inevitably sided with the Office of the District Attorney Kathleen Rosenby, and was quite amusing and helpful in presenting characterizations and opinions of various personalities there. "I'll be the first to admit she's a hard-liner." he stated carefully. He also was, he laughed, judging clients guilty right from the start, based on gut feeling, so there was little to say or do to change his opinion in the next fifteen minutes. "Like you," he said, gazing into her hazel eyes, "You look guilty as hell, but I can tell you don't deserve to be shoved out in the cold, because Gambit apparently made promises to you to shelter you long ago. You're his daughter, for Christ's sake!"

"Thank you so much. I'll do what you suggest. I'm sorry I can't pay more." Heading to the library, she wrote up a rejection letter, then mailed it marked *certified* to Big. Feeling much saner, she walked home, to discover that Duvey was gone, and Big had changed the locks, barring entry downstairs.

She called on Helga's cell phone, from the neighbor's porch. "Sorry, Mom. Uncle Ben gave me a key to the front door, but told me not to give you a copy. I can visit there and remove my stuff, and you can come in while I'm there to get yours, but we can't live there now."

"How about this? I saw a lawyer, and we have a month to move out, legally." she said.

"Really? That's great! I'll be right there. Sorry, Mom. I'm at work. I'll be home in about two hours."

Next, she tried to call Daddy Gambit upstairs. She heard his television blaring in the back room, but he did not answer. Giving up, she sat in her car, on the driveway, running the motor to keep warm. If she could not pay insurance, at least she could heat it up! Duvey drove up in his black Camero at about 9 p.m., to let her in, then left, without comment.

After a fitful night's sleep, Channah arose the next morning to find a note on the kitchen table.. "We are very sorry." the letter stated. "But you're not Special. You know Dad expected certain things from you and you failed to deliver. He is justified in seeking a new tenant, as he spent $23,000 renovating the downstairs to make a legal two-family income residence for his retirement."

Blah, blah, blah. It went on and on, or so she thought, furiously. She had made an investment emotionally, staying on and keeping that apartment so that "someone familiar is downstairs--family--if you have a heart attack, Dad." No First Alert would ever be needed while Channah was alive. She was deeply grateful for his letting her live

Expose: The Reckoning by Channah Gambit
upstairs free for three years, to work her way through graduate school without having to pay rent. He had encouraged her, and she had encouraged him to resist Big and his wife Pauline, and remain independent and free, dying with his boots on.

"God, this whole incident is evil!" she said to Mellow's friend Pat at the drug store. "It is all the fault of Big and his greedy wife. They can't wait until Dad is six feet under. Then, they'll have their chunk of the estate. Where's the Pepto-Bismol?"

"Over there." Pat pointed behind her. The cashier tried not to listen, as they stood in an aisle. "How much cash would that be?"

"About 350 grand." Channah said, embarrassed at her anger.

"Gosh." Pat said. "I've talked to Mellow recently. Sure wish I could help you, but I don't want to get in-between you both."

"I understand." Channah rode a ten-speed home slowly, struggling against the wind. She hadn't retained Joseph Bee, and kicked herself mentally for that. She reminded herself that it would have taken the last bit of savings she had.

She thought about him, and all the people who were drawn to work for the District Attorney's office. It was like a revolving door. The Law Enforcement system in Nassau County was corrupt and berserk, harming peaceful, ordinary citizens who committed small infractions. As her own ordeal began, she would notice, in the manner of her arrest, that there was some kind of hidden agenda, particularly in the case of the Sheriff's Office, the conduct of Edwin Really and his cohorts. Now, she was hearing an echo of some deep realizations she was having regarding Family Court. They seemingly permitted petitions to pass which were full of specious lies and contrivances! How corrupt!

As January slowly passed, there was no official response from either the F.B.I. Or Elliot Spite's Complaint Unit in Albany regarding the crime next door. "Might have witnessed it." she told herself, frustrated. "I'm not getting any mail anymore except bills!"

Later, while she was held for four months at the county jail, Efram Kopf's marriage plan fell through, his fiancee left him, and they sold off the property at a loss, leaving Long Island. Channah speculated about the back door key and body parts disposal while the weeks passed in jail. She even confided in an elderly jail mate. She decided that the homicide had most likely been the young man with a shock of unruly hair she noticed. "I never saw him leave after the party that night." she told herself, remembering. His profile was indelibly marked in her memory, as he bore a striking resemblance to Stephen Randell, her ex-spouse, when he was 17--the looks of a man she had first fallen in love with, right after their high school graduation. "No wonder I remember him. It could have been my own son." she shuddered.

How did this whole thing begin, this *mess?* She asked herself, packing another suitcase, just in case she needed to retreat to a motel room.

Why did I have children? Where are they when I really need them? What is family for? She was staring at the cherry paneled wall in the den, the one on which, a few short years ago, she had hung several heavy items: the Bachelors Degree, her Masters Degree from Adelphi printed on parchment, and several New York State Certification

Expose: The Reckoning by Channah Gambit

Certificates, under heavy pressed glass. Such pride had burned in her chest at the time! There they were : tangible proof that a person could win despite poverty, a broken marriage, loss of custody, and domestic conflict.

"Gosh, take away anything you wish from me--my sofa, my birds, my computer--but don't ever try to take away my achievement--because that's all I've got." she said out loud. Then startled that she was talking to a framed photograph of her son, daughter, and ex-husband, she stood, slowly beginning to remove the diplomas, one by one--at first, slowly, then in a sudden frenzy, carefully folding them into towels and placing them into a valise. The photograph went in, on top, and she snapped it shut, locking it.

Expose: The Reckoning by Channah Gambit

Chapter 6: Strange Attacks

Channah has always been a rather mercurial, temperamental individual. Stability is not something she can attest to comfortably for she has suffered many hardships since the loss of her children in a custody battle and she was aware that she came from a horribly dysfunctional family.

When she was released by Detective Barney, she came back to a situation which was untenable. For one thing, someone in the family was still determined to evict her. Though knowing that she was down to few pennies, without a job, without savings, her own nearest kin did not so much as allow her a can of soup. They were oblivious upstairs spending their time watching television from morning to night. When they weren't doing that, they were opening doors to her apartment and shouting at her regarding small things like using the washer/drier incorrectly.

She had been suffering steady malicious mischief in the apartment for years, beginning January, 2003, when she moved in. She often found articles of clothes missing, placed there, or things like hair brushes and scissors. One time she had found her aloe plant died. It was sprayed or drenched in something which smelled like vinegar. By this time, she had a list of 8 key holders to her apartment. Dad had had two prior tenants, one family and one an Italian-German couple. He gave a key to the next door neighbors in case of fire, one to her brother, her sister, and her brother's best friend, a volunteer fireman.

Her son and daughter each had keys. She had no idea who was demonstrating spite towards her. She kept a careful journal. Just before the arrest, she finally got fed up when her towel disappeared and two strange ones surfaced there and took all her careful records of thefts down to the Complaint Unit of the District Attorney. William Brown, the Director there, listened carefully to her and looked at the affidavit she had.

"We can't be sure who is doing this, but formality dictates that you take out a protection order against the landlord, who in this case, is your father. He is responsible for what is happening on the premises." She did so.. Shortly after, her brother and father quickly put together a heavily worded, long winded document accusing her of mental illness and asked for a counter-protection order.

While this happened, she returned to the house after her first questioning. She was seriously upset and perturbed. Other things were going wrong as well. Her source of security after all the months of pilfering was her safe vault box at Commerce Bank. Originally, she kept her certifications, jewelry and records there, but recently, she began to use it for other things like her Will and affidavits on two happenings in the apartment.

One day in January, she went to her box and found a tissue inside. Someone had entered the box and tipped her off to it. She was livid. Dora, the customer service representative, referred her to the manager, Elizabeth Fergesi.

"No, we don't have an extra key." She stated. Later, Channah was to find this was not the case. The vault box 3-key system was illegal. Something was seriously wrong. And, once again, someone was on the attack against her, using techniques which reduced her to fear and created a situation conducive to producing paranoia.

"But I'm college-educated!" she told herself before going to bed nightly. "This is just too much to maintain appearances."

She was suffering from the almost daily demands of her father who would no longer allow her to come into his apartment. Big hired a locksmith one day to change all the locks in the house right after her January calling in for questioning. Strangely enough, her own son was the only one with a key to her apartment and possessions. He was the only one and sometimes he resisted letting her in. After all, he was planning secretly at the time to move out.

As a result of all this hostility, she was sometimes staying over at motels, using the precious little credit she had left. Channah began to consider seeking the help of more distant relatives.

Regarding mail, that too had begun to be pilfered in November, 2005. It started with regular delivery of her mail to the upstairs apartment, forcing her to retrieve it after dad examined it. It progressed to a period in December when there was no mail delivered for almost 3 weeks. This was most unusual. Therefore, she rented a box in the local post office. Still no mail. In the coming weeks there was little or no mail in her box. She was accustomed to receiving 4 pieces a day. A lot of legal mail was not coming in from attorneys she solicited or creditors. So she finally went to the Assistant Postmaster and complained in January. Nothing happened. She went to the former D.A., now practicing law privately, to get the correct advice. He told her to request an internal Post Office investigation. A Ms. Harris took the evidence from Channah and began her investigation. Channah pursued this for the next five months, but never got a reply to her inquiries. Mail delivery returned to normal after she was arrested in March, 2006.

The apartment vandalism was intensifying. Shortly after the Barney arrest, Channah found out someone had broken her new Lexmark printer. She took it down to a local computer store and asked them to analyze the damage. They told her it was totaled and offered her $40. I took it.

She did something foolish at this point, I admitted to herself that she must take it down to a local computer store to cash it in for money. Channah asked them to analyze the damage, they told her it was totaled and offered her $40. She took it.

That was the least of it. In February, she discover, to her horror, that someone had taken her futon apart and stolen it, replacing it with another cushion made up of shredded recycled carpet remnants and covered instead in black Haitian cotton. Someone had covered that with the old Kelly green slipcover, thinking she would never notice. She retaliated by taking this apart and storing it somewhere, marking it for evidence for later. Evidence of what, though? Channah was one scared lady. No one cared, no one watched, no one corroborated anything.

In January, while she was away on a trip, someone accessed her Commerce bank checking account and emptied it, so she thought, of about $1,900. By this time, her fear had reached the point where she was messing up her checkbook math. She was spending all the money running away to motels and on trips to visit distant relatives. Channah could not find a job and was walking into town. There was some kind of stone wall she was hitting, and not even part time work was coming her way. It was partly her fault because she had been a butterfly during her graduate school years, working odd jobs in unrelated fields. Everyone remembered that she was a teacher, so why was she coming back? They had congratulated her and wished her good fortune when she left.

In July, a scam artist had penetrated her email and kept telling her. She had won $6,000,000 and needed to give her personal identity information. Channah almost gave in, but decided to report it to the Assistant District Attorney who had it investigated. She printed out the correspondence which was traced back to Germany and turned over to European authorities. Concerned at the loss of vault box and all the trouble with the mail and with the apathy and hostility of family members she took all her legal papers including birth certificate, marriage license, children's birth certificates, mementos, and purchased a steel legal box with key lock. She placed in it her evidence against the school where she had resigned, her original complaint to New York State, her recollections, and the bench summons which was a warrant from the night of her arrest. Channah added microcassettes detailing everything she could remember about that night, all the violations of her rights and the injuries she received. One thing more, the documentation which proved that she did not have a working cell phone to make the alleged false report with 911.

Channah was leaning on her conversion to Catholicism. She was panicking, having PTSD, and not recognizing the strange attacks as symptoms. She was going to local churches and asking for sanctuary until finally someone helped her at the cathedral which ran her diocese. A kind priest permitted her to leave the legal box with him while she raised the money to ship it to someplace safe. St. Agnes would not hold the box for a parishioner from a local church but they were sympathetic. Channah was frantic. She decided to leave the country temporarily. She was disillusioned and fed up with local law enforcement. She felt as if she had been targeted, and that Barney had been bribed by her irrational brother and father. She chose Montreal, a city she visited once in the 1980's. She found a cathedral there and using Babelfish, wrote a letter in French and sent it. Channah phoned, initiated a proceeding, and in early January, she shipped her legal box to Canada after retrieving it from the cathedral of St. Agnes rectory. She truly breathed a sigh of relief. Later, she discovered that it was not a panacea, that lack of the summons in her hand as an excuse would not save her from being in contempt of Court. She had not noted the hearing date. Channah knew nothing of legal procedures, and did not have an attorney. Even her son was alarmed. He was receiving phone calls from the police once in a while, reminding him that she had a hearing to go to. He found her numbed, exhausted and starving. Channah had lost 10 pounds walking back and forth. He could not give her lifts all the time. He was the only one occasionally stuffing $10 into her hands for food. He was her lifeline and her daughter was not available and unresponsive.

Something else was hampering Channah, and that was the lack of a phone. In early December, while making a call on the Meadowbrook Parkway, her new cell phone was sucked out the window. She did not bother to stop. because she had a clause in her contract to replace a lost phone. That was not to be.

In the 12 weeks after that, she was unable to obtain a new one with her own phone number because Sprint provided a reclaim number with an unacceptable identification pass code. There were technical obstacles which just wouldn't permit her to get a phone back. Channah reported the loss around 12/10/05. Shortly after that, parties unknown found and began to use the phone. When she called back in January, 2006, Channah discovered that someone reactivated phone service. She was terrified, in light of the misdemeanor she had been charged with. The full directory contained the phone numbers of most of her friends and loved ones as well as business contacts. The mailbox proved to be full. Again, due to a technicality, she could not access her messages from an external trunk phone. Time slipped by. In January, truly alarmed, Channah asked service to deactivate the phone again and tag it as a possible identity fraud problem. So for at least 6 weeks, someone had her phone and full access to her family connections. Since she had someone prying into her family in July, she thought it might be the same con artist that had informed her that a relative "Lou Gable", a dead engineer working for a Zenobia Bank in Kenya, had saved a huge sum over the years and died of a heart attack. Someone knew enough about her family to mention a plausible relative. She thought there must be an insider, but she was naïve.

Channah took her last bit of cash and purchased a cheap pay card Nokia cell phone. It proved to be a *scam* phone very quickly. She purchased 40 minutes and wound up getting 10. When Channah called a phone number, it scrambled the number and she got a wrong one. It was no better than a beeper. She was totally frustrated. And then the police came along and stated she called in a false report, a 911! That was irony.

Returning from a stay at a motel due to a confrontation over garbage with her father, Channah was cornered in her apartment by her son and daughter who had come home for a visit. They told her she was going nuts and needed help. Her sister quickly drove over in her car. They told Channah she would be taken by ambulance to the Nassau County Medical Center and put into involuntary hospitalization. She could not believe it, the big certified College Graduate with a Masters degree! A 54-year old woman, being treated this way after all the attacks on her privacy, identity, property, professional career, and credibility! She quickly ran into the driveway, gaining entry to her car. Jamo, quite powerful, grabbed her arms from behind, trying to pin them to her sides in a police-type motion. The police cars were down in the road. She managed to drive over the grass and get away, leaving the four traitors in the driveway. They were well-meaning people who had betrayed Channah totally.

Expose: The Reckoning by Channah Gambit

Chapter 7: To Flee, Take Trips

Confused, frustrated and feeling totally unable to return to Long Beach in order to find some employment, she decided to get away to get a clear picture of her family situation. Channah drove up to Westfield, New York and visited Peekskill, a place her maternal grandmother had grown up in.

There again, something strange happened. Near Westfield, she checked into a motel run by a Hindu gentleman. Falling into a deep sleep, she did not so much as turn on the television set. When she awoke the next morning, she discovered a large wet area next to the bed, on the carpet. Panicking a bit, she flipped on a radio while showering.

"We are sorry to report that there was a murder in the vicinity of Westfield last night," an announcer's voice stated. "A young woman was found dead in bed, her head split open by what appears to have been either a sledge hammer or machete. The night time desk attendant is no where to be found, and police have launched an investigation into his current whereabouts. Anyone with information regarding…" the voice droned on, as she started to dress. Carrying her satchel out past the front desk, she glanced there, only to discover there was no one in the cubicle. Shaking her head to clear it of dreams, Channah threw the satchel in the rear seat and turned the ignition. She was a bit nervous, and shivered with cold. She had left Beeritz quickly, in order to avoid her kids, Mellow, and Big.

Driving into Westfield, she parked the car carefully behind a street of stores. There was snow on the muddy ground. The sky was gray and threatening. Passing into Westfield had been exciting, since you had to cross an ancient iron bridge with black iron girders criss-crossed into the sky. It dominated the landscape. The town's architecture, like many upstate New York towns, was vintage forties. She walked into an Army Navy store, seeking a garment. Finding what she needed took a record ten minutes.

After that, she headed up toward Boston. Driving through the countryside near a scout camp on snowy country roads, she skidded into an embankment. Before doing so, Channah noticed that a gray car had been following her quietly for several miles, although she was moving slowly. The other car had stopped as well. An hour passed. Then two. The other car just sat there. Inside was a couple just watching her. She got out and took a walk to clear her head.

Another car came along, a woman picked her up, and drove her to the closest gas station. Along the way, she observed a couple arguing and relaxed. After a two hour delay, the tow truck driver and Channah came back. Her vehicle was undamaged and the other car was gone. Returning to roads leading to Westfield, she stopped in a small parking lot to buy more items she felt she needed. Once again in the Army-Navy store, she quickly found a canteen, a pocket knife, and work boots.

It was a good twenty minutes later when she came out and discovered that the car was gone! She retraced her steps and tested her memory. It had vanished! She walked around town for 2 hours, looking high and low. Finally, a pedestrian led her to the local precinct. A brusque attractive young rookie drove her around in his patrol vehicle. There it was! She found her car parked in a totally different lot.

The police officer was rather dubious, but kind. "Why don't you check into another motel and get some rest!" he told Channah.

"I know you doubt me, but I'd like a report to be made, just the same." Channah told him about the shadow couple she had seen on the roads about town. He believed her.

"Miss, is there any reason why the authorities on Long Island might be looking for you?" he asked. He had given her some steaming hot coffee at the station, and she cupped it in her hands, sitting on a bench.

"No."

"Well, there's nothing in our state database regarding that." he said. "So these must have been idle curiosity seekers. It's not a good idea to travel alone."

"I hear you." She smiled. He was young, and very well motivated. He'd go far.

"It's a good thing you came in so fast." The officer told her. "If someone commits a crime in your car, you would be liable to charges."

"I'm trying to think back to when I bought it. I've always had two keys." she said. When the car was purchased in 2003, Channah was given two computer chip keys.

A month later, when she returned to Beeritz, she took the time and trouble to phone the dealer, and speak to local police. Actually, the dealership should have provided three. A gray key was missing. Since the keys are not ever copied, and the doors had been securely locked, there was a clear case of intrusion. No jimmying was evident and the car had been driven.

After the Westfield episode, Channah was in a state of near panic. Her anxiety attacks were extreme, and she resolved to turn around,. getting back to familiar territory.. It was far worse driving back to Long Island because she had nowhere else to go.

Once back, Channah wasted no time, and visited two local churches. She viewed her family as a passel of demons, and asked for sanctuary. The first, St. Bernard's of Levitville, where she had been baptized long ago, simply had no facilities. The second, Our Lady of the Miracle in Point Lookout, would not. Her demands on the Diocese had been too strange and intense.

"There's no simple explanation but I feel as if I'm someone's prey, and I'm being stalked." she told Father Gepito. He shock his head, and said mildly "Young lady, it's time for a bit of counseling. We can't have a woman staying here."

"I've got to get to a new town, and find some employment." Channah said, the week after her car was heavily damaged by the road accident. Barely able to open the driver side door, she grabbed the car insurance policy, leafing through it.

Thankfully, she had purchased it with a provision for a free alternate vehicle, good for months. Using the Nokia and sitting in a coffee shop in East Long Ditch, Channah phoned Entreprise. They picked her up two hours later, providing her with a first class, mint green SUV. With jubilation, she returned to Beeritz, pulling a number of suitcases out of the garage. Finding the cartons of precious books, she threw them in the trunk, panting with exhaustion.

Within an hour, she had gassed up the van at a pump in Point Pleasant, and headed out on the open Parkway. "Good planning has certainly paid off again." she told herself, listening to the radio. She was not all that well, however. Migraines had dominated her consciousness ever since Westfield, so that she took Ibuprofen every four hours. Additionally, she had developed something like acid reflux disease. "Ever since that time I tried to catch a Greyhound up to Albany at the Port Authority, I've had a problem eating." she thought. Stopping in Glen City, she purchased a pint of cream and slugged it down. By the time she reached the Throggs Neck Bridge, she felt less queasy.

Channah was fatigued and weak, and couldn't keep her concentration up. She was too scared to stay over at a motel, and, although she had credit, reluctant to use it. The time of year was the coldest time of winter, and she could not sleep overnight in the car, even should she want to. The heater was excellent, as she drove upstate, keeping to the right lane, watching the white stars shine in the sky. She had difficulty with the fan, finding that it made her drowsy. Periodically, she turned the heater off and cracked her window. Revived, she would shake her head. The trailers and heavy rigs on the expressway were terrifying. Some had twelve wheels, and barreled along at 85 miles per hour. Even in the SUV, she could feel the jet stream of them as they passed her. Another problem was the headlights. Many of the were covered in bright amber beams which blinked, winked, and hypnotized her, mile after mile. The radio was not working as a distraction.

Finally, she found a need to stop around Poughkeepsie. Bringing herself into the parking lot of a Motel Six, she checked in to Room 5, locking herself in. There was no heat, and it had not been prepared for someone for a long time. Throwing her coat, sweaters and a spare blanket on the bed, she fell in, although she did have some delusions starting about being mugged, or murdered there, difficult to ignore or suppress. Some fantasy that she would die soon floated through her mind. She was flabbergasted to find that the shower ran only ice cold water. She bit her lip in frustration.

Next morning, she came down to a free breakfast, which turned out to be a buttered roll and acid black coffee, much overheated. There was a fine view of Lake Peekskill. The only other guest was a man who closely resembled Teddy Roosevelt.

"Hi, I'm Fred." he said, brandishing a hand. His palm was warm and calloused. Dressed in a corduroy tan suit jacket and brown slacks, his presence there seemed incongruous with cheap surroundings. "Where are you bound?" she asked him.

He slathered his roll in orange marmalade from a packet. "Oh, I'm visiting my son at Vasser. He's one of the few male students." His laugh was warm and liquid. "And you, where are you going?" he asked her.

She adjusted the collar on her red sweater. "Oh, I don't know--I'm heading up to Albany, to find work."

"Isn't that a little unusual? A woman traveling alone?" he said. She noticed how intent and intelligent his dark brown eyes were, as they regarded her.

On each table was a lit candle, although it was morning. She thought of how absurd it was that they were burning, and cupped her's in her hand. "I've got to admit it's a longer trip than I thought it would be." she said.

"Why not visit Vasser?" he said. "Got any children of your own."

"I'm alone. Yes, I have two." They continued to have a nice conversation for fifteen minutes. Then he rose to go.

"Goodbye. I wish you luck." he said, going out.

She went over to the clerk, retrieving a strong box he had placed in the safe for her last night. It contained important personal documents she had removed from the

Expose: The Reckoning by Channah Gambit

Commerce Bank vault after her discovery that someone was going into it without authorization. Although the day was new, she had had little sleep, was still numb with chill, and exhausted.

She consulted a map, discovering that Albany was still quite a distance away. She was afraid to do it, but could not admit that to herself.

Channah drove another ten hours in the direction of Albany, along the Northway. The only vehicles on the road were trucks. The moonlight played with shadows, and the moon rose early, bright and full. She watched the sky. For strength, she drank coffee. At a gas station, somewhere above Peekskill, she emptied the van of several household plants, leaving a Pathos donation for the supply outlet attached to Mobil. It was beginning to wilt in her SUV, and she didn't want to be responsible for it any longer.

She looked up into a fog strewn sky, with fog rolling in within the valleys between hills and villages. At some point, she began to sing hymns, :*Moon River, Que Sera, Sera,* and many others, to gain courage. It seemed years since she had started heading toward the state capitol, and it wasn't getting any closer. As she looked at the moon, with a slight headache, she suddenly saw a profile in the clouds: Andrew! It was the visage of a former therapist--the very one who had counseled her to leave her first husband. There he was, looking down to her, but in her dreams, he was transferred into Saint Andrew. She enjoyed the humor of the fantasy greatly, watching him gaze down on her beatifically mile after mile, with a gentle smile playing around his lips. Man in the Moon indeed!

Finally, fatigued and scared stiff of the truck traffic, she got off on a clover leaf and began to head back, resolving to return to Long Island and somehow make a go of it.

Channah couldn't see further than ten feet beyond her car in some spots, the fog was so bad. It was almost 3 a.m. She then had an accident on the south road of the Northway, at a ramp above Lake George. She was exhausted and drove into the embankment, a stone shoulder with a steep incline. Channah was lucky she did not get killed, but did suffer whiplash and a partial concussion. It was a nightmarish incident.

The car slithered over twenty yards down a sharp incline, with the brakes on but locked. Careening along a wall of fitted stones, the left side crushed in, the driver mirror was ripped off, and she was violently thrown into the steering wheel, knocking the wind out of her. It gradually came to a halt, leaving a long trail of black rubber behind. Ploughed steeply into an icy snow bank, the car was trapped and could not be thrown into reverse. Channah, a bit dazed, could not open the driver door. She managed to find her cell phone, and call 911.

The crisp staccato speaker from the New York State Highway Patrol came on. "I can't tell you where I am. I am at some exit ramp, near Lake George." she said.

"Don't worry. We've got your signal. We'll triangulate. Be there within an hour. Just keep warm."

A tow truck and two patrol cars showed up eventually, complete with a young suspicious state trooper Officer Brown. He pryed her out of the car.

"Let's see you walk a straight line. You might have to submit to a drug test." he said, seating her in the passenger seat of his car. He used the computer terminal there to file the report. "You say you teach. What in blazes are you doing up here, driving alone?" he demanded. "I might have to take you in."

"No, no, that's not necessary." she protested. "I don't need a hospital! Just a bit of whiplash. Can I please have my car back.?

The other officer was a woman, and Channah got out to talk to her. Brown was totally offensive and nasty. "I'm really okay. There are hotels in Lake George."

"Well, let's see, here, stand back, there's traffic." the woman said. "Are you sure?"

"Yes, I'm fine. I'm headed back to Long Island." Channah said, averting her eyes.

"Well, okay. I'll talk to Officer Brown." She walked back to the car with her, as the tow truck driver did his job with a chain or two, backing the SUV onto the road once more.

"You sure are lucky. You had a close call." Officer Brown said, somewhat mollified by his partner. "Here are the keys. Just sign this, and you can go. Lady, try to use some more sense next time."

She spent about five minutes getting the engine going. They told her they would follow her for a few miles. The night was macabre, all black, blue and freezing gray, with yellow fog which hung low to the ground in spots, disguising the shoulder and the road behind and before. She had been fortunate. The next two exits were for industrial parks, only used during the day and ghost towns at night. Soon, a sign for Lake George appeared.

Once again, Channah found a motel, a Howard Johnson in the deserted garish ghost town, deserted in January right after a blizzard. Parking on crusty ice, she walked in to the lobby, ringing a bell. On the coffee table in front of an acid green sofa was a basket of plastic fruit. She had reached out to eat an apple, as she was starved.

A bright, wide-awake lady with auburn tresses came out of the office and greeted her. She quickly took her credit card. The room was at the end of endless, empty corridors. Inside, a safe permitted deposit of precious things.

The bed was wide enough for a honeymoon night. Channah slept in the chill sheets after a luxurious bubble bath with hot water. The soliloquy started almost immediately after the tub. "What am I doing here, an educated person like me? Why did I allow myself to be driven out of my home? Who is the person who has been attacking me, and my things?" her thoughts spun around in her head, making little sense.

She glanced from behind heavy maroon drapes on a ghostly winter scene, with high drifts, scores of empty motel rooms where nothing but black glass existed, and no light of any kind shown out to relief the arctic solitude.

Sometime around 4 a.m. Channah awoke from a fitful nap in one corner of the bed. She panicked late in the middle of the night. Dressing, she fidgeted with the combination of the safe, unable to recover her belongings. Finding her way down the long empty halls, she passed a disheveled, slovenly blond bimbo, leaving a room while dressing in a maid uniform.

At the front desk, she accosted the redhead.

"I just phoned home on Long Island. It seems my father has had a heart attack. I have to leave immediately! He's been taken to the hospital."

"I'm so sorry to hear that!" the woman said, real concern showing in her eyes, without a trace of disbelief.

"Is there any way you can refund my stay?" Channah asked.

"Surely." the lady said, after a moment's thought.

"Unfortunately, the lock box of mine is stuck in the room safe."

"Oh, those are time locks. It can't be opened until tomorrow morning."

"My gosh. I'll have to leave it then." Channah's mind raced, while her heart fearfully beat in her chest. "I'll have to abandon it. Is there some way you can ship it to me? I'll pay for that now."

"No need," the woman said. "I'll have it removed tomorrow morning, have it placed in the manager's safe, and you call me later!" she smiled at her.

Channah thanked her, watching her process the credit. Taking her wallet and sticking it into her purse, she braved the freezing cold wind blowing from the front door. Skittering on the ice, and pavement which was inadequately salted, she found the SUV, forgetting for a moment the damaged driver's door. Fighting with the frozen locks, she managed to put the suitcase in, then entered through the passenger side.

Once inside, she ran the engine for a while, warming the frozen motor.
Heading out, she traveled back onto the New York Thruway.

This time, her nerve did not fail, and she managed to make it past the Tarrytown Bridge. She fled from herself all the way down to New Rochelle, too scared to get sleepy. Besides, she had had a few hours of rest.

Once near the metropolitan area, she visible lightened her mood, stopping at a 7-11 to buy orange juice, an egg sandwich, and coffee.

"I really had a close call up there." she thought for herself..

Ultimately, her flights, due to PTSD, did little damage to anyone other than herself. It is true that, after her arrest, her driver's license was suspended on the basis of Trooper Brown's report. It would be over a year before she was authorized to drive again, on the say-so of her physician.

A few short weeks of abuse later, she fled once again, seeking solace from distant relatives. Channah traveled down to Washington, D.C. in the SUV, through Maryland, Delware, Pennsylvania and New Jersey.

"I have no home," she told herself. "I am in danger." Through endless rural and suburban vistas, punctuated with stops at roadside rests, she wandered. Down in Washington, she stayed at The Red Roof near Chinatown, with a credit card fueling her, providing gas, food and comforts. Although she was not pursued, nor injured, there would be one more *close call* down in Delaware, on the frosty road.

The heater plagued her with air which made her sleepy. Somewhere down there, in the middle of Osh-Kosh, she pulled into a dealership and chose to sleep at the wheel, around 5 a.m. in the morning. Unfortunately, with the motor off, the temperature in the SUV dropped precipitously, to below freezing. Unable to keep conscious, numb to the danger of exposure, Channah came perilously close to freezing to death.

An alert motorist, driving by, spied her in the windows. He stopped, shining his headlights into it, honking his horn loudly, and rousing her.

Cursing at her stupidity, Channah caravanned after him, gratefully, until they came to a Windsor Restaurant. He continued down the road, never to be identified.

Expose: The Reckoning by Channah Gambit

In Washington, she enjoyed a night trolling at the motel bar, where she was not befriended. Cousin Lucille, phoned in Gaithersburg, Maryland, declined to assist her, apologized, then hung up.

With tears in her eyes, Channah thought to herself "Why are they all turning against me like this? Why doesn't anyone like me?" She had breakfast in the motel restaurant, then packed up. She could not remain in Washington. She did not have enough money.

Traveling back up the Eastern seaboard, she marveled at the country, taking stock of ugly Baltimore, and the many empty industrial wasteland ghost towns in Maryland. It turned into a pastiche of alienation, a T.S. Eliot *Wasteland*, or a Jean Paul Sartre *Nausea*, with a gradually growing feeling of failure, of impending humiliation and defeat.

During a short return to Nassau County, she went down to the Department of Social Services in Charles Lindberg Plaza and applied for a place in some battered woman's shelter. Channah later recalled sitting there for over 3 hours, having handed in her paperwork and not having any call for an interview. One night, she sat in her car for a few hours, trying to decide what to do next. There was no more credit left on the last card.

Regarding the hearing on February 20th, she had the whiplash and partial concussion both untreated due to lack of health insurance to use as a plausible medical excuse. In January, she consulted with an attorney specializing in school law to advise her, *pro bono*, regarding leaving her last teaching position. Maybe he could help her now. Advice? He had examined the bench summons and told her:

"It's not legal. It doesn't mention a courthouse. You have a medical reason and you don't have to show up." Channah wrote up a medical excuse and posted it to her door in early January. In the weeks following Sheriff's Officers never showed. They never came to give her a summons or to remove it. Additionally, it was mailed to her attorney friend and his name and number were left on the door. She thought she had done all she had to do on the basis of sound legal advice, however, the attorney forgot to advise Channah to mail the medical excuse into the Justice at the District Courthouse. He did tell her that the District Courthouse was 99.9% surely the place she had to be. As a result, a warrant had been issued for her arrest. In another peculiar irregularity in law enforcement procedure, no officers came to the premises to find her or called her. Additionally, no note was left at her door, nor was Daddy Gambit, the landlord, contacted. Instead, there was one cryptic phone call to Duvey, telling him that she had to come in to explain something or she might be arrested. Channah found it peculiar that they contacted her son first.

Bankruptcy was rearing its ugly head so she had purchased a program to file. She filed, spending a last dime on photocopying six sets. Her credit cards were used up and she had no where to go. Channah took the apartment apart in a fit of panic. She put pieces of furniture out at the curb for charity and tried to give her valuable books on deaf education to the local church so that they would not be garnished. The local clergyman thought that she needed to see counseling. They refused her gift. She had to remove it and bring it home. She was sure she'd lose everything. Channah had no one left to confide in or to tell the incredible details to.

Expose: The Reckoning by Channah Gambit
Where was a White Knight?.

Expose: The Reckoning by Channah Gambit

Chapter 8: Home Vanishes

Joseph Bee, a decent former District Attorney, did not help Channah *per se*, but he became a witness of sorts to the conflagration her personal life was becoming.

Sometime around March 6th, she had packed up most of her library to donate to a charity in Israel, and she gave away quite a lot of personal objects in an attempt to clean up the premises before she left for good. She completely forgot about the pending charge which she believed was already dismissed, the contempt of court related to her Dad's counter-petition for a non-harassment Order of Protection.

On a Tuesday, she held a tag sale of household items on the lawn, although it was February. Neighbors dropped by. By the fence, her bike sat padlocked to a tree. Daddy Gambit came home, driving the big white car up the driveway. Walking up to the tree, he broke the padlock with a tool, wheeled the bike to the garage, parked it, then closed the electric door. "I'll call the cops if you chain anything to my tree again!" he yelled at her from the steps.

The following Thursday, for spiritual medicine, she hung a wooden crucifix made out of rulers from the sill of a window in the foyer. Big spied this as he was visiting. After bringing groceries upstairs, he and Daddy Gambit walked down the front steps, opening the garage with the remote. They entered Channah's apartment, where she was seated writing at the dining room table.

"Out you go!" Big said.

"You take that damn thing down!" Daddy Gambit said. "You're Jewish." he walked over to the window, removed the crucifix, and broke it over his knee.

"Get out of here! Get out of here! You're driving me crazy!" screamed Channah, shooing them out the door. Such was her vehemence that they both retreated. She called the local precinct. Although the Sheriff's Officers and patrol men visited the house several times during these weeks to defuse domestic squabbles, nothing about a warrant was mentioned.

Much later, when she was incarcerated for lack of bail, she met a lady from Queens who had been similarly treated, her warrant on a parole violation ignored for 9 years until she gave someone sass and strings were pulled. It seemed that law enforcement liked to have some irons in the fire for those who did not behave as expected.

The simple pressures of living and malnutrition were keeping Channah in a delirious stupor while she was constantly harassed by Mellow and Big. Jamo and Duvey sent strong messages.

"You're crazy." Jamo said, hanging up on her when she phoned.

"Your misfortune is due to your own actions." Duvey chimed in, as she sat at the delicatessen table, eating a bowl of soup. She was confused, perplexed and hurt regarding treatment received at their hands. They were all ogres or hobgoblins in her mind.

Psychological health was not a strong point with the landlord, either. He was doing strange things at odd moments. The garage had suddenly acquired some reels of what looked like piano wire. Her dad had started collecting oily turquoise drop cloths. He broke a padlock off the inner garage door and forced entry into her home, during evenings. He would vent his spleen, spouting obscenities, then retreat.

For her own protection, Channah wrote records of forced entry.

She actually wrote next to broken locks with numbers and dates, to match to journal entries of certain incidents. She finally wrote a letter to the F.B.I. A lot of what she said was pure bunk, but a lot of the details of disappearing mail, stolen bank accounts, illegal entry of her car and bank vault, were mentioned. She waited for a reply, having spent her last $18 on first class mail service, insured and registered.

The letter read, in part: "I had the scare of my life sometime around late February regarding a neighbor, Efram Kopf." As days grew into weeks, the silence from the Bureau of Investigation was unsettling.

There was more she had witnessed in ensuing days, unmentioned, regarding the Kopfs. The day after a party upstairs, some carpenter arrived and ran a buzz saw for what seemed like hours in the garage there. Her feverish mind, in Post Traumatic Stress Disorder mode, imagined that Efram Kopf was disposing of some body and having it truncated. She saw many strange people coming and going to that house and knew that he was the son of Mellow's friend. What was he up to? Had he also been entering her apartment to terrorize her, using her sister's key? Had he been given his house rent-free as a payoff?

What about that key discovered in Duvey's room! Had Big or Mellow planted it there, to make Channah suspicious?

Now panic stricken, she could barely control her emotions. One night, in a fit of paranoia, she smashed the windowpane next door with a screw driver. Knopf met her in the morning, for a hard confrontation. "You'll have to pay me back for the damage." he said, eyeing her from under his brows.

"You'll be part of the bankruptcy." she said.

"You know, technically speaking, you've broken the law." he said.

"I'm not the only one, Efram." she said.

"Now what do you mean by that?" he asked, but she just walked away.

Channah couldn't seek counseling from the hospital without health insurance. "The charity center at Nassau County Medical Center is a dump!" she told Jamo during a heated exchange. "I'm shocked by your appearance, Mom!" Jamo said.

"Why don't you give me some money for groceries?" There was silence at the other end. " No one will give me a part time job, let alone an interview." *One last try to get a job*, she thought. *I have the rental SUV for a week or two longer before it's repossessed so I'll go to Massachusetts and seek work in Boston. It was good for my daughter to live there, it will be good for me.*

Before she left, one more incident occurred with Daddy Gambit, who had the local police wrapped around his little finger. If he even just saw her, he would call the police, and start screaming that he would have her arrested. She had returned the SUV, since borrowing time had expired. There were still Greyhound buses at the Port Authority willing to take her. She fled, traveling by train into Manhattan.

Up in Boston, she was unable to find sanctuary with a Christian organization she was fond of. An overnight in a *7-11* with some strange characters did not leave her in good shape. She had no telephone number for a local cousin, Larry. He was unlisted.

Expose: The Reckoning by Channah Gambit

Her daughter was on Long Island. Should she go to Montreal to collect the box of personal papers from St. Catherine Du Monde Cathedral? A woman her age, who was unattractive, starved and exhausted, could not find a driver willing to take her, not even another woman. She trudged the streets of Boston, weeping at times, going from church to church seeking shelter, growing more scared and wary of the police. A suitcase of unnecessary clothing was discarded. Channah dumped an expensive sleeping bag near a trash can. The last night ended with an overnight sit at the Boston East 24 hour bus hub.

She decided to return to Long Island and face the charges, to clean up her debts, and to rescue her son from the horrible family who had failed her before it was too late. That was the best thing she could have done but it guaranteed she would suffer an ordeal. She begged charity selling AAA maps for cash to get the bus fair and train fare home. On March 5th, she arrived back at her house at 4 in the morning and crashed on the bed.

Expose: The Reckoning by Channah Gambit

Chapter 9: Crime *Accompli*

It was a cold day in January. She had been malnourished for weeks, and felt faint sometimes. Recently, she had gone on a job interview at Salisbury, for Nassau Boces; a teaching position. Driving aimlessly around, one snowy gray afternoon, Channah pondered why her own children, both working, refused to give her money.

Relying on church pantries was counter-productive. Driving aimlessly around, she passed close to Eisenhower Park, making a left at a road close to Post Road and Old Country. Her anxiety mounted with each traffic light. *How can I survive? Someone wants to destroy me. My own family hates me.* Her thoughts raced around her head, over and over, like a gerbil stuck in a cage ring.

The two injuries to her head had taken a toll. The first had occurred in October, 2005. She thought back to that day. Channah had been on her prep break, and visited the gymnasium to check on the day's schedule with a substitute teacher. Coming back along the basement hall, she was catcalled by a special ed student, African American, seated on the steps watching the gym students exercise. He was a high school student cutting classes, and words were on her tongue to make him go back to class. In the hallway, as in all hallways at The Tertiary School, was a fire door, supported by a steel frame featuring a girder through the center of the space. Channah walked directly into it, struck her head, and ricocheted off, falling backward onto the floor. The force of impact was taken by her glass frame, which drove into her head and brow, particularly on the right side.

She got up, brushed herself off, and screamed at the kid. A tall, ugly boy in a jersey and sweat pants, he immediately left, taking the steps upstairs in a hurry. She walked on to the teacher's lounge, where she found Jon and a colleague on break. Her forehead felt hot and funny. There was a throbbing pain in both eyes. It had seemed nothing, but that was due to instinct. As time passed, she began to develop a black eye. Channah traveled into the main office, and Ginger flinched on seeing her. "You look terrible."

"Do I really?" Channah said, touching her face.

"You'd better go upstairs to the Infirmary and have the Nurse look at it."

"Okay. What about my class?"

"They're at gym." Ginger said. "Devorah will watch them."

"Alright." Channah said. She went to staircase B, climbed twelve flights, and visited the nurse's office, all the way to the rear corridor up there.

"Doesn't seem to be anyone here." she said to several students who were there, waiting. They all looked perfectly normal, and were sitting and chatting, chewing gum and content.

Channah felt terrible. Visiting the bathroom, she looked at her face, noting with alarm that pain was mounting geometrically. She took the elevator to the main floor, returning to Ginger's desk.

"Do you have any Excedrin?" she asked.

"Oh..certainly." Ginger gave her a cup of water from the cooler, and she took three.

Expose: The Reckoning by Channah Gambit

"I'd better go see my supervisor, Mrs. Peaches." Channah said.

"Why don't you go sit down for a minute. She's right in here, having a conference with Mr. Woodward."

"Sure. I'm not one to argue." Channah sat in a soft chair in the waiting area. Mrs. Peaches came out after a while and took a look at her.

Channah was apologetic. "I'm sorry. I've given myself a shiner."

"You have to fill out an accident report. There's also a statement. Was a student involved?" Mrs. Peaches' voice showed less concern than a sense of duty.

The next hour was spent in filling out forms and signing releases for the Board of Education. "I am really feeling poorly. I would like to go home. I don't think I can finish the day." Channah said weekly. Her eye had puffed up to the point where she could not see out of it.

"Let me get Mrs. Peaches on the phone." Ginger offered. They spoke briefly, and Channah went upstairs afterward, retrieving her coat and briefcase from her classroom locker. She had been replaced, by Mrs. Peaches herself, who sounded dubious regarding the necessity for the early leave-taking.

"I'll be in tomorrow." Channah said.

"Well, have yourself looked at. Take care." Peaches said.

The drive home, passing Kennedy Airport, was bumper to bumper traffic, taking two and a half hours. She made it the local hospital, went to the Emergency Room, and had her wound inspected by a young intern who stated that it wasn't a partial concussion. She doubted it, accepted his prescription for triple ibuprofen, and went home to rest. It was the beginning of a disenchantment with the job. There was definite loss of short term memory in the ensuing weeks, as well as an inability to concentrate or focus for long periods. Her glass frames, driven into the cheek, caused some hemorrhage of blood vessels, producing some scarring. The swollen eyes took over 3 weeks to return to normal.

The second cause for disorientation and befuddlement, the car accident on the New York State Northway, where she had skidded on some black ice and run up to an embankment, occurred while she had no cobra insurance coverage, long after resigning from the Tertiary School. Although there was no direct hit to the head, the shock of impact forced her forward into the steering wheel with such force that she suffered trauma and whiplash. Unable and unwilling to treat herself, Channah suffered a post traumatic stress disorder, which included inability to sleep, some visual hallucinations due to anxiety, and feelings of loneliness and confusion. The pains of the whiplash distracted her when driving. She used a simple heating pad and ibuprofen to treat the symptoms, which method was simply inadequate. By January, Channah was suffering from persecution mania, and was a bit self-destructive. She was punishing herself for resigning, then failing at the new position. She felt like a failure, and had internalized her sister's hatred for her, turning it inward in an impotent way.

Driving along some way fare, Channah believed that her children were in as much danger as she was, from unseen forces in the environment. Someone wanted to destroy her. Everything would go wrong. The cycle wouldn't end until she was hospitalized, her hard-won career destroyed. She began to hear her daughter calling to her. She could hear her son, begging her to come to him. She braked the car, pulling to the side of the road. Someone wanted to harm her children! She must use a telephone. Even her telephone had been lost on the parkway! She took out a memo pad, scrawled a note, and put it in a mailbox, returning to her vehicle. *You must stop this. You must let go of my children. Stop turning them against me! Tell them to help their mother!* Returning to the car, she started the engine, deciding to make as much trouble for her antagonists as possible. She stopped in Long Ditch, calling in a 911. She told the dispatch the address where she had left the note, and said that there was a crime occurring on the premises. Then she hung up. Returning home, she ate a scrap of bread, all she had, with some peanut butter, and fell into a doze.

After she awoke, she forgot completely about what she had done. Nor was she aware at any time that day of the implications of her actions. It had temporarily alleviated the terrific anxiety she was feeling.

Unknown to her, the owner of the home, away on vacation in Florida, had a visit from the Westbury Precinct of the Nassau County Police Department, who found nothing. They located the owner in Florida, informing her of what had occurred. It did not seem as if anything had been stolen, nor was their forced entry. They got the story wrong from dispatch: the call in had suggested a threat to the homeowner's children. That was the way the original complaint was framed. 911 dispatch had a trace put on the telephone used in the call, which seemed to be Channah's Sanyo LG cell phone. With that information and a computer printout, an investigation was begun, on the basis of a complaint initiated by the homeowner, initially named "Christine", upon her return the following week.

Channah continued in the ensuing weeks to imagine she was being persecuted, chased, or pointed in the direction of destruction by Mellow, Big, Daddy Gambit, Jamo, Duvey, and all the next door neighbors on either side, including the Harrisens and Knopfs. She was under the misapprehension that a murder had occurred to the east, and that Efram knew she was a witness. At any rate, he was mad at her for breaking his window. .

Channah was arrested on March 6th, 2006 for doing something illegal on January 13, 2006. There were 3 misdemeanor charges. These were PL 240.50 03 AM, *Falsely Reporting an Incident*; PL 215.50 03 AM, *Criminal Contempt;* and PL 120.45 01 BM, *Stalking,* which was dismissed and reduced to PL 240.30 01 AM, *Aggravated Harassment.* At first, the Stalking charge was listed as a Felony in the District Courthouse computer. Channah spoke to another inmate, Sherry, who had also been a teacher. She discovered that she could not return to her profession with a felony on her record. It reduced her to tears. However, after weeks, she found an error had been made, and this fact gave her false hope.

Expose: The Reckoning by Channah Gambit

Chapter 10: The Questioning Event

As Channah came to her own home at 4 a.m., she was aware that the Lord had sought fit to return her safely from a most dangerous journey. Her back ached and her vision was blurry with exhaustion. The apartment was in shambles, furniture disarrayed from her efforts to place sentimental items and personal belongings somewhere else safe. Attorney Joe Bee advised her that no eviction notice had been sent and the letter from dad had been a scare tactic, and illegal. She did not have to move yet.

Her brown hair was scraggly, uncut for months and turning gray. The furrowed brow was deeper, and removing the spectacles revealed clouded brown eyes, if she bothered to look into a mirror. She had not worn makeup since she left St. Joaquin.

Channah had been trying for weeks to lock her larger personal belongings in a closet closet with chains and padlocks. She would have to leave them there temporarily, until her lifestyle stabilized.. She had found out that the Sheriff could seal her room and stay the landlord from emptying the contents by the curb. Seals she had placed on the doors were of duck tape only. After a fruitless trip to Mineola to find the Sheriff's Office, she was told that they would not come. Another trip to Long Beach City Hall led to a similar admonishment: that there was no way to legally seal papers, books, or belongings. Channah was discouraged.

"The Sheriff only evicts people, lady." a spokesman said.

An attorney met her on the stairs at the Courthouse and told her how. He stated that she should make a paper or cloth seal, write the date, add her signature, and it would legally close the compartments. Anyone who broke it without my permission would be a lawbreaker. Unfortunately, Channah was suffering from Post Traumatic Stress Disorder, with panic attacks the norm for the days. Frequent break-ins through doors inside and out occurred daily, without signs of forced entry.

Need I say more? she thought as she walked aimlessly through the chill rooms. *I'll make do. I'll do the best I can. Why did I buy so much? You can't take it with you when you're gone!*

She used markers and drew lines across the tapes onto the walls. *At the very least, it will be evident if someone goes into them and tries to reseal the tape. Damage to property will be the next charge* The lines drawn were also on the walls.

"Mom, what the heck are you doing?" Duvey said, there to retrieve some clothing. "What's the point?" She didn't answer him. He watched Channah with raised eyebrows, saying nothing more. To a bystander, tension was evident between them.

"Can you give me a lift to town today?" she would ask.

"I'm sorry, I have to be back at work in a half hour. If I lose my job, I'll be stuck. Dad is making me pay rent." he said, frowning. "I need to go to class, and my grades are failing. It's your fault." he said curtly. She found out from his friend Mike that he was cutting classes, despondent and claiming stress.

At any rate, back from motels, she was now back temporarily in her own bedroom. She spent a fevered hour restoring precious belongings to their spots, putting clothing away in drawers, and pretending that she had a home and could rest in own own queen-size bed. *There's now a bigger wrinkle.* she told herself. *These belongings are listed for the bankruptcy, and no longer mine.* That night, she indulged in a crying spell.

As Channah lay there in a remorse-filled fever, she went into a reverie, recalling Knopf's antics recently. Would he come in through the door with a hammer? Was he the culprit doing all the damage?

On a recent Monday, a carpenter friend came to Knopf's home and spent hours buzz sawing away. Fear ran through her veins! *What is he breaking up? Firewood or a corpse?* the panic attack said, whispering to her. Of late, she was afraid to think at all let alone sleep. Every Tuesday, she would hop the Point Pleasant bus to Munroe street in town, visit a church-run food pantry, and bring home two bags of staples. Lately her diet consisted of bread and water, sometimes an egg, and beans and rice, without condiments.. Duvey, under considerable strain, permitted visits to the deli for a hearty dinner once or twice a week. On that Wednesday she saw him, looking so young, alert and toned in his black and white waiter's uniform. "I'm here!" she said. Duvey's brow, so much like her own, furrowed. He ignored the comment, had his friend Mustapha plunk down some pea soup, and avoided her table. "I'm crushed." she said to him, preparing to leave. Duvey silently removed his wallet from his pocket, peeled off two twenties, and placed them down on the table, then walked away.

It was 8 a.m. on Friday, and Channah heard Daddy Gambit shuffling around heavily upstairs. The sound of a flushing toilet echoed through the ceiling. He was heard making a phone call, talking loudly into the speaker. Daddy Gambit was half deaf. *He never stands on ceremony. He's coming down again.* She steeled herself for a visit. After 2 hours, he headed out, came down to the garage, and opened the electric door. Then, footsteps were heard outside, as he came around to the front of her apartment. Using his passkey, he opened her front door. He started to scream at her from the Florida room.. "I'm having you arrested. You are eating me out of house and home." he said. Quickly, he shut the garage door and left.*He can't be serious. I've done nothing. He wouldn't dare!"* she told herself, shivering in a thick wool sweater.

Although Channah was exhausted she decided to act on the *worst case scenario*.. Summoning strength, she strode quickly down her walkway. Heading east, she made her way down the boulevard. *I need to find sanctuary* she thought, her heart in her throat. *He's Jewish. He won't be able to follow me into Our Lady.*

There were sirens coming down the boulevard, as she reached Silver Springs Road.. She could make it to the home of a former best friend, Barbie. Feverishly, she rang the doorbell. Helene stood there, listened at the screen, but did not invite her in. "I'd like to help." she said, after listening for ten minutes. "My friend is ill, and a neighbor is driving him to a doctor's appointment. Get into her car, and she'll take you where you have to go."

"Thank you so much, Helene." Channah said, looking guiltily at Barbie's mom's face. The woman was not happy at being brought into the middle of a domestic conflict and said so. "Goodbye." Channah said, as the front door closed in her face.There was a black car moving down from the beach, which paused at the driveway. Inside, were an elderly couple. Channah stepped in and they moved away.

"Thanks." she said. There was a man sitting, wheezing, all bundled up riding shotgun. She looked out the rear window to see a patrol car pulled up at her family homestead, with Daddy Gambit's car parked in front of it.

They reached Point Pleasant, and she got out quickly. Waving goodbye, she walked swiftly to the Rectory, south of the church.

"Hi, I'm Veronica." an elderly woman said, letting her in. "Pastor Cole is not in."

"May I wait for him in the church."

"Okay, I'll find you there. But it's unheated. The door should be open." Veronica said.

She spent time at the prayer stand before the Madonna, praying. Sitting in a pew, she ignored her growing hunger. After an hour, she slipped out to a quick shopping mart and bought a hard boiled egg. Frightened, Channah skittered across the boulevard, hurrying into Our Redeemer. The wind blew in gusts through the street, throwing her green hood over her head. It propelled her along faster, whipping around her legs in their ski pants. *I look a fright. I can't go to a motel tonight. What will I do?* she thought.

Veronica peeked in and beckoned to her at 3 p.m. Walking in single file, they returned to the Rectory, where Pastor Cole waited in a rear office.

"Now try to relax, Channah." he said. "What is the problem that couldn't wait."

"I can't return home because my family is after me." she said.

"Now that can't be the case. You are a grown woman. Do you have any children?" the Pastor asked.

"No, I'm estranged. I have no children." She started to weep. Pastor Cole handed her a handkerchief. She blew her nose. Channah was warming up a little, and undid her coat. "Please, Father, give me sanctuary."

"Sanctuary?" he said, startled. "Why, we don't have that here."

"Could I possibly stay the night." she said, explaining that Dad was acting irrationally and had phoned the police, contriving an incident.

"Young woman, I can see you need counseling. We can't offer that here, not now. You normally see Father Salle, on Sundays, for spiritual direction?"

"Yes. But not lately." she said. She clutched her handbag in her lap. The room had a warm glow to it, coming from overhead fluorescent lighting recessed in the ceiling. The décor was lacey and pastel. She liked the embroidered pillows on the sofa.

"I am sorry. You may stay for a while inside the church, but when night falls, you must be gone." He rose from his chair, to indicate that the meeting was over.

Channah closed the storm door and walked briskly back to the church, against the wind. *I'm so disappointed. Why won't they help me?* Long hours passed at a pew while she debated what to do. *Will the police find me in Point Pleasant?* she asked the silent statue of the Madonna. Luckily, they did not. When she thought it was safe and the crisis was over, she crossed the boulevard and took the local bus home. Seated at the wheel, the driver glanced at her curiously. Her face was smudged with tears, her hair blown and scattered around the front of the hood. *Thank God!* she thought, as she got off at her stop. Only her son's car was in the drive way. *Duvey must be back again for more belongings.* He immediately rose from the kitchen table when he saw her.

"Mom, where have you been?"

"I was hiding from Grandpa Gambit." she said. "He sent the police here."

Duvey's face was pale, his eyes gray and stormy, as she looked into his face.

Expose: The Reckoning by Channah Gambit

"Mom, mom, it's for your own good. You have to go in. They are coming to arrest you." he said.

They heard the front door upstairs slam, as Daddy Gambit came out of the house to stand on the porch. Both walked quickly outside. They saw Helga Hansen, on her porch. She ran down and gave Daddy Gambit her cell phone.

Shocked, Channah ran into the house, locking herself in. Duvey got into his black car and drove away. In a loud voice, Daddy Gambit called the police from the front stoop. Mellow drove up in the driveway in an unfamiliar gold car. She parked, stood on the brick front porch and could be heard calling for an ambulance. *I'm trapped.* Channah thought, wildly looking around the entryway.

Shortly after that, 3 policemen showed up in two patrol cars and handcuffed Channah, throwing her roughly into the back of a vehicle. She watched her home and family shrink and then disappear, through gritty, tired red eyes. Her arms ached with pain and she felt both helpless and terrified. The Gambit family had planned her capture very well.

As she later discovered, prior to the arrest, Big and Daddy Gambit went into Family Court and had the record of a Violation to his outrageous Order of Protection modified. New perjurous details regarding tampering and theft of cartons was written in. Big dictatetd allegations regarding mental illness to the Court Clerk, demanded they change the *non-harassment* language to *stay away*, a more extreme form of control.

It was now a District Court Order of Protection, as well, coordinated with a second Order of Protection from a Westapple complainant named Tabatha Sand, indicating that Channah stalked her.

Big's legal move was orchestrated in perfect synch with the added charges. It painted her as a bi-polar threat to the world, a psycho who might harm anyone at any moment. It implied that she could not be counted on to act responsibly. *Big is building the way to having my rights revoke, so that he can involuntarily confine me.* she thought, frantically. *I know this Counter-petition is one huge act of revenge to get even for my even filing my own petition against the landlord in the first place. But I was advised to.* She tried to talk to the cops in the squad car, but kept spluttering.

This is how she was brought into the First Precinct station house in Hewlett, where she was finally addressed. Both the stalking and calling in a false report misdemeanors were based on incidents that a detective claimed had occurred around February 8, 2006. *That's much later than when it really happened, in January,* Channah told herself while seated on a bench in an interrogation room.

` *One charge is identical to the bench warrant Barney questioned me about in January. But they've changed the complainant's name,* she thought helplessly. *It's contrived!*

As she was later to discover, any one of the misdemeanors carried up to a year in prison and a $1,000 fine, left to the discretion of the Court. *But of course I'll get off.* she thought. *I've never been in trouble with the law before, except for that time at the university. Hmmm.* She paled, remembering past history. *I'm even more certain this is contrived, because it is the same darn charge they tried to build against me out there in Suffolk.* she thought. *I can beat it!*

Expose: The Reckoning by Channah Gambit

After being looked over by a desk sergeant, she was led into a questioning room. Castaglio, a cop who identified herself as Susan, searched her with practiced care, wearing the ubiquitous turquoise gloves. The omnipresent Diamond Technologies fingerprinting machine would appear later.

"Young lady," Charles Solo said, "I'm here to get a narrative from you." he said, pulling on his white moustache with one hand. He had finally showed up, after performing duties upstairs.

"I don't know why you think I'm a stalker." she said. Channah's rear end was sore from sitting in a captain's chair there. She tried to stand, but the handcuff to the chair made it impossible. "I'll tell you my side of it. You see, I had a partial concussion, and was anxious about my kids…" her story went on for long moments.

When there was silence, Solo filled out a form for a minute, signed it, and walked out. "I'm sorry you did what you did. I'm not going to write this up. You'll be given the opportunity to defend yourself. You cannot eat or drink here." He walked out.

Nuzzo went through the wallet, counting plastic cards and itemizing them on a sheet. All her personal belongings, including jewelry were stripped from her and stuffed into a manilla envelope. Nuzzo and Castaglio gossiped through the whole procedure.

"Please let me call someone. Can I have some pizza?" Channah said.

"You can make one phone call but I can't remove the cuffs. I'll dial." Castaglio said while seated at the table munching pizza.

Channah's stupefied mind came up with the name of the attorney: Damito, the one who had advised her regarding appearing for the hearing in March. "I don't have the number." she said.

Susan Castaglio looked up the number graciously and dialed it. The receiver held in the uncuffed left hand, Channah got a recording, leaving a message. The attorney did not respond to any contact for weeks. Later, she discovered this was because he was *never paid a retainer*. Supportive documents she sent to him, including the medical excuse for not appearing mysteriously vanished from his office. His secretaries claimed they did not exist when she spoke to them weeks afterward, still trying to reach him from the holding block.

Channah, still in the captain's chair, felt her right hand become paralyzed from lack of circulation. Hours went by, as she watched officers going and coming. *These officers look cynical and mean.* she thought.

"Sorry, there's no food for prisoners." Nuzzi said, taking another slice.

"May I have a sip of water?" Channah asked. Castaglio sighed, got up, and brought her back a paper cup from a cooler. *Her whole attitude is that I am an annoying bitch.* Channah thought.

"Aren't I supposed to see some badge identification, Officer." she said.

Susan looked at her with a smile, her eyebrow arched.

"I don't have any." she said, laughing and looking toward Nuzzi. "I left it out in my car. I'm not normally with this precinct."

"Yeah, I left it in my car." she repeated to the other officer, ignoring Channah. He nodded his head and they broke into laughter.

When Solo came downstairs, she tried a couple of times to tell them her side of things, but he interrupted her. "It's pointless, young lady. I know you are a teacher, a good citizen, but you're being charged" He said. "I can't help if Damito isn't home." The stodgey, short geezer left the room after handing a carbon copy of her statement to Nuzzi.

"You'll get a chance to explain at your arraignment." Castigano stated.

As she went into the hall, Channah heard *Susan* addressed by an officer as *Mary*. All during her stay at Nassau County Correctional Center, N.C.C.C., she'd observe Sheriff's officers and patrolmen routinely switching badges with one another, mixing up inmates' ideas about identity and cultural background, denying them the right to know authority and the reality of their situation. Channah felt from the start that something was deeply wrong with the system. It appeared to be run illegally.

The processing of her arrest was typically slow and tedious. Her belongings were taken, not listed piece by piece. An attorney did not come. From the hall clock, she noticed that the hour was growing late. She was taken in a patrol car to a holding pen at 1490 Franklin Road by two young rookies sporting heavy guns. *I am in god knows where* she thought as a bald one drove them through dark winding suburban streets in the night.

She was brought to a non-descript brick building without any sign and led in to the front desk. A group of white whiskered policeman, including the desk sergeant, were intent on watching Conan, the talk show host on the overhead flat screen television. They asked Channah her name then took her into a holding room where she was chained to the bench. A young terrified man in sneakers and sweats was seated at another bench. Although already in his thirties and going bald, he fidgeted in wide open laced basketball sneakers. When a patrolman came to take him away, he started and groveled.

Channah sat and stared off into space, dressed too warmly for the heated alcove. Everything was dirty from use. Eventually, after about an hour, she was led into a room with a Diamond Technologies fingerprinting machine and printed by a walrus moustached technician.. For some reason, it kept malfunctioning, and would not keep her prints in memory. She was told there that the prints from the precinct had accidentally been erased. The ordeal lasted almost an hour. Sometimes they scanned her finger over and over again, never getting an approval from the LED display. She was made to stand on blue shoe marks on the floor, and I photographed, both forward and profile. *I am now a classic cliché felon.* she thought.

Channah was then led down many winding corridors filled with rows of aged gray-painted cells until she came to a door in the wall which led into a short concealed hall. This was a remote area reserved for women inmates. There was plain plumbing and gas fixtures in all ceilings, and filthy frosted barred glass windows. It smelled of a urinal.

They finally came to a line of cells, and she was escorted into cell 1, right next to the door to S.O. Guber's sitting room. Once there, she was uncuffed and they took her glasses away. *I need them to write, read and recognize things. Everythings a blurr!* she thought helplessly, sitting down on a metal shelf there.

Later, in retrospect, she'd recall what she had learned in Graduate School about the Aid to the Handicapped Act, the so-called IDEA legislation prohibiting withhold of prosthetic devices. *How can this be happening to me? How can law enforcement do this to citizens? Accommodations in public and government places have to be adapted to the handicapped!* There would be no relief for over 36 hours of solitary confinement.

What is the point in denying me sight? My rights have been violated. Her educated mind would run around in frantic circles, her remarks ignored, and she would not be given the right to register her alarm.

S.O. Guber or *Ms. Frieda* as she asked to be called, took a dislike to Channah from the start. *It's because I'm brainy. I'm confused.* She was forced to sleep that first night on a small bare shelf without a blanket. Cell 1 measured roughly 2 feet by 9 feet long, in a hallway whose dimensions were about 6 by 12 feet. The outside door clanked shut, and this remote corridor was erased, disguised as a cell.

During the course of that long night, Channah would hardly sleep and would notice that Ms. Frieda would make mistakes. For example, once she forgot her keys, leaving them in plain sight on the radiator across from the cells. Guber would sit in her control room and ignore them for hours.

Shortly after Channah's entry, a young Syrian woman was placed in the same cell, dressed in identical clothing, green and black. The overhead television camera monitored every move. If Channah tried to place her beige sweater over the bars to block on an incandescent spotlight, Ms. Frieda, watching from inside her pad, would come out and shout at her to put it aside. All night long, Patsy and Channah took turns with the bunk. They were both exhausted and felt cramped. Channah sometimes sat on the cold concrete floor, observing the marks and messages left by years of former inmates on the walls. A group of prostitutes came in, and were thrown into cells 2 and 3. They were quite young, gaudily dressed, and chattered away for long hours. Ms. Guber came out once more toward morning.

"Yo, Penelope. You in here again?" she asked a tall redhead dressed in punk costume.

"Brenda, what are you doing time for. When are you going to leave that Gary?" she asked a platinum haired transvestite next door in cell 2. He had a low voice, was emaciated, and gesticulated through the bars, his wrists covered in long black hairs and bangle bracelets. Channah recoiled. She was extremely drowsy, disoriented, and dizzy. They received some bologna and cheese sandwiches from Guber. Chewing the bread, she threw the spicy meat down the toilet and flushed.

Guber, glancing in her cell, frowned. "Hey, you better eat it. And don't put that sweater up on the bars. Yeah, I know that it blocks the lights, but knock it off."

Her tone became sweet and simpering. She continued to gossip with the girls, ignoring Channah for the rest of the night.

"At least my girls like me." she said as she walked down the aisle, feeding everyone. Someone came and was placed into cell 4. A favorite, Lucy's cell door was left deliberately open.

"I don't really have to be here." Lucy explained, "I just wanted to visit." and they all laughed heartily at the joke.

Channah refused food. S.O.. Guber, in the morning, surprised her with a bagel and cream cheese instead. She could not eat, nor did she trust Guber enough to accept food. Her head was throbbing, and she felt as if someone had punched her hard in the face.

S.O. Guber informed them all that the first arraignment hearing was set for 9 a.m. At 8, girls were told to prepare to go to court.

"Your prints were lost once more." Ms. Gruber said. "You cannot go unless you get fingerprinted again."

Channah exploded in frustration. "No, it's been done 7 times already. I must go to be arraigned." she said. Guber just chuckled.

At 9 she led the other girls away in 3's, handcuffed. Channah was not permitted to go. She began to despair as hours passed. At about 12 noon, she was fed again and decided to comply. Lucy, who looked a lot like Natalie Wood, had left in the morning, wearing her mink coat. "You are abusing my rights." Channah suddenly yelled. Guber, you're just making up an excuse to keep me here. You are denying me my rights under the law." She looked at Channah placidly and returned to her office. It was close to noon. A phone call came in. She took Channah out right after that and brought her down to the fingerprint room. "I'm sorry, sweetie, but it has to be done." she said.

There, Channah was put through a long scanner printing session. She also had to sit and answer questions about her mental health on a questionnaire. Four officers busied themselves with booking tasks, making her feel almost important.

Finally, she was led back to the remote corridor and cuffed to 2 other women. They all followed the escort to the waiting paddy wagon and climbed in.

She would later write a friend about the delirium session at 1499 North Frank Road, in that hidden away from the world place where she had the first breakdown. "I remember listening to the sound of a buzz saw singing for an hour on the 3rd floor above. I remember that most of the guards there looked blond, Teutonic, and vaguely like Albert Einstein. I remember reaching out to clutch the hand of the young woman being held in cell 2, who was terrified as well. I remember, most of all, being very, very scared that someone would leave me there forever and throw away the keys."

A lot of defense statements ran through her mind while she drifted in and out of sleep, while seated on the floor of Cell 1.

It was impossible to communicate any of these ideas to an ally while she was being booked that night. They would barely be heard at the arraignment hearing, nor conveyed to the Legal Aid Society attorney hastily put in charge of her defense.

The night was spent sleeping fitfully under Guber's care once more. She was then paddy wagoned down to the District Court Building with four other prisoners, all handcuffed together.

In a basement holding cell, female prisoners fielded questions from several Legal Aid attornies. They were confined in a cool, cement floored room. It had no toilet, nor were there benches to sit on.

The Arraignment was held on the second floor, with so many participants that seats were unavailable. Channah was held solo in the hall, guarded by two female officers. When she entered, the scene Judge Antony Packins' courtroom was pandemonium.

Her name was called, and, with handcuffed hands behind, she was led to the defendants' podium. At her side, Laura, a LAS attorney, replied to the Judge.

Expose: The Reckoning by Channah Gambit

There was a shock awaiting her in the discovery of a newly granted Order of Protection from Hebba Sands. It was coached in the most extreme terms as a *Stay Away,* just like her father's, rather than a *Do Not Harass.* Additionally, because a misdemeanor was misrepresented as a felony, her bail was set high $1500.

Channah froze as Laura was called away by a guard. Left alone at the podium, she was unable to present circumstantial evidence regarding the stolen cell phone. She could not mention on her behalf that her Miranda rights had been violated twice.

In the audience, Mellow watched silently. Daddy Gambit, Big and Mellow walked out. They capitalized on the situation, punishing her severely by cutting her off and not making bail.

Channah was returned, handcuffed to another holding pen, to await an outcome. She spent two terrible hours fielding jeers and questions from other inmates. "I'm waiting for my family to post bail." she said. The Court had appointed a L.A.S. attorney to her case, as they were informed that she was destitute. "My son will come. His boss will lend him. My daughter will come and bail me out." she thought, watching the minutes tick by on the big institutional clock there. The Legal Aid attorney did not show. Inmate after inmate was released and left. Now there were but two female inmates left.

"You're being taken to Carmen Road, soon, Ladies. You'll have dinner." Officer Kirkpatrick said. The curly haired brunette was not without sympathy, but her ice blue eyes were cold. Bologna and cheese sandwiches had been offered that afternoon, and rejected. There were some pints of milk on a bench. Channah's stomach turned as she drank from one. It had already soured. A filthy steel toilet stood behind an open partition. She relieved herself several times.

It was now after 7. All male prisoners had either gone to the Sheriff's Correctional Center in Westapple or made bail. A sharp command issued from Kirkpatrick, the barred gate opened, and Channah was led to a cold observation room. Once there, two African American guards commanded her to strip completely. They examined the soles of her feet, looked into her mouth, and made her move her tongue around. Almost satisfied, they then made her bend over, and fluff her hair with her hands. Finished, one said "Get dressed."

Returning to the holding area, Channah found her right hand cuffed to another prisoner. She was given a lapel badge to wear, with her new number and photograph. They were walked sideways through several long corridors. They climbed up a steep set of steps into the rear driveway, where a paddy wagon was being filled with last minute stragglers. As she seated herself on a steel bench, her shoulders slumped. *I'm living in hell tonight.* Channah thought.

Channah would spend the first 6 weeks of imprisonment making fruitless telephone calls, awaiting release which never would come. The classic *one phone call out* would be a misdial to a cousin, never returned.

Channah sensed that her professional career was over, as the paddy wagon bumped and ground over Westapple roads toward Carmen Road...She had been told by Laura that one of the charges indicated was a felony. Another inmate, a former day care teacher, had taken a liking to her in the holding pen, and told her that although technically speaking a teacher could return to the workplace as a professional certified by the State of

Expose: The Reckoning by Channah Gambit

New York with a few misdemeanors, employers simply chose almost always not to hire. *It's over.* she told herself, looking at the ugly faces to either side, then glancing away. *I've got a felony. That's much worse.*

It would be six weeks of negligent legal representation and computer glitches before the felony would be relabeled a misdemeanor.

Expose: The Reckoning by Channah Gambit

Chapter 11: Holding Cell Preparation

As Channah lay exhausted in her cell with *Natalie*, she could not think, nor use the potty, nor eat. Until she was actually allowed to go in for a late arraignment, she kept up her faith in the attorney. Unfortunately it was in vain because she had not paid a retainer and he hadn't the faintest idea that she mailed him anything nor was he a noble person.

At last! Still forced to wear handcuffs, and attached side by side to a quietly sobbing black woman busted for being a hooker, Channah passed through the Scylla and Charipdis of the fingerprinting center for the last time, the fifth to be exact. She had once again, been told that her fingerprint records had vanished. They asked her some peculiar questions, like "Have you ever tried to kill yourself?" and told her how good she was being and actually patted her on the back.

Channah had no idea what was to happen in arraignment court, but received unusually lax treatment. First of all, Legal Aid came up and agreed to represent her and asked a few preliminary questions, such as

"Are you guilty?" Channah still did not know the charges she would be facing.

Next, she was brought upstairs to the courtroom, Honorable Judge Antony Packins presiding. It was a madhouse, scores of people crowded into a room and no seating available for her. That was the result of an action by an officer named Patty, who needed to seat a young man where she was. To this day Channah wonders why she singled her out. At one end of the session the Judge sat behind his bench, with a man closely resembling a local assemblyman nearby. She stood out in the hallway as instructed a few inches away from the wall. Channah asked for a seat but that was denied, and two female officers watched her closely as if she was a violent criminal and not a poor unemployed, ill-fed teacher who had been tossed out by a family she formerly cherished. Finally, they allowed her to return and sit in the back row to watch the circus. As her name was mentioned, Channah looked around, wishing desperately to see the face of a family member. No one. She was called to the defendant's box and stood with an unfamiliar Legal Aid attorney at her side. The judge rattled off 3 misdemeanors, and she went into shock. Three! Then to her utter astonishment, the Legal Aid lady was called away and never returned. For her arraignment, Channah had no counsel. This just couldn't be justice or legal. The Judge quickly informed her of a protection order from one Hilda Sandstorm in force, and the other surprise was that one of the charges was a contempt charge for violating a protection order from her own father, already filed in district court, although it had originally been a non-harassment order of protection in family court. The Judge asked her how she pled and Ishesaid

"Not guilty". He set bail at $1500, and decided there and then that she would need a competency test, better known as a **7.30**, to see whether she understood the charges. This was due to looking at her, it certainly could not have been from her answers because there were none. Thus, Antony Packins, in a few swift motions, avoided hearing circumstantial evidence such as Channah had no cell phone to drop charges, and managed to eliminate legal counsel. In so doing, he reduced her professional career until it hung by a thread, and managed to throw her into prison for 112 days.

Once back in the holding cell in the basement, Channah waited with 12 other

Expose: The Reckoning by Channah Gambit

screaming, cursing, malevolent and primarily African-American women, who would become her companions for the next 3 months. Bail? Surely her sister or brother would bail her out. Hours passed as she paced after stomaching a hot spicy bologna sandwich which turned her insides to yuck. Nothing happened. To this day Channah remembers her shock over two things: First, seeing dear Ms. Detective Englemann wearing a different name badge, and a black ribbon on her pigtail. An officer informed her that she was just a parole officer. The second shock was the fact that her attorney never came.

Time came for a strip search. Clutching the protection orders and some other paperwork, Channah was led by two black bimbos into a side room with glass walls. They removed her cuffs and I began a ritual *The Antler Dance*, which would be repeated *ad infinitum* while in jail. There is nothing quite as demeaning as this ballet, and nothing so shattering to the ego. Afterward, she would retain a serious tendency to be biased against both black women and officers. They snapped on those ubiquitous turquoise gloves, and they checked her body over from stem to stern. They made her squat, cough, and turn, lift her arms, and open her mouth. Channah had to stick her tongue out and lift it to the roof of her mouth. She had to hold her head forward and rake her hair with her fingers. Their eyes were impersonal, unkind and cynical.

"Get dressed." One stated. It was a warm room, so she was lucky. Later she would discover that they were searching for evidence of drug use. She was under suspicion for everything from that moment on, and lost all pretense of dignity or feeling of innocence. Channah became a white skin suit on a hanger, a *ghost*.

They were moved once to a smaller cell to await transport to a place called the Nassau County Correctional Center facility at Carmen Road. Once they were there, they were thrown into holding Cell 1, to await processing for admission. Ten of them sat there. Channah listened to Michelle, a white small pit bull in cornrows covered with a French white kerchief, brag about her recent bust.

"I know my boyfriend's going to be there in the morning and see me." Michelle said.

"Michelle, who you kidding? You just got sentenced and you be going up New Bedford for over a year." Molly said.

"You crazy bitch, why you go deal crack cocaine?" another said, and they all broke out in raucous laughter. Channah shook slightly.

"We going to Block D." Michelle said.

"That be the Drug Crimes Area." Molly said almost proudly.

"I don't belong there!" Channah said.

"What you in for?" another asked.

"I just disturbed the peace and scared someone." Channah said.

"Honey, you don't belong here. You got a boyfriend to bail you out?" Molly said sympathetically.

"No." Channah said.

"Leave her alone. Anyway, they put all crimes in the D Block now because they don't have enough space in the regular buildings. So it don't mean nothing." Michelle said.

With more discussion, it was clear that most of them had been in before. They were no longer handcuffed, and shortly afterward, were fed spicy *mystery meat* bologna sandwiches. The sentries came around eventually at 9 p.m. They were walked down to photographing, fingerprinting in black ink this time, time number 7, and then to *wardrobe.*

"Okay, ladies. Take it off. Take it off. Take it *all off!*" Officer Aero said suggestively, twirling a whistle on a string.

"Stick all your personal garments into the brown paper bag provided you, and put all your clothes on the hanger provided you. And do not keep anything else." she said.

Thrown into stalls, Officer Aero made them strip down again and do the *antler dance.* Each of them received a maroon garment bag made of expensive satin with a number on it. All put their street clothes in, and received issue, but it wasn't like the army and they were very short-changed. Channah had a laugh inside, recognizing that the bags were *saint* colored, traditionally such a deep burgundy being associated with goodness.

Likewise, at the 1490 facility, a zipper hood to an expensive ski jacket had vanished under Grind's watchful gaze. It was necessary to be careful.

That night was the start of a period of total comblessness for her. It would be 112 days until she could groom her hair properly. Her eyeglasses had been confiscated at the time of her arrest. They were withheld from her for 38 hours, counted during which time the world was a blur.

This seemed the greatest travesty of all, on a par with having her arms painfully pinned to the back in a jolting van, or with having one phone call, and not being able to dial it correctly, or use a telephone directory the first night. Channah would have called her attorney and retained him if she could have phoned him. Instead, she received false directory assistance with 411, and ended up misdialing a cousin, who never responded.

They were about to enter Isolation and face the rudest abuse of all. It would go on for 36 hours extended to 48. But now, after being propertied, photographed, fingerprinted in ink, and wardrobed, fed, issued one towel and blanket, 2 uniforms, a tee shirt, a pair of flat cloth shoes with vinyl soles, and a small toothbrush, they were dead set on sleeping, nothing but. Up the elevator to floor 2, to isolation in block c. Thrown into a double tier of holding cells, most with 1 bunk. The new inmates began to snore almost immediately. It was March, and the weather outside was frigid. The cells were rather warm, about 68 degrees. Channah would come to appreciate the value of wool blankets the next day. But, for now, she was in shock, blind as a bat, unable to process, lost in a wild rough new world, and totally incommunicado with the outside world.

It would be over 27 days before she would meet with an appointed attorney. It would be about 48 hours before she would receive her glasses once more. There would be no phone use throughout her stay, either by design or incompetence. She had checked in with a total of $13.53. That would stand by her with Commissary for the entire time she was in prison. It would not be added to by anyone from her family, friends, or associates. No one would come to visit her with 2 exceptions.

Channah's had discovered something like her father's doghouse, his ultimate dumping ground. Daddy Gambit had tossed her into a garbage can to continue his campaign of degrading and destroying strong women. Many things would happen while she was there, injuries of spirit, mind and body which were not in keeping with ideal law enforcement practices. Each time they did, Channah would register the fact that something like an alternate agenda was being adhered to, and the veracity of it would lean her into paranoia, another side effect on top of PTSD. How many other women had gone through this? In short days she would meet M Dot, another casualty in the domestic violence arena, with a history amazingly similar to hers, a parallel case of abuse and punishment doled out by family leading to arrest on contrived or trumped up charges.

She would find herself extending the spectrum of knowledge of human nature. She would grow to understand, make acquaintance with, and communicate with "career criminals". But, for the first month or more, Channah was too scared to do anything more than cower. Dealing with it intellectually, she would consider the N.C.C.C. a coercion system, a *Guantanemo Bay II*. She would also think of it as a *Trojan Horse* or *Heartbreak Hotel*.

Expose: The Reckoning by Channah Gambit

Chapter 12: Isolation

Isolation was meant to ensure that all inmates were well, held *incommunicado* from enemies of the State, such as pimps, complainants, and vendors for users and such, and suitably malleable to be handled. Lucky ones could dial out and call lawyers. But Channah found, with new eyes, though blurred, that the purpose was to break them down, emotionally and physically. She found her resentment growing with each hour due to rough handling.

For there was no heat for the full 72 hours—and it was still winter. Additionally, there was cold air blowing in, from an a/c central system, into each cell. The privations were severe. They had no combs to groom themselves. There was a box of sanitary napkins and toilet paper rolls that was all.

The cell she held in C block, on the top tier, showed signs of ineffectual prisoner modifications. Someone had tried to block the air conditioning using newspaper or toilet paper attached with toothpaste once. Channah kicked around there for a few minutes, then walked back downstairs.

She walked over to the bin by the front sliding gate. No one else was moving around the area. She could relax. She was freezing and knew she couldn't read the small print.

She riffled through the bin. There was a newspaper or two in the block but here, in March, none were later dated than January, 2006. It was deliberate delay, intended to limit their knowledge of the news outside and that was the first thing which characterized the confinement to one as something out of a Russian gulag. For it is Communist to deny news to the populace or to make it useless information.

Lying on the cold hard cot for hours, clinging to a flannel blanket for sanity, her college courses in psychology played sonnets in her head. She could analyze jail isolation in psychological terms by training. There were behavior modification techniques not unlike those in brainwashing being employed. The hours of cold desensitized and numbed the women. There were hours of forced silence because they were held for these in single occupancy cells. There was nothing but boredom, nothing to read, no sounds of conversation so many just slept. Hours of sleep would lead inevitably to weariness and depression.

While she lay there in the cold, fighting for her sanity, she lost track of goings on around her. Often, lights were off or the power did not work and the monotony and dimness caused the mind to shut down. *This is intentionally built into the penal system. What a weird world is this!*

The guards were unusually severe, prone to physical remonstrance and crude.

She avoided the sentry desk after her first mistake. She learned that every opportunity to speak was denied, or an inmate had to wait 5 minutes while they did some scribbling or just sat and stared. Very little constructive direction was given.

Looking down from tier two, she observed that most women were forced to do menial tasks, like *Swab the decks* with harsh detergents in order to earn the right to watch television. *Especially the older ones, the ones the guards know or who have been here before. They are hunkering down the most.* she thought.

On the second night of isolation, Channah watched a news show repeated from the previous evening. *Bizarre!* she thought. Television was Communist too, in that it was wireless programming, edited and censored from a room on the second floor emanating from a central station. These were soap operas, or even stranger, violent or science-fiction movies with bizarre aberrant themes perfect for destabilizing and provoking inmates further. Commercials were fakes and telephone numbers culled from ads were non-existent numbers. That was deeply unsetting and Orwellian, to her way of thinking, as Channah analyzed this, trying to comprehend.

She thought back on the first trip to D block from the arraignment hearing. After they chain ganged in from the paddy wagon, Channah was forced to stop at a short hallway of windows. Behind one stood a young guard.

"You have the right to make one phone call. It's your turn." he said. She didn't say anything.

"Go ahead. Don't have all night." he said.

"But I don't know who to call. I need a phone number." Channah said.

"Oh all right. I'll get you information. She heard the operator. She asked for the phone number of a cousin Joe who lived locally. The crisp automated voice spit out the numbers and she tried to remember. Reaching around the ledge, she couldn't find a pencil.

"Can I please have a pencil." she asked.

"No, sorry. That would be considered a weapon. You dial out now. Hurry up!" he said. *You bastard!* she thought, glaring into his green eyes as he gazed at a clipboard. She dialed Joe. He loved her from way back. He'd come down make bail and she'd be out of here tonight.

"I'm sorry. Your call cannot be completed as dialed. Please check the number hang up and dial again." automated said.

"Times up. Next!" the guard said.

"I dialed wrong. I need to try again." Channah said.

"I am really sorry you misdialed. That was your fault. You had your one phone call. Next!" he said.

"Look. I misdialed. I have to get someone on the phone! You can't be serious!" Channah said. She had no glasses on, and his face was a pale blurr. She felt like hitting him with Dioxin.

"Now look. I'll tell *you* what to do, okay. *You're* the one who did something wrong to end up here. There will be pay phones in isolation. Bye." he said. She was not sure, but thought she had caught him winking.

She would not regain the right to dial out for almost 4 weeks. That was the *Chinese water torture* routine She began to notice. Services were intentionally delayed by jail employees. Alternate attempts later to communicate with someone via a social worker acting as a middleman would be stymied at the big communication center which programmed the lines.

If an inmate was deemed *harassing* by those listening in and monitoring all outgoing calls, the central station would program a block into specific dial outs. She found, over the months, that she had been so characterized in the system, enabling someone to essentially restrict her ability to call someone on the phone to nil. The severity of restriction in her case was unacknowledged by the internal investigative unit, or the grievance officer.

The Certified Social Worker. got in trouble for doing it or for acting as an advocate. Boiling resentments, weeks later, would be addressed in the regular cell blocks with *gripe sessions*, group meetings, which led to no change in conditions. The workers were looking for insider information to use against inmates to spot potential unrest and uprisings in prison mainly.

The women in isolation lived mostly on a treacle substance, vaguely purple, called *coffee*, in the morning. They ate bread, slightly acidic, either white or brown, which caused painful bowel movements. The cereal was the most edible substance once a day.

The oranges were rotten, green, and acidic. The sandwiches for lunch were always some *mystery meat* bologna, heavily peppered and disgusting. Dinner was often pasta covered in a jelly substance, like congealed cartilage, or in an acidic dressing which could not be forced down the throat.

Channah lost weight rapidly in jail. In November, she weighed 175. By the end of March, it was down to 145.

The drinking water was dirty, and had a scum to it—in the sinks—and it was rusty in the bowls of the toilets. Many seats were covered in filthy gauze, which could not be removed. She worried about sexually transmittable disease. Someone had violently barfed in her cell. There was a pool of food waste still congealed on the floor. She had sprayed it up on the ceiling near a vent, and it looked like a Jackson Pollack. It seemed to contain iron filings—and these turned up in the pasta salads—had no taste, like metallic pepper. So from the start, being a meticulous eater, Channah was predisposed to be paranoid about food or eating. This turned out to be a major means of control, or demoralization, the diet.

There were all types of systems to get better foods, if you faked illness. And that was the 3rd clue it was a Socialist design—that only by feigning illness, or being labeled *sick*, could a dissident obtain a good diet, or good conditions to live. If you filled out a sick form, you could get kosher or pregnant or bland diet later. This was not an option in the first isolation days. Just like the way the Russians threw political subversives into hospitals back in the 1960's, Channah mused.

If you were sick, you could not leave your cell at all, as you might infect others.

Walking aimlessly around one afternoon, Channah spotted a slight African American woman brought in, still dressed in street garb. In black and red, her form shown vibrant in the surrounding gray green and brown drab quarters. Two guards wheel chaired her in and left her on the floor in a cell.

"She's going through withdrawal from crack cocaine." Phoebe told Channah. They monitored her progress, as she spent the next 72 hours passed out on her cot.Channah never saw her given food or medication. Her name was Ace and they moved her across into the Medical Observation quad the following day. Little did Channah know that she would be short to follow.

Expose: The Reckoning by Channah Gambit

Inmates avoided the guards, who liked to shake them up, yell, or lecture. Channah found nothing to do except watch blurry television blaring constantly in her ears.

God, what did I do to deserve this? I'm freezing my butt off! Other women are being bailed out. Why not me? Where's Duvey? Where's Jamo? What must they be thinking? She thought these things mostly in the hours she was locked down in her cold clammy cell.

There was one woman she'd remember, Kimmy, who was a striking brunette with black curly hair down her back, and with bandaged wrists. She said,

"Put my hands through a window". She went down to medical early, she was *salved*, allowed to call extra and bailed out after a day.

"Don't feel bad about her." Officer Nudge said to Channah one day. "She deals drugs. She belongs here." His dark brown eyes looked sternly at her from behind long lashes. "You worry about yourself only. And you look out for yourself too." he added.

"I'm really in need of my glasses, please?" she would ask at the table in the proper manner. Guards showed pity to her, but the other inmates just looked away.

"Why you old toad! You poor excuse for a man lover! You got something to say you go and say it now." foul mouthed sister number one said to sister number 2.

Channah and all the other women backed off, starting toward their cells.

"You say your man done time? You want to make something out of something?" foul mouth 2 said back to foul mouth 1, who then threw her bucket chair back. Up until then, they had all been watching Andrew R. Broccoli's "Goldfinger" on television. Watching this fight would be more fun.

But, the sentry guard stood up and started the horns blowing. The screen went dark and they took out their nightsticks. Nudge started poking Foul Mouth 1 up and away from Foul Mouth 2, but neither one saw anyone else but the other.

"Into your cells, ladies. Lock down for bad behavior." They all went in obediently and the doors slid shut.

"There goes an enjoyable evening!" Channah said through her slot.

The others were foul-mouthed, primed for a fight, entering into arguments and bragging about their crimes, often in for violent assault.

That was another evil of the prison structure. White collar crime, first-time offenders were mixed in with the career criminals and felony sentences.

But some kind of initial sorting was going on, done by the guards. They were analyzing them for ease of handling, and spotting *easy medicals,* those who seemed inordinately scared, or possibly suicidal, or weak, or victims who needed to be tracked out of the general prison populace. In this filthy system, the criminals won more freedom, less observation, less labeling and manipulation, and had less medication forced down their throats. They were just *bad*, a distinct advantage! That seemed backwards to Channah. Sedating them would have made things much more bearable for her. That, she guessed, was where they'd cross the line into a Khrushchev state. That's where everyone gets called a criminal and medicated into oblivion, a double whammy.

The medical coercion and brainwashing techniques she saw clearly delineated in the manner with which they performed initial medical evaluations.

Expose: The Reckoning by Channah Gambit

On the second night, they were awakened at 2 a.m., and a group of four was taken through the beehive labyrinth down a left-hand corridor, through a yellow door to a medical suite. Forced to sit for hours, she was summoned past 3 guards at a glass booth, into an examination room, to meet a Chinese American doctor. He was gentle, kind, and astute. He took a little time to ask her medical history, noted that she did not use drugs, or have any psychiatric problems which were noticeable, and then released her. He did not weigh her, or take blood pressure, or do any physical exam. It would be 2 months before Channah was weighed.

About a day later, she was awakened roughly at 3 a.m., by a flashlight-carrying guard at her cell door, and hustled out, to the right, to a red door, oriented exactly in the hall as the first one had been in the other wing. Inside, it had identical furniture, identical handwritten signs, and identical placement of personnel. It was a different office and different doctors were there. The parallel setup slightly disconcerted her especially when she was asked, while very groggy, whether she had been in before. Channah knew enough to say "No", and it seemed to displease the medical technician, who had expected a different answer. This seemed to be a deliberate parallel, to throw off the memories of inmates. That was her private speculation.

She supposed that was standard in prison architecture, not to let criminals know a real layout, for they could plan an escape better. But the parallel signs and furnishing were just too deliberate. They seemed to serve the purpose of masking some medical practices involving prisoners which were going on there under the guise of medical exam routines, or sorting them into a yellow, and a red group. The difference seemed to involve blood-taking and injection activities. Some prisoners, for reasons unknown to her, and not guessed at, would be called at *reveille* each morning to go to medical for about a half hour, around 8:30 a.m.. From talking to prisoners, she learned that it was for either blood taking or injection. If you were *true*, you gave blood in the red door exam room. If not, you were a *yellow*. The blood taking was explained as a venereal disease test, required of all prisoners. If you did not comply you would wind up in isolation in your cell indefinitely. Urine specimen would have sufficed for that or so Channah thought. At 4 a.m., on that second day of exam, she was asked for blood by a technician, a *Maude*, a steel magnolia with salt and pepper brillo afro, for blood, for a TB test. If she refused, Channah would not get to use a phone or see prisoners or visitors.

Maude was surprised when she was lucid enough to mention a previous TB exam, and name the Chinese doctor.

"I just had a TB test for a job, and it was a negative. You can have urine. No blood. Contact my physicians at home. I am going home soon." she said. First, Maude's mouth fell open. Then, she turned her back on the inmate. Channah's suspicions were aroused when she declined to take down the name of any family doctor, or call him. She immediately saw that it was a system of coercion. She was weary, and befuddled from isolation, so she could not recall her doctor's phone number.

This was privation, another denial of human rights which they employed. There were no phone books in the block. Channah could not get a doctor or lawyer on the phone for the first few weeks. In law library later, there would be ancient phone books for two local counties, from over four years back. Some names of friends she knew were omitted, although she knew they were printed in the book at home.

There was an unwritten policy of misinformation as if she was an intelligence agent from a foreign government. In some ways it felt like a micro-Guantanamo Bay. Even later in regular stir when she was allowed Mondays to get to the miniscule law library on a regular basis, she found that wrong addresses were posted on the pillars for such things as the Nassau County Bar Association or the Human Rights Commission. These mailed envelopes would return weeks later stamped **unaddressable**.

What was the purpose of this policy or procedure, this denial to an accused innocent citizen of true information?

Channah could not organize her head or plan a strategy in response to her crisis or develop some means of recovery when her appointed attorney did not come. What was that stacking the odds against her when she had not been convicted about anything?

At any rate, having disarmed the blood takers in the red suite, showing competence by noticing the parallel examination areas, she won an uplifted brow, the turn of *Maude'*s back, and a quick return to a cold cell. ChannahI earned a profile for being too glib, as well.

Attacks on inmates in isolation and elsewhere were therefore environmental, medical, dietary, and communicative. They involved distorting means of obtaining information, making it unreliable, or denying it through censoring. Sometimes it was just technical trouble.

That is not the true purpose of a segmented isolation from the general prison population. The purpose is to spot trouble which requires separating out an inmate from that. Medically, a baseline physical status is supposed to be set, and some testing for communicable disease is done.

There were some acts of mental cruelty displayed by guards she witnessed. These appeared to have been taught by rote, from commanders or superiors. Some guards, like Putman, were just ingenious.

His favorite tendency was to sit at the guard desk with his feet propped up on it. As you came near, he lifted one big boot up and held it toward your face. It seemed to mean

"I will stomp you, vermin!"

Taunts were legion. But why rub it in to a group of tired, scarred women that they don't even have the right to groom? A guard came in, sauntering casually, a hair brush displayed in her pocket. It is easier to manage a group with low self-esteem.

Another one, whom Channah actually began to dislike intensely, did her shifts with 4 pens prominently displayed in her belt. Anyone who asked to borrow one, and there were several, was denied.

She observed, during meals, as they struggled with acrid Kool Aid or acidic water that guards <u>always</u> brought water bottles, coffee cups, or soda drinks in with them. These were always displayed prominently on the desks, like Poland Springs liter bottles.

The *haves—have nots* program set up a demoralizing wall.

"We're good—we get clean drinks. You're evil—you get shit!" It seemed to message silently, through visual props.

"We're better than you; we abide by the law." This message, similar to parading prisoners down a Chinese street, derisive slogan-printed placards around their bodies, smacked of Red Communism to her. Such actions browbeat them subtly, day in, day out. Bodily injury through ingestion of substances and behavioral signals happened.

One other dramatic device, involving uniforms, was cruel. This was the placement in the front *public* bin of a pair of prisoner's slacks. The bin was there to provide extra things, or books, or free supplies up for grabs. If you were to pick up these slacks, which Channah noted happened in every block she was in, you would discover, much to your chagrin, that someone had cut them completely up to crotch, so they were a useless garment. The prisoners had no scissor, no sharp object, so it had to be the guards. To her it signified an insult, and *rape.* She witnessed some poor prisoner, who had handed in her one pair of slacks to be washed outside, forced to wear a pair of these all days, with a towel draped around her middle for modesty.

The guards had their favorites. Even in isolation, the *Alphas* stood out. These would approach a guard and request something like if she would get them the other pair of their slacks, from the wardrobe room. She'd take care of it within hours.

There were the girls, back for the umpteenth time, who knew the ropes. They would be allowed to quickly join food service, and get double rations every meal. Channah was denied the right to join it, or volunteer, her entire stay, because she was a newbie. This sort of stuff was typical prison corruption.

She saw much more than that going on. Once, a guard, Zulu, who resembled Rambo, came in to guard them during dinner. They had been in solitary, freezing in their cells, for 36 hours, due to no apparent behavioral problems. The dinner that night, brought in from his family, was *Chicken Marsala.* It had wine and roasted tomatoes in it! Although it was full of cayenne pepper, they were eager and allowed seconds. How she loved that man! After 4 days of torment and starvation, it was a treat.

By the next morning, many of the inmates had *Montezuma's revenge.* Rambo never returned, and they had graduated.

After isolation, Channah felt like a victim. She was on her guard with everyone. It was as if an older, reptilian part of her brain had kicked in. The sweeter teacher personality was submerged.

As a result of the treatment she received at 1499 Franklin and trauma, she suffered temporary brain damage. Channah had a cognitive breakdown happening. Although she was not stuttering, she couldn't recall such things as Big's phone number in Queens, and spelling was messy. There were emotional symptoms induced by the lack of a bailout by loved ones she had alienated. These did not clear up for about 10 weeks.

Expose: The Reckoning by Channah Gambit

Chapter 13: Block B

When Channah was admitted upstairs as a regular prisoner, it was because no one had come to make bail. She had been arraigned on 3 misdemeanors, and been given a protection order from the complainant, who was unknown to her.

The charges were : 120.45 Stalking 4th degree, a B misdemeanor worth up to 90 days in jail; Criminal Contempt in the 2nd degree, against the family, with up to a year for a sentence; and 240.50, False Report of a 911, a Class A misdemeanor, also with up to a year as a maximum sentence. She discovered these through the computer printout I received at the arraignment. However, there was a glitch in the system, and the 240.50 had been labeled as a Class A Felony. Through informal talk with an officer, she had been given the notion that she would never teach again with that felony made a conviction, as a felony would automatically destroy her certifications. Channah was terrified, then depressed day to day at that prospect. The misinformation did not change for about a month, not until she had seen my legal aid attorney, Matt Silverwitch, twice.

They were brought upstairs with no handcuffs to block B, 3rd floor, and unloaded in, with supposed restoration of phone privileges. Her head was pretty cloudy. She could not remember her pin number to phone out unless it was in front of her. Was it from the partial concussion or shock? She had no account set up with anyone outside. It was *global net.com*, as she was told by Jackie some time later, so her limits to help herself were severe. Her cousins had never responded to a call for help, nor had the attorney, Theo Dumo. Channah could not recall her sister, brothers, daughters or son's phone numbers.

In the first couple of weeks, almost a third of the prisoners were bailed out and left. Even more distressing to her was the lack of a telephone directory. She had no pen or pencil to write a number down. She was scared of other, more violent, prisoners. Some women, with short afros and mean actions and remarks, were dominating the tables, the televisions, the phones, and the jobs. She just never thought of asking one of them to call a friend to make an outside third party call. After about 6 weeks, she was driven to attempt that.

The charges were minor, but they had been inflated out of proportion by her brother's adding wood the fire, his power of attorney on Daddy Gambit's Order of Protection, reflected badly on her at the worst possible time. In protecting her dad, also her landlord, he had heaped abusive labels into the public record, and these in turn encouraged the police, she imagined, to suggest to the complainant, Hilda Sandstorm., to put herself under the protection of a second one, coached in the stiffest possible terms. In no time at all, Channah had been depicted as a violent mentally ill women by others.

The treatment she had received at the hands of NCPD was not unusual, her attorney told her months later. It was pretty much status quo for the county. The fact that key people she leaned on emotionally failed to bail her out crushed her spirit, and she very nearly snapped. The fact that relatives, phoned from outside person-to-person collect, hung up silently, bewildered her. It was just so coordinated, like a Busby Berkley routine. After such out of character behaviors, she could not look back on her past, and began to mentally burn bridges in the weeks ahead.

Expose: The Reckoning by Channah Gambit

B Block was home free after isolation downstairs on the second floor. There was a lot of steam to get rid of.

They milled around until someone started an argument, then they were thrown into their cells for an hour or two. This pattern repeated several times a day.

Channah looked at the women with wide eyes. In her book learning, she'd have referred to it as a *population. This population seems rather savage and bisexual with a lot of over development of sexual features.* She told herself. They were split into all races, with Blacks predominating. She looked at the faces.

One dubbed Golda Meier was at the head of a table which was her sisterhood, and no one elses.

At another, a female Louis Armstrong, short and dark, held court.

A tall trashy blond put her arm around the waist of an old crew cut matron. Channah winced.

Different strokes for different folks. How do I get out of here.

"Hey, you stay out of my way." this redhead elbowed Channah aside on the staircase.

"Excuse me?" Channah said.

"And don't you answer me back!" the inmate snapped at her.

Channah couldn't believe it. She walked over to the desk for security.

"Hey, you can't just approach the desk. You gotta ask permission to stand there." Castelli, a tall female officer stated.

"Sorry. Is there any chance of my getting my glasses back." Channah said.

"Who are you. Gambit? Yeah, Gambit, I'll see what I can do." Castelli snarled.

Channah saw lots of movement, but mostly blurred colors. She could not watch television. The ocean of colors bored her terribly. She would stay in her cell if it was warmer. She trotted around, a gray flannel blanket over her shoulders for warmth.

There was a major fight between two old women the first night they were there. The sirens sounded, and they all were forced into their cells. It lasted for two days of isolation. No exceptions.

_A guard, noticing that she tended to stay in her cell, choosing not to converse with most other women, decided she was *anxious*.

The first week there, as she would recall, was freezing cold, with the inside temperature hovering around 65 degrees, and a lot of *lockdown* occurred, where they were isolated in their chilly cells, even for meals, because of fights or arguing. The cold a/c air, wet and smelly, blew in through the vents. One paced, or sat on the floor near the door crack. The cells were very expensive, with big, well-oiled, rolling glass and steel doors.

Channah's cell had blotchy walls, as a bored prior inmate, Melissa, had dotted them all with toothpaste. Orajel, in a little 3-inch tube, clear colored and orange flavored, was available for hygiene with a little bristly plastic thing you stuck on the end of your index finger. She brushed with this finger puppet.

There was one gal, Patrol, who had been a worker before. She had connections, and obtained a slightly different brand of Oragel—blue green, sudsing, and mint flavored. Channah was jealous from the start, and used hers as laundry detergent and shampoo. It made her scalp burn. She had a wash day to do the towel, washcloth, sheets, underwear and a spare uniform. The block noticed the toothpaste and a jet black lady, Black Maria, who had reputedly nearly killed her boyfriend in an assault, sat at her table playing cards with her chums. They disparaged Channah on it.

"Almost an infraction, not allowed. Most of us use soap power purchased from Commissary." Patrol announced.

A new friend Phoebe, was a small white woman who tied her hair into *Buckwheat* curls with pieces of scrap paper. Their first day out in the day room, she befriended Channah.

"Come back to my cell." she said. Walking there together, they started up the stairs.

"NO, NO." the sentry said through a bullhorn. "You can't go up there unless your cell is there." Channah walked back down.

Phoebe returned and placed a miniature Gideon bible in her hand.

"Keep it. I'm in for a 14 month sentence and they are going to isolate me in block F soon. At least I will have my bible to read." she whispered.

"Thank you for this. You shouldn't have! What's the F block?" Channah asked.

"Oh, I just like to get into fights. They call me a pit bull. I don't take shit from anybody." Phoebe said.

"Unbelievable." Channah said. Phoebe was about 5 foot 2, a light delicate blue eyed blond. It was impossible to see her beating on other prisoners.

There was a prisoner on the floor who looked like Roseann Barr. She had been watching her talk to Phoebe.

"Hey, you come over here. I want to show you something." Channah followed her warily to a full table. The women, mostly Black Africans, were sitting around arguing and complaining.

"Watch this. This is how the poor gals live!" Roseanne said. She took a bar of issue soap, sat at the long dining table, and pulverized it into powder against an edge. It curled up like mozzarella cheese, then she broke it up and stuck it in some toilet paper.

"Hey, that's really good to know." Channah said. Roseanne handed her a bar of soap. She wouldn't let Channah leave until she had practiced it.

Some there had means. While other inmates placed huge commissary orders on Sundays for more than $20, she had very little. To stretch it, she used what was given to her free.

After a day or two, food got no better: bologna sandwich lunches made of pink *mystery meat*; breakfasts of boiled eggs and bread, or cereal heavily sugared along with milk, oranges and coffee; dinners of meat, potato and puddings. She picked up the habit of hoarding cereal and fruits, and using it as barter money.

A Roseanne Barr-type disliked Channah on sight, and yelled at her about something. A guard took notice and wrote them both up. This meant that a report of the incident went into the journal and they might get locked down for several hours or worse. Next thing she knew she was called down to the basement to the medical observe offices to see a hospital psychiatrist.

She spoke to the ratlike Muslim doctor Quakez under duress not trusting his faith nor his motives. The guard had written her up as *possibly suicidal,* a technicality which gave him the right to take her rights away. He could force Channah into the hospital, or feed her medicine, or put her in solitary confinement in the medical wing.

"I'm sorry," he said, in a soft firm voice.

"You might be suicidal. I believe you when you tell me you are okay, but we don't want you out there like this with those rougher girls. So I am putting you into A Block, the Medical Observation block. And I am going to give you something to calm you, okay?"

"No thanks, doctor. I'm not taking the meds." Channah said.

"But it's so that you can make phone calls with the social workers! Things are better there. It's a softer environment, and you'll fit in. That's really why I'm doing it. In a few days, I'll make a phone call for you, okay?"

"Okay." she said. "I have a clear enough mind and I won't take any medication."

This was the first of a dozen attempts to maintain autonomy. It would come to the point where the chief social worker, Powers, would leverage her into taking medication so that her daughter would phone her. .

Chapter 14: M.O. Block A

The guard walked Channah to the elevator, she went to her cell, threw her belongings in her sheets, and returned downstairs. She submitted to a body search, spread against the wall. Her things were looked through by two guards. They passed out inner glass doors a few feet away to an identical block to the right: Medical Observation or *the nuthouse* block.

There she met Merry, a white, snub-nosed girl with frizzy hair set into cornrows. She was enjoying a hot game of *Spades* with the group Channah came to think of as the *German Alpha Circle.* The leaders of the block, quite blond and buxom Jen, svelte, shapely Denny Purge, and small-featured, ugly little African-American Wondra, were at the television set, facing the beehive with the corporal stayed, visible through the thick ¾" shatter-proof glass as he watched all the monitors in his inner office. It was surrounded by a quadrilateral corridor, with four blocks fronting on it.

At an outside long trestle table sat the Black clique, comfortable, grooming each other's hair, and watching Desmond. Channah was moved into cell 1, adjacent to a main wall, her new haven for the next 115 days. It was next to the laundry machines, the non-stop trundling noise of which would accompany her silent lockdown hours and nights of down home recreation in the chilly, windy, group inner space.

It featured along the outside rails, 24 solitary cells in 2 stacked ribbons or half circles. There were 2 shower stalls behind vinyl curtains, lit by fluorescents downstairs and above. The wraparound stairs to the upper tier were forbidden to downstairs inmates, as were those hot water showers. A couple of closets for cleaning tools and buckets, a table near the door for food service, an old beat-up wooden desk with drawers for the constantly changing guards, a few black easy office chairs in leather, and the whole block in drag grays, steel gunmetal gray floors and turquoise steel hardware. That was her home.

Her room was alright and fairly private, so she quickly put her things away and got out before all cell doors slammed shut in unison. Their *in's and out's* were every half hour. You had a choice then where you could go. They were under the watchful eyes of surveillance cameras at either end of the hexagonal block, with those loudspeaker phones over head for the monitor watchers to shout out orders. Under the front chow table was the universal bin of junk, torn slacks, recycled books and outdated newspapers, Modess pads, tampons, rolls of toilet paper, discarded shoes, and clothes up for return to wardrobe. It contained newspapers dating from January.

She entered toward evening, after dinner at 4:30, after the obligatory hour of lockdown for no other purpose than apparently digestion, or to give the guards some easy vigil time.

The game of Spades, a unique feature of NCCC prison culture, took her weeks to master. Channah was now watching faces in the *Alpha* group, looking for a welcome. There would be none.

Then she just sat in a chair with them and asked if that was okay. It was. Merry lifted up an eyebrow, surprised that she'd bother to ask. She said she was in for

"Slashing up my boyfriend's arm with a knife during a fight." Channah immediately

Expose: The Reckoning by Channah Gambit
dubbed her *Nancy Whiskey.*

Insert lyrics****

It was not customary for these crude devious women to practice the niceties of etiquette like Miss Manners. But, she learned soon that there were a lot of unwritten rules of the block she'd be forced to keep or get set upon.

Right now, it was all pure curiosity.

"What ya in for?" they asked. Channah told them, briefly.

"Aw, you shouldn't be here! Get bailed out already!" they said, in unison.

"No. Not going to happen." she told Crystal. Wondra was a piece of work: an unstable, highly aggressive, cunning careerist. Far from ugly, she was like a miniature Cleopatra, with a straightened wig hairdo which never changed. She wore only white, and turbaned her head in a strip from a sheet. All she did was write letters back and forth to her boyfriend.

Jen., a nature type with a strong, athletic physique, carried herself like a Russian Olympian with very few traces of feminine grace. Although she was extremely attractive to the guards, she was a bitch. Still, she spent time playing up to them. The rest of the time, she did Word Finder puzzles with a pencil stub. As she was on food service, doling out food to each spot, she had a privileged place at the central trestle table, bolted permanently down and painted acid blue. Her fresh complexion with a sprinkle of freckles across her nose, made her look as innocent as Doris Day. But, Jen kicked butt when someone did not follow block rules. She was in for some rather heavy assault felony. Jen was vague about it when Channah questioned her.

"I'm sentenced already. I got 5 months, and get out in August." She said. Right above me in cell 13, she took upon herself the job of protecting and caring for me.

"Call me "MAMA" she said.

In jail, women adopt other women and become mama. It is an affectionate term, used instead of a name to show who belongs to whom.

Jen had her sit next to her. Lucky lady, she had a fiancée coming to visit her regularly, and a good phone connection with him, placing calls home every night. She offered to make a call for Channah, if she could get a number. Channah tried to call my son at the deli without success that night.

Denny to her left held the top seat at the head of the table. A rule was not to take that, but leave it always to her. Denny was beautiful, with clear blue eyes, perfect skin, straight blond hair in a pull-tie ponytail, and white canvas sneakers without ties--a status symbol brought in from outside.

Denny was watching television a lot in those early days. Her speech revealed she was intelligent, spoiled, and used to being pampered. Her fierce aggression led to rebukes, condemnations, and vicious spells of epithet-hurling, often at Channah. Channah quickly learned her other side, that manifested in little girl vanity sessions where she sat for an hour or two with brush and curling iron, doing her hair, using a door glass as a mirror. At these times, she was almost friendly. Denny was in the process of a divorce, and it had her in a prissy mood. What charges she served were unknown, but that was a March to August sentence of five months. Quite likely, a repeat offender status rumors said.

Expose: The Reckoning by Channah Gambit

Their temperaments led them all to fight frequently. But, they'd quickly end it because, as it was understood in the *Sisterhood*, any loud fight would end the night early with a punitive lockdown to avoid a more serious write up for breaking the Sheriff's code, with extended days of jail time.

"If the guards like you, they'll just put you in your cell for 3 hours. That's better." Jen said.

Channah heard a loud banging, as of a hand slamming a door window. It was cell 8.

"Ice! Shut the f--k up!" someone yelled from the black's table. A girl by her side looked her way with scorn. Channah looked from cell to cell. There was another black woman in isolation in cell 2.

"That's *Special*." she was told by a woman named Menda Mader over at the other table, friendly already with crinkly eyes which lit up her Javanese face with warmth.

For the entire 120 days Channah was incarcerated, she saw Special spend 22 hours of each day in her cell. She walked over to gaze in. A huge, 250 pound *Aunt Jemima* with a huge mass of hair uncut and uncombed, seemingly never, sat with her back to her at the desk. She craned around, and she caught a glimpse of a face which made her think of a cross between Quasimodo and a hippopotamus from *Fantasia*. *Special* was the ugliest black lady she had ever seen. But she was warm, maternal, and her toothy mouth broke into a warm smile. She began to rummage in her top bunk and took down a box of Wheaties, which she stuck through her slot to Channah.

"You must be crazy to be here on M.O." she grinned.

"Thank you." Channah said. She began to explain when the huge Officer Sharaz a Muslim-type black man shouted out at both.

"No one allowed near solitary. You'll end up in your cell for a week if you don't stop. Somebody tell her the rules!"

It was different in M.O. Of course, no suicide tempters like shoelaces, belts, rubber bands or emery boards were allowed. Nothing sharp, nothing allowed in your room would be tolerated. Channah was told all this in a whisper. If cosmetic razors came around, you had to shave outside the cell.

Twice a day, medical carts came in to dope the inmates, or treat them as prescribed. They all obediently stopped what they were doing, as there was an announcement on the loudspeaker from Corporal Zizzer.

"Medication. Medication, *ladies*." They all stood in their doors peering out. As each person was called, her door slid open with a clang, and she came forward with a cup of water. When she took the pill, she was forced to open her mouth and lift her tongue so the nurse could check she swallowed it. After forty minutes, this was all done, and free time resumed.

She got into a great conversation with Ice, who was about twenty. She was extremely thin and had an angular, savage beauty in her face. She told Channah that she would have to get a tattoo. It seemed that everyone who had ever been incarcerated passed a rite of passage, and had to mark themselves *on the street* with a tattoo of choice, so that others in the *Brotherhood/Sisterhood* could recognize that they had been underground. She told Ice that it was against her faith, but she wrote a line on her right hand with a pen to make her feel comfortable.

Expose: The Reckoning by Channah Gambit

"What are you in for?" Channah asked her.

"A man in his forties come up to me and call me *Nigger*. I pulled a knife, slashing in the face twice." she told her. As a result, she lost her right to liberty for approximately 15 years without parole. Ice had been sentenced already, and was being shipped *up country*, to either Bedford or higher upstate for storage. The woman was so aggressive she could not be trusted to mix with other inmates. She was under-medicated although she was high strung. Channah talked to her about the movie *Million Dollar Baby*.

"I'm going to call you that." she said, and Ice smiled.

"You gotta get yourself a nickname now that you've been here." she told her. Channah ended up being called *Artist* eventually.

At the *Alpha* table, an argument had ensured regarding who had to clean up the showers. Denny looked at her then called her over.

"You do it tonight." she said.

They forced Channah to. She said "No.", but she then got yelled at and harangued. Denny made jer put on a pair of plastic gloves, and she set up a bucket of industrial strength Clorox. With a mop, Channah swabbed the filthy, scummy and moldy walls. It was *Initiation Time*. Four pairs of eyes watched her every move, and she was corrected and asked to put out more effort. Then she threw the plastic waffle mats back in. Denny helped her turn the showerhead on to rinse everything off.

"Use the left stall only, so we have less work." she said. They then started a heated discussion about cleaning rules, while an oblivious guard read a *Glamour* magazine and ignored their raised voices. Channah wondered at that time why they did not have only women guards watching female inmates, as sometimes people walked in stages of disarray and disrobed, doing personal hygiene things.

As for cleaning rules, some wanted the last girl showering at night to have the job. Jen and Denny stated that they should all take turns, a different girl each night. Twenty minutes elapsed. She had been told the return the gloves to the garbage. Channah had been warned against hoarding Clorox or rags, or about 10 other things.

"M.O. block is a blast!" she told herself, falling to sleep the first night.

Expose: The Reckoning by Channah Gambit

Chapter 15: Consignment & Food

With the $13.73 Channah had, she needed to pay out for phone calls, for postage, envelopes, pens and paper, to try to raise the bail. She was mystified by not having been bailed out. Her attempts to get a pushy social worker named Carol Muck to make calls for her were soon to backfire.

Every Friday they'd plan our purchases like frantic army ants. On Saturday mornings, after Catholic services, they'd hand out blue checklist sheets. She was feeling mighty needy, because no one had brought her any undergarments, and she'd been wearing no bra for weeks. This was due to her being arrested right after a nap. She'd been wearing mighty strange attire—a pair of stretch pants, a thermal ski shell on top with nothing under for comfort, and a hooded sweater.

So here was a freebie, they'd shorted the wardrobe checking in and she'd been washing out the panties every few days. So she checked off the free socks, undies, and bras. But they just would disregard it the first few weeks.

Commissary would come around on Tuesday mornings. Reynolds was a tough female officer in her sixties who favored jodhpurs and high black boots. With short sleeves, she'd trundle and push the large cart of commissary goods, a big lumbersome shelved thing into the room.

"Clear back the tables. Make room." Officer Ripper would yell. The Day Room would be cleared. Then Reynolds and Ripper would take brown paper bags out of a bin, and put them on one table to the left. All prisoners would have already gone back to their cell doors, to wait being called.

"All right. Calm down! Calm down! We'll do this right. Just take what's coming to you and go back in." Reynolds said. She called out orders by their prisoner names.

Channah had very little money left by April. "Gambit" Reynolds bellowed. She walked up to her and was handed a brown lunch bag.

"Well what do you know. You got something!" Ripper said, peering at her and smiling rakishly. Walking past the washing machines, she opened.

"Wow!" Channah said to herself. She had received a free golf pencil, a pad of lined paper and two free envelopes. That wasn't all. The comb was there too.

What a way to get the ball rolling! She looked at herself in the cell mirror, which was hazy because it was made from unbreakable polished steel. Her hair was growing out in waves and sat every which way down her neck. Tangles made her grimace as she raked her head. It took an hour before she was satisfied. The paper and envelopes lay on the steel desk forgotten temporarily. *Damn comb cost me 75 cents!* she thought.

I have no intention of buying the peanut butter. I have no money for food goods. Forget it! No Kool Aid for me. She began to learn to barter early on. An egg and a mini-box of cereal for an envelope. A poem for some paper.

At first, other girls were nice to her, and sometimes gave her one. But, she soon noticed her collect calls to cousins led to auto-hang-ups, or non-acceptance of calls. She needed to find a sponsor or advocate to help her and racked her brains to figure out who to write to for money. The plain truth was, she had no friends out there, only acquaintances. She had squandered the past 10 years going through undergraduate and then graduate school like a Gollum without a social life. The few she could think of were social workers at an alcohol rehab center she worked at in 2004 and a second cousin in Glen Cove and her psychologist therapist in Lynbrook.

On Monday, after a good weekend, she went to law library—a small room with some 150 books on loan status. Channah used the telephone books for the entire ½ hour they were there. She copied down the address to Newsday's Letters to the Editor department.

"I'm going to compose a bail letter." she told herself. Sitting at the library typewriter, she wrote the following:

"Dear Sir/Madam:

"I am a poor woman who cannot make $1500 bail being held at the Sheriff's Jail in East Meadow.

"My family decided to make an example out of me, and I have no friends to lend me the money for bail.

"I am a former teacher who is down on her luck.

"Please send me some money! It should be sent to my commissary account at the facility. It will be applied to my bail. I will be released on my own recognizance.

"Thanking you in advance for your generosity, sincerely, Channah Gambit."

"Hey, you better let me see that." Officer Pulcrid said from his desk. His stern grey eyes looked her over appraisingly. "It's my job to read everything and all the photocopying too." he said. He took it from her outstretched hand. She recovered the computer. Standing behind the table with it's glass top, Channah counted to 90 before he gave the letter back to her.

"I can approve the letter, Gambit. You can mail it off to *Newsday*. It ain't going to do you any good." Officer Pulcrid said after he read it over carefully.

She planned to give it to Matt Silverwitch. He might send it to friends outside as well as Newsday. It was an appeal letter, sad and desperate enough to touch many hearts.

Sheriff's Officer Pulgrid did not know law

"How might there be a bail fund for you? Let me see if I can figure it out." Pulgrid said. Channah looked hopeful and stood attentively by his large computer console.

"I mailed it last Tuesday." she said.

"They might allow checks which come in from *Newsday* readers to be pulled out of your commissary account. That account is under your prisoner number, by the way. Did you put that in the letter?" he asked.

"No." Channah said glumly.

"Well, then, you might as well give up, because the money is going to get misplaced."

Expose: The Reckoning by Channah Gambit

"I hope not." Channah said.

"Well, let's be optimistic. Suppose it is left in that account. If your son or daughter were given Power of Attorney by yourself, they might withdraw it and pay the bail for you. Yes. That is the only way it can be done." Pulgrid said. He felt such satisfaction that he sat back beaming and folded his hands across his ample paunch.

"Officer Pulgrid, it has become obvious to me in these last few weeks that my family *en masse* has turned their backs on me just when I need them the most. It's my brother's contrivance to have me be punished by the State *ad absentia*." she said.

"What about those kids who love you?" he asked kindly. She looked at his ugly old face with the beak nose and the Brill Cream hair and thought he was an angel.

"Obviously, my kids are too scared to help me." she said.

After leaving him that Tuesday, Channah continued dealing with the bail fund struggle, but the more immediate problem was food. How could she think straight if she was hungry all the time?

Shortly after she came to Block A. (Medical Observation Unit), Denny Purge decided she didn't like Channah and showed it by offering her bad food.

Denny had taken a boiled egg back to her cell. She cracked the shell and kept in there unrefrigerated for several days among her bed linens.

"Channah you look starved. Are you hungry?" she said one Thursday evening. Channah looked at the big blond Swede warily.

"Ah, yeah." she said.

'I have something extra for you! I don't want it! Why don't you have it instead?"Denny said with her big turquoise eyes wide open and inviting.

"What is it and why should you give me anything?" Channah asked. She stood next to Denny and looked calmly up into her eyes.

"Why I'm just trying to be friendly. Wait right here. It's a hard boiled egg."

"Okay…." Channah said. She watched Denny climb up to the top tier and enter her cell. *Now, what's she being so nice for?* she thought. Climbing down the stairs, Denny carried the egg right over and plunked it into her hand.

"Charming. Thanks." Channah said. She grabbed it and swallowed it without salt. Denny waved her way and went to the magazines at the front table to sit.

Channah, walking back to herself, caught a rancid odor under her nose. It vaguely smelled like an armpit. She saw Denny whispering to Menda and Ouija there, and then they all burst into laughter. Denny looked her way and then covered her mouth with her hand.

Well, well. Another initiation ritual! Where did this egg spend the night? I can only guess! Channah felt nauseated for a while but kept it down. After that Denny was her enemy.

Even when the food was fresh, it was odd. The morning coffee was heavily sweetened. It had sediment in it, and sometimes was purple-brown, not purple. Were they doping inmates up? Channah often wondered, for about a half hour after drinking this, she'd fall on her cot in a weak swoon, as the sugar went to her head. Maybe it was a light dose of Thorazine, or artificial insulin, her blood sugar level apparently was dropping rapidly. She would not put it past that medical room. All the girls seemed to get knocked out after breakfast, and the compulsory hour of solitary was followed by few venturing forth around 8:30 to use the *day room* area. A lot of inmates refused to be medicated and thought they might be getting deliberately sedated simply for *more easy handling*. There was simply no way to test it so Channah stopped drinking the coffee because of the food coloring as well.

The notion came to her that there was some lunatic in the kitchen, down deep in the basement. It was rumored to be run mostly by black male inmates, She learned later. The manager, Blanche Mange, came in as dietician to talk to some chronic gripers. She studiously ignored Channah for at least 10 minutes. Wondra got a *pamper* menu of choice foods and extra portions usually reserved for pregnant inmates. She complained to her incessantly. Channah just had to laugh.

The problem was often acidity. They used a solution of something on pasta salad which turned her mouth to fire. Potato salad at lunch, turned blue from iron utensils, she assumed, ran drippy with a vinegar-acetic dressing which gave her the runs.

She could not fathom the processed synthetic meats they served! Although she often realized that otherwise she would starve this was, crudely put, *mystery meat* an inmate joke. The meats were pink, a lot like human flesh in appearance, or what you'd call pork, but they had no recognizable taste. If anything, it was pepper. The tuna salad was gelatinous, with what looked like flecks of cartilage in it, or turnip. There was some good in vegetables, green beans or boiled carrots were army issue, canned quality.

The trays would get wheeled in and the gals who were on the diet team quickly went around the tables, putting them in place. A sack of oranges, a few slices of bread at each setting, a warm pint of milk sat down. The women behind bars watched. Some sized up whether they were getting enough or not.

The gates opened and they charged the tables. Gert stood up with her beef stew and traded some potatoes with Ouija for an extra dessert. Special hoarded bread, as did Sally. Ace had a special platter and shared nothing. Channah traded off her *mystery meat* for some peas. Some extra white bread on one table was torn into by two inmates at once, which resulted in an argument.

"Pipe down or you'll eat in your cells!" Robertson yelled.

The dessert was sometimes pudding, either chocolate or butter scotch. Channah was forced to admit that, on some occasions, she had it, and on one occasion, shortly afterward, felt like her esophagus was on fire. She spent hours on her cot in June, as a ball of fire moved down into her stomach, then bloodstream, in extreme pain. Channah seemed to have a high threshold for it, so she did not request to go to sick call. Afterward, she wrote up the problem on a medical form and submitted it.

As the weeks passed, these occurrences struck her as paranoid so she tore up a lot of medical forms and grievances, because she wanted to seem competent, *even if it killed me*. In the early weeks, Channah was very think, and she ate everything. But she started to have a daily acid reflux reaction, so she began to get fussy. It made her head foggy and her vision blurry. A lot of inmates complained about that, and instead of eating the menu, hoarded bread. It was as delicious as cake when you were truly hungry but even here too acidity was a problem. The white bread in clear plastic with turquoise markings was particularly bad. The rough brown bread was just a cause of a stomachache. The best bread was served from other bags in the breakfast menu only.

"Don't ask me why there is a difference or why my body doesn't like it." Channah thought.

She was suffering from sheer nerves and stress just being around hardened professional criminals, relatively moronic and mentally ill inmates. Her acidic stomach, she thought, might have been attributed to aggravation as well. Days went by where she just ate breakfast cereal and skipped two meals, drinking milk instead. Her weight steadily diminished.

Most everyone felt the hunger by 9 p.m. Channah and others would get up from watching movies. There'd be some girls being quiet in their cells, reading or writing.

"Have you got anything to eat?" Action asked Ace.

"Got any bread? Any cereal?" Sally would stand by Special's cell, talking through the slot.

"Sure I got! What you got to trade for it?" Special would say. Under her mattress would be ten boxes of Wheaties.

"You got any dinner left?" Gert would ask the Black ladies corn-rowing their hair over on the other side.

"Sure. Here's a potato. Here's some roast beef. Hurry up! Hide it! I want some shampoo for it!" The Wheaties were a top trade item. Corn puffs came in second.

During May, a generous kitchen aide brought in a carton of clementines. They were grabbed up by many hands and placed on window sills for days.

"I'm sick of these damn things. Giving me a stomach ache. Got an egg?" Demo would say plaintively at the *Spades* table.

"No. Be happy for what the Lord provides." Cassie would say, her eyes looking up sternly from under a head tied in a sheet rag.

Who would ever think that food served in a public place in our modern-day society could be so bad? But it was, and she didn't recall later much that was palatable. Channah starved, or spent her days drinking milk.

The economics were easy, to trade for what you needed. But after week after week, women got surly and preferred the pleasure of denying Whitey. Envelopes, pens, and finally, paper dried up.

She rarely received mail. After 2 months, that really floored her. She used food barter to make friends too. It wasn't necessary to give the strong *alphas* food to protect her, or to be left alone. It was a *soft* block, except for the need for constant lockdown of chronic fighters or nut jobs. The doctor who had assigned her there for *additional* services did not keep his promise to her to permit her some extra phone calls. But the environment was better.

After weeks of negligence, Channah started to doctor the pasta. She found that, if she soaked it in milk, then rinsed it in water, she could manage a mouthful. Wondra was getting her *special cuts* dog food, and her meat seemed like sliced turkey. Channah's was not. She lived vegetarian, then she grieved it all in writing. These grievances came back, **nixxy,** stamped in red *unclear, vague wording*, except once.

Why would the Sheriff of Nassau be purposely *sicking* people with food, inmates asked each other? Why was it so strange, particularly the meats? And the texture was bizarre! On certain days, it seemed that the meat had passed through one of those wood shredder machines. They were eating something that had been torn up, that was white like albacore, but it was dry and rubbery, and had no taste at all. The food was also sometimes pulverized into microscopic pellets, like commercial fish food, mixed in some acid mayonnaise or gloppy milk sauce that was slightly sour. Was it dog? Horse?

Then, around March 13th, something happened Channah felt the need to explore. For lunch, they were served a type of sushi meat, coated in a glistening viscous sauce. When she ate it, the bouquet evoked the presence of her daughter. A strong feeling of nostalgia involving her came over Channah, as if she was right there, hovering near her. Channah started to masticate, thought better of it, and spit it out. She was at an impasse. The sushi reminded her too much of human flesh. She was already anxious. Subconsciously, she believed she was eating someone's puke, or someone's toe from the Nassau County Medical Center had been ground up and mixed in. Channah started to gag.

For, after all, the style of food was degrading, and made her feel like a dog. Her self esteem was low. It was something like those army experiments during Wolrd War II, where they changed the colors you normally ate to see if it had a demoralizing effect on the troops: blue milk, purple steaks, pink soda. None of them could relax about eating, and fretted about it. What was to stop them from pissing in the food downstairs? Was there shit in the chocolate pudding? By now, Channah really disliked the guards, and the heavy handed treatment she was receiving from the authorities had made her quite distrustful.

EVENT - searched for a crayon after mass by bernie.

They would not let her change to "kosher", like Demo there, who was Jewish, unless Channah also changed her religious affiliation on some form to the same. At that point, she would not be permitted to attend any Christian service. A Syrian lady in her late sixties actually had professed Jewish just to get the outside packaged meats delivered. The whole system of technicalities was just so ridiculous Channah gave up.

The bizarre sushi incident, which had evoked her daughter's presence, told her she was seriously depressed. She was still reeling from the berserk betrayal of Mellow, Daddy Gambit, Duvey and Jamo. At times Channah fantasized that her children were in danger, or that they might end up dead, an aftereffect of the car accident, and what she had witnessed at Efram Kopf's house, she believed, next door. She left the dinner table, wrote up a sick sheet, and handed it in. The next day, she was prescribed something like Maalox and began to receive from the medical cart tray.

The dietician met her at the medical room, and Channah told her she had had an encounter with something putrid. She begged for a change, telling lies about food allergies, which were true in childhood. She put her on the scale. It said 142. She had been 175 in November.

"I've lost 33 pounds." she said.

"No, that's not true." Mindy replied, showing her a nurse's check-in sheet where she had penciled in 154, a guess the first exam with the Chinese doctor. She regarded Channah for a moment.

"Alright. I'll tell you what. I don't know what to do other than to give you a *bland diet."* the dietician said.

"Thanks. I won't need to starve. But you should contact the F.D.A. and have them look at the menu. The foods are very acidy." she said. Susan just raised her eyebrows and pursed her lips. True to her word, the next day, Channah had a Styrofoam tray, a sign of distinction with different foods from all other inmates. It had no condiments, was bland, and it sustained her. Everybody wanted a piece of her tray, every day. Even then, she distrusted the meats and dumped them into the garbage. She learned to eat eggs for protein.

The last thing annoying was milk. There were two kinds, red and white whole milk pints, and 2 percent skim in blue and white containers. For some odd reason, the skim often hit her with acid stomach about an hour after, and she felt somewhat sleepy.

She remembered, one day, drinking a pint of "white and blue" that had been resting on the inner window sill for an hour, then walking out to outdoor rec. The drink made her vision blurry.

Milk was welcome when compared to the fountain water, or the water from the pump sink in her cell. That was hard water. She knew because her hair and laundry, washed there, never soaped hardly at all. It was also rust colored and smelled bad. Sometimes, at certain hours, if you drank it, you developed a sore throat.

You could drink the purple coffee with the heavy sugar which was like a drug, milk that made you feel sleepy too, that was slightly acidic, or there was *bug juice*. This lunch and dinner beverage served up, seemed like Kool Aid, made from jello power, with super concentrated red dye #8. It was full of citric acid, and synthetic sweetener.

In all this, Channah found that after about 8 weeks, she had built up a tolerance to the beverages, and no longer recorded perceptual changes when she ate or drank. She was just perpetually vigilant and cautious of what she put into her mouth.

It is not fair nor right that a correctional center population, without the option to choose what they eat, should be subjected to this sort of messy diet. Bad enough, they are treated there like children, without the autonomy to wear a belt, and their normal lives have been stripped away from them. They are degraded and humiliated by the food—and that's not a part of the sentence, in the meaning of the law.

Many women there were just suspects not yet convicted and not sentenced. Some, like *Special,* seemed to be there because a kind officer had decided to put up a homeless person for a few winter months in public lodgings. *Special* had witnessed a crime, and refused to testify against two neighbors out of fear for her family and she was in lockdown for months.

Light offenders, or nuisances, or homeless Charity cases that were guards' *pets* were degraded and humiliated by living conditions there. It was unacceptable to Channah's self-esteem to eat swill and it lowered daily. She was becoming slightly paranoid and anxious by being there and felt set upon by the State. No judge, when he gives a 90-day sentence is suggesting that an offender should be poisoned, have her health ruined, or be made ill because *she is bad*. Offenders are paying back society and learning a lesson simply by losing their liberty. For her, it was much worse because she felt I was innocent yet forced to rub elbows with career criminals, with unsympathetic and hardened guards stonewalling her every moment in every conceivable way, pulling psychological stunts to break her spirit down further, in the interests of making an inmate *easy handling.*

Some longtime repeat offenders showed signs of long time spent there—in breakouts of rashes like rosecia, or peeling skin, or *ghoulish* wooden behavior.

M. Dot, a felony in room 24, almost never ate for she could not abide it. After weeks, when she was so malnourished that she dozed in her cot most waking hours, nothing was done on her behalf. When Channah commented to Officer Goul that M.Dot might die, she was ignored. The sick inmate clearly needed intravenous. As Channah observed, one day, she rolled out of her bunk up high and landed on the floor, smacking her head. They took her to the hospital, she received 8 stitches, and they brought her back the next day—without giving her drip, or feeding her. She did not file a grievance for treatment she received. She was on heavy medication. The guards did not like her, as she was uppity and cursed. If she stated anything negative, she would be put into lockdown, sometime for as long as 2 weeks. She would watch her, when she was up the first month, pacing her cell, talking to herself, and gesticulating in the air. She told tales that her father was abusive, and her own husband had discarded her, taking the children and home, she said.

As for Channah, regarding the encounter with the menu after filing 4 grievances which were *nixxied,* she received that gift of butterscotch pudding in June, suffered *the burn,* and stopped trying. It was so bad, that acid indigestion, that she had burning eyes, a huge migraine with heat in her head, and muscle cramps. She truly believed at one point she was dying. It happened twice to her, with sweet dessert foods she was thoughtfully served in her designated chair.

Channah recovered from that in June, but was weak. She wrote up a complaint which mentioned she believed she was poisoned.

The next day, two well attired Officers came into the Medical Observation quad and spoke to Potter at the sentry desk. He pointed at her, then gestured her over.

"Take a seat at that table and talk to these two men." he said.

"What have I done?" Channah asked. It was right after recess, and the inmates were wasting time before dinner.

"We are very concerned about this complaint you made about the puddings. I'm Officer Brown. This is Officer Green. We are very concerned for your health. We want to look into this carefully." he said. They were both seasoned law enforcement types, well grizzled but still muscled in their late fifties. One sported a walrus moustache and both had bright gold stars pinned to their chests.

All three sat down. Channah described her agonies caused by the pudding at her spot that past Monday night. Brown listened attentively while Green took notes. They both stayed for fifteen minutes, then stood up, thanking her for her cooperation.

"Wow. Can't believe how nice they were!" she said to M. Dot., down for one of her rare visits.

Inmates were called out shortly afterward in groups of four, to speak to the Lieutenant confidentially in another room. Even Carol Muck, the social worker, spoke to all food service workers with access to the trays each day. No diet change was made universally.

Expose: The Reckoning by Channah Gambit

Jen the inmate above Channah in cell 13, was suddenly pulled off food service and spent a day of disciplinary lockdown in her cell. She had been busted and they all heard her sobbing through the cement ceiling. It appeared that an irate, irrational, prejudiced inmate was responsible, not the N.C.C.C.

Why should inmates, not prison personnel, be in charge of food distribution? Judge for yourself the conditions at that place if you are a guest. No food in the form of gifts from visitors was permitted. Only commissary food, at exorbitant prices, things like peanut butter, Tang, chocolate bars on Pop Tarts, sustained the female inmates.

Channah, in a few short weeks, spent all the money she had come with. It was not replenished by family, with nothing put into her commissary account the first and last time Jamo visited. She was at the full mercy of the kitchen there because she was poor. In the block totem pole, Channah was at the very bottom, and disrespected for it. She had no clout, no way to bribe anyone. She did not thrive, or enjoy anything much. She just existed. Channah just stayed alive.

Expose: The Reckoning by Channah Gambit

Chapter 16: Litigation Tangles

Sheriff's Officer Flan didn't like Channah. Why wasn't clear—but here's a little tale that shows it. She had started to look forward to her first hearing on March 14th. She was called down, the evening of March 13th, to be served by a Sheriff's Officer Flan in the hall. It was her filthy brother Big. He had made a note of a technical loophole in their Order of Protection skirmishes: The Family Court Order of protection had been nullified by Judge John Skinner when she appeared late on January 22nd. The District Court Order of Protection was a contempt and a new, more severe, protection order from her doddering dad, who had become a kind of malevolent puppet on a string to Karen and Big, did the dandling. It was implied that she had stolen from garbage deposited in front of his house.

After the fact of this contempt charge, she would be again served the OOP; the modified one, and added on more remarks about her *mental disease*, clearly labeled, and other things put permanently into the public record.

Channah was in a quandary the night of March 13th as she had two hearings happening simultaneously in two different courts the next day. The first was for the misdemeanor charges. The second was the OOP defense, to show why it was not necessary to have one in place, should she choose.

Flan was a type of career Army jock. He looked like fine military material, with aquiline features—you might think, a worthy sort of soul. After he had served her, it caused her a heart flutter and shock due to the sheer brutality of being kicked when she was down by a brother and her own family, she asked him something.

"Will you," Channah stated politely, "Inform the clerk of the court, Rozzie Scribes, of my dilemma?" He assented and went off. She was wary of this procedure, so she racked her brain for a solution.

The pillar in the Law Library had the 800 telephone number for the District Attorney's hotline. Desperate to adhere to legal proceedings, Channah wrote it down on her wrist before they returned to the Quad.

"Good evening. I am Channah Gambit, Prisoner Number 08971234 being held at the Carmen Road Facility D Block in Section B. Please note that I have a Family Court Hearing on Monday, April 1, to respond to a petition for an order of protection by Dan Gambit. Unfortunately, I am also being taken to District Court in Hempstead that same morning to appear before the Judge to answer misdemeanor charges."

"Also, I do not have the means to avoid that since I am jailed for lack of bail. I have no money to phone the Family Court Clerk, Rozzie Scribes, to tell her about the schedule conflict."

"Therefore, I am taping myself here, on the advice of an acquaintance, Joe Bee, who used to be an Assistant Attorney, to put myself on record that I attempted to comply with both judges' requests for me to appear. I am not seeking to risk gaining a new Contempt of Hearing judge brought against me. I am, once again, Channah Gambi, Prisoner Number 08971234 and this is Friday night at about 8:06 p.m. Please do the right thing on my behalf. Thanks! Good bye!" she said and hung up.

Standing at either side of her were Rose and Ginette. They both looked completely baffled. Rose burst out guffawing, slapping her thigh repeatedly. "Honey, you have a lot to learn. That ain't going to do anything but make more trouble for you." she said. Then she walked away.

Rose scratched her forehead absentmindedly. "You better off calling your boyfriend and having him call." she said. Channah sat down in one of the plastic chairs and just stared fixedly at the big black clock in the bubble for about ten minutes.

A few weeks later, when she actually got to chat with a phantom, Mr. Silverwitch of the Legal Aid Society she was told bluntly that she had committed the incredible *faux pas* of asking her enemy to be her advocate.

"If you do it again, you will be charged with contempt against the District Attorney he said. Channah calmly explained that she had been advised to get it taped *somewhere* and had tried to comply.

"I was trying to meet the demands of the law." she stated.

"It took me a while to talk them out of giving you another count of contempt." He replied,

"That was a very big mistake."

"But I have a friend in the District Attorney's office Steve Tedle, Assistant District Attorney" Channah said.

She had a few sheets of paper and a postaged envelope from sketching portraits last week. The next morning right after breakfast she began to write Tedle a letter.

"Dear Steve,

"I need you to be a character reference for me, as I am being held at the Carmen Road facility for lack of bail, brought up on a few misdemeanors."

"I am sure you recall the time I approached the District Attorney's Office regarding a scam from London, claiming I had won the National Lottery.

"After a lot of phone calls back and forth, I am sure you will recall that you requested I print up all the emails I had had from the British scoundrels. Remember?"

"I mailed that to you UPS back in September, 2005. You were so appreciative! Now you can help me once again."

"I am totally innocent of wrongdoing on these 3 misdemeanors. I am a good person. You know that! Please agree to stand before Judge Mess on my behalf, and say I am a person of good character. Use your influence with Kathleen Darby to let them to release me without bail."

"Steve, I am really counting on you. I come from a dysfunctional family. The misdemeanors grew out of a domestic conflict and some injuries to my head. I didn't hurt anybody."

"I could sure use that $6,000,000 promised to me by that Louis Gambi now! I will be looking forward to hearing from you."

"Sincerely,"

"Channah Gambit"

After weeks of waiting, Steve Tedel never responded.

Expose: The Reckoning by Channah Gambit

Channah called up the other free 800 telephone number for the Legal Aid Society and asked to speak to Ken Belsen. In an unaccustomed routine, he picked up the phone almost immediately.

"Ken Belsen here. What can I do for you?" he asked. She marveled at the intensely masculine, young and energetic tone of voice on the other end of the wire.

"Mr. Belsen. Hi? This is Channah Gambit and Matt Silverwitch is my attorney."

"Yes, I know. What can I do for you, Ms. Gambit?" he said laconically.

"Could you please contact Steve Tedel, an Assistant District Attorney for me?"

"Why do you want me to contact him, Lady?" he asked.

"He's a good character reference. I was the victim of identity fraud on the internet last September, and got to know him then. He's got proof that I'm a good person, and that someone was trying to hurt me." she said.

"How was someone trying to hurt you?" he asked.

"By giving me $6,000,000 in order to get a copy of my birth certificate and social security number. They actually wanted me to fly to Zambia."

"Oh, you were the winner of an inheritance? That's a scam." Belsen said.

"Right."

"Look, Gambit, I'd like to tell you straight out that having *any* contact with the District Attorney's Office is stupid. They are your enemy right now. He didn't respond?"

"No. That's why I phoned Legal Aid." she said.

"Well, he's not going to. He can't help you. He's on the opposite side. I can see why you are up for that 7.30 competency test! Goodbye!" he said, and hung up.

Channah stood there blustering for a few minutes. Then she started weeping. Walking to her cell, she threw herself on the cot. She wouldn't speak to anyone for the rest of the day.

While resting there on her back that Sunday, her mind wandered back to their first meeting with a representative from the District Attorney's office. It was back in July, 2005. A very clever internet email phishing scam. Channah had won the U.K. National Lottery!

An email had come in, telling her she had been submitted in the lottery through some engine website or other. About $250,000 was hers, if she would just establish her legal identity.

It was replied to, and then she went so far to send Western Union a telegram, to the box office in Northern England. She had begun to provide personal identity information. When they asked for checking account access, mom's maiden name, she slowed down. Calling the London U.K. sweepstakes office long distance, she learned this was a mirror website, an exact replica of the real one. In all, she had spent about $16 on nothing.

Later that July, she received another email from a "bank official" in Zambia. The Zenon Petroleum Company was looking for heirs of one "Al Gambit", who had bankrolled his shares of the company while working as an expatriate engineer there. It was her family surname, and there were 2 Als in her family tree. Channah had quickly gotten sucked in to a correspondence.

Expose: The Reckoning by Channah Gambit

More cautious, she researched the company information. It was all there! Her legacy was a cool $6,000,000 waiting only for her.

Channah filled out the official bank form and sent it back. When they told her she would actually have to fly to Zambia, she slowed down, for she had no fare. Then they asked her to scan her passport and send it.

She caught on that she had been conned! Channah reported the scam to a website run by the Federal government. They referred her back to local authorities. She reached Steve.

When they had first spoken, he had seemed to personable on the telephone, so engaging. Channah had fantasized that maybe they'd go out together.

That first week she visited the Department of Computer Scams at the Nassau County District Attorney's in Mineola. He turned out to be terrifically handsome, tall, lean and brunette. Such a masculine figure! It was just that he was also matter of fact and professional. He sat her in a bucket seat next to his desk and told her what he wanted. She looked at him with widened eyes.

He had her print out long form, with all embedded codes, the correspondence and send it to him. He told her he was in the Department of Computer Scams at the Nassau County District Attorney's office, and advised her to change all her mailboxes and passwords. At least, she would not lose any more identification information.

After a month, in September, just when her job problems began to coalesce, Steve wrote a nice note to tell her thank you.

It turned out that he later traced it back to a location in England. He turned the investigation over to them. They used Interpol and, ultimately, the scam was traced to Germany.

"This really will mean a lot to my career. It might even mean a promotion." Steve said. "I want to thank you for doing all the photocopying. We got the son of a bitch! At least you only lost $65.00. Think of how many Americans might have been taken in!"

"I was glad to help. Maybe we could meet sometime for coffee?" Channah said.

"No, I'm sorry. That would be awkward you see because I just got engaged." he said.

"Well, goodbye Steve." she said.

What a fraud, what an advocate! God bless the Nassau County District Attorney's office! she had thought. Someone had certainly been trying to steal her identity in 2005. They had finally impersonated her on the cell phone, making crank calls. She'd prove it! But now, lying on her cot reminiscing, Channah doubted it and came back to reality. Steve was now her enemy, and no White Knight.

As for March 14th, her morning revealed no call to head down to District Court. The first hearing was postponed, a pattern which would be repeated for weeks of non-existing conferences. There she was, attending neither one, getting no where, nothing done. It was like dwelling on a circle of Hades.

The following Monday, she went down to Law Library, the favorite treat of her week. Channah asked Officer Pulgrid to bring her name up on his computer.

"Oh," he said, "You have a new contempt charge in Family Court! Your bail is now raised another $500 to $2000. You missed a date in Court." Flabbergasted, she said

Expose: The Reckoning by Channah Gambit

"I've been screwed by Flan!" to him, *screwed* yet one more time by the rotations of the rotten wheels of the State.

A day or two later, Officer Flan had a tour of duty. Channah saw her advantage, and went up to him.

"Why didn't you do me the favor of informing the court secretary as you promised?" she asked sweetly.

"What are you talking about?" he said.

"You served me papers the night of March 13th." she said, "Remember?"

"No, I didn't." he said, looking her straight in the eye. Then he left. For the entire remainder of her stay there, he insisted he did not know anything, and gave Channah the *fish eye* if she approached him.

Her contempt charge was a burr in her side. She wrote a long, blow by blow letter detailing the whole thing, asking that the penalty be dropped, to Scribes, the Family Court clerk. The contempt charge was not her only problem. It remained on the screen for over two weeks, and then it was dropped just as mysteriously as it had been put on. Channah never discovered if the reason was that letter. The oppression had lessened.

A prisoner cannot be faulted if he or she is incarcerated and has two simultaneous court actions on the same time requiring attendance, she learned from Pulgrid. Perhaps that was it.

The buggy computer, supposedly tied in with the central station at the district court building, regularly unrecorded court dates, or set them different from the courthouse.

It was with a grateful sigh while visiting law library a week or two later, Channah discovered that the charge labeled felony had gone back to being a misdemeanor, at least in that system.

Now there was something worse looming on the horizon, a 7.30. She was deemed *too nuts to understand the charges* by the arraignment judge, Antony Packins, and her own court-appointed L.A.S. attorney, Matt Silverwitch. He would make that abundantly clear the first time they met in the visitor's pen.

Yes, even before her attorney met her, he was already in the mindset that she was guilty, deluded, and unstable using labels which corresponded with words which were spoken by Detectives Englemann and Barney.

Silverwitch was quite well-informed, but would do little to relieve a neophyte in trouble with the law, or to inform her of the charges, or to make himself accessible either by visiting or by phone.

This isolation and inertia continued for days on end.

Her incarceration for lack of bail for up to 120 days wouldn't be termed *severe*. Channah survived.

How would it all turn out? What would Channah be like after the end of the ordeal:? She would look back and notice many physical, mental, and emotional differences. It was almost as if she was a different person.

**Afterward, she had asthma back after a lapse of 14 years, hay fever and allergies. Her constitution would remain less strong. She'd tires easily after hour walks.*

**For about 4 weeks after release, her feet swelled up when she stood for long* *periods or wore conventional shoes, to the point of losing a new part time job which required standing.*

**She had lost 20 pounds and had bouts of fear, stress symptoms, and sometimes delusions of being harmed. In short, she became an emotional mess, or a basket case in certain ways. She required medication, which was not necessary before, and talk therapy.*

**Channah would not be able to practice her chosen profession for years due to the stigma of a record, a loss of approximately $50,000 in income. She had incurred a bankruptcy.*

**All this was a rather hefty price to have paid for 3 misdemeanors—for some harmless disorderly conduct which harmed no one, or for making a phone call on bad judgment. That would appear to be the case. There it was. Even though she had not yet been convicted, she had already been punished.*

**Beyond that, she had lost all personal familial relationships except one, with her son. Relatives didn't resume ties. Her personal belongings were spread between two transient homes. They would be auctioned off, despite her protests. She believed she would be losing the inheritance promised to her by Daddy Gambit long ago. Background checks for even menial poor-paying jobs would lead to a lack of rehire in several instances. Any jobs she'd find would be precarious perches, which well might disappear should the boss discover those convictions through a background check.*

If she went to a jury trial over the issues, she might get a return to jail, if convicted, by an annoyed Judge, for up to a year. So, she weighed the odds.

You can say Channah brought it all on herself through her own behavior, or that she earned it as her two children contended. She would attest that she was a good, nice, law-abiding citizen who deserved to be treated well and to be left alone by the State.

After a long muse, she decided that it was worth a gamble to go to jury trial to clear her name and be able to return to teaching.

Expose: The Reckoning by Channah Gambit

Chapter 17: A Matter of Cross Tides

In Medical Observation block,. Sunday morning hours were spent isolated in cells, reading or dawdling. One day on her thin hard cot, Channah allowed her mind to wander back to recent months, and a recap, seeking some insight:

Channah guessed one of the reasons she converted to Catholicism was the lack of a religious upbringing. She had not been Bat Mitzvahed. She was a self-taught spiritualist through most of her early years and married life. A mystic, artist, and poet, she habitually speculated on the meaning of it all. During the marriage, she adhered to the rules and holidays along with her husband. During that marriage, they held a little shabbot dinner every Friday night, that was all. She raised her children in the faith.

With the divorce, and the loss of custody at first, she fell into a hole of despondency. Her faith did not serve her well because she had no training in seeking support from a greater source of strength.

An encounter at a local church led to her Baptism months after the separation. By the time she became a member of her family household again, as a graduate student from 2000-2003, she kept it well hidden. That old crab landlord was intolerant, although a non-practitioner.

When the domestic troubles heated up in 2005, she sometimes went to Communion, or sneaked away to confession. She even found a Jesuit priest who guided her, but could not wear a crucifix around her neck even though she was urged to. She was too afraid she would alienate her children. She was afraid of losing their love.

As time passed, after the divorce, she thought about *coming out* as a devout Catholic, and even bought a missal to read every day.

In October, 2005 the job pressures being what they were, Channah resigned. She found herself needing spiritual guidance. Several yelling sessions with Big and Karen had led to no offer of support. Fighting with Duvey had pushed him back to living with his dad Stephen Randell in Long Ditch. That fight had cut into her heart and made her deeply unhappy. Now she turned to the Church in Point Pleasant for solace guidance and a sanctuary. She found the Church of the Nativity closed. A second interview with the Pastor was denied her. Visiting a temple in Long Ditch with the young handsome rabbi was pleasant.

"I understand you are thinking of converting back?" he said, tapping his spread fingers together in front of his face. He was allowing her a half hour of his time one afternoon.

"I really am confused. I want to belong to my people. My own family hates me." Channah said, starting to weep.

"I see. Well, what can I do to help?" Rabbi Gutenberg said. His copper bifocals shone and he frowned slightly.

"I wish I could find a safe place to stay for a while. Maybe then the viscious attacks would stop. Is there some family in your congregation which would let me stay over and use a room and perhaps spare some simple groceries. It's only for a month or two until I can find work. Then I'd feel safe." she said.

Rabbi Guttenberg pursed his lips. He leaned all the way back in his chair and rocked, staring fixedly at his computer screen. "No. We don't have anything like that here. There is no family that can take in a woman your age. You need to seek some counseling. I can recommend a very fine therapist in town." he said. He began to click and point to roll up the list he had. Channah's eyes began to slide big tears down her cheeks.

"I cannot afford a therapist. They cost a lot of money. I simply need to get away from them. They are so evil! They won't even give me food." she said.

"I feel sorry for you, but you don't belong to our congregation. This is all I can do. I am helpless." Rabbi Guttenberg said. He closed his study door behind her.

It was that way also at the Church of the Madonna in town. They had a food pantry which ran in the Community Center. She knocked on the rectory door and was seen by Father Antony. They sat in a parlor decorated from the 1920's. It had a wood and chicken wire pen in the corner containing a large brown and white rabbit which was quietly nibbling lettuce.

"What can I do for you, Channah." Father said.

"I need sanctuary. My family rejected me after I lost a job and I cannot even stay there. No groceries, no car and no friends. Father can you help me?" She looked into his kind blue eyes, his partially bald pate and thin build in the priestly garments. He smiled at her and his eyes suddenly had crow-feets in the corners.

"I see. We don't have sanctuary in the Roman Catholic Church at all anymore." he said. "So that's out of the question. I advise you to stay where you are for as long as possible."

"Father, where did you get the rabbit?" she asked.

He smiled broadly. "Oh, him! He's my pet and a gift from some altar boys I teach." Father Antony took a moment, walked over and fed the rabbit a carrot. Then he returned and sat down.

"Take advantage of our food pantry while you can. Stay there at home and don't travel around. Although the Lord seems to be protecting you from harm on the roads, you are spending all your remaining credit on motel rooms. I will pray for you. See Delores in the Community Center. Tell her I told her to give you two bags of food."

Channah was sobbing out of frustration.

"Thank you." she managed.

"You must trust that you will survive this ordeal." Father Antony showed her out after about an hour.

The last thing he mentioned to her was "Seek some counseling." After this she filled her arms with groceries and came home. Tuna, potato buds, canned beans, Campbell's soups, half stale bread, peanut butter, tea bags and cereals enough for several weeks went into the kitchen shelves. She did not seek another place right away to stay.

It was a notion Channah had picked up from reading many books, the *sanctuary,* a refuge from a hostile family. But, she was denied at the local church where she had been sponsored for conversion by the local cathedral and by the local churches in her hometown, 3 times.

Channah seemed an unstable woman and was advised to seek counseling. As she grew more embroiled in arguments with Daddy Gambit, more fearful at what she witnessed, she made some wooden crucifixes and hung them around the house to her son's raised eyebrow and silence.

At that time, it had become a grand design of Daddy Gambit's addled pate to drive her out of the house. He needed rent money to pay taxes and living costs. He hated her, seemingly, in thought, word and deed. Both Karen and Big shunned her when they visited him. She was starving, but they would not give her bread. She recognized their cruelty, so she turned more toward Jesus Christ but the Church turned a cold shoulder.

In January, she lost personal papers. She shipped them up to a cathedral in Montreal. Believing that distancing herself from Dad was a great idea, she wanted to emigrate there. Channah had just enough money to ship her family mementoes and other precious legal family papers away.

Her mailbox was empty for over 3 consecutive weeks that month. She phoned Joseph Bee. "I'm really busy, lady. I can't see you right now. You have to walk over to the post office and ask them to launch an internal investigation. That's your right."

"Thank you Mr. Bee." she said. Channah biked into town. It was a dark blustery November day. The ride was against the wind and lasted two miles. The post office, a one story brick building on the corner opposite a large shopping center, was rather empty since it was late afternoon. Locking the bike to a front railing, she climbed the marble stairs and pushed open the heavy copper plated door.

"Mr. McNeil. The postmaster will see you now." she was told by a swarthy dark-skinned Dravidian who looked like Peter Lorry. Behind him Naomi the mail clerk was shuffling through some envelopes which she stuck up on a shelf after rubber banding them. In the dark foyer the only sound was a blaring flat screen television showing post office ads. Mr. McNeil appeared like a small walrus at the door to the right.

"My mail is open on the back and I don't receive any for weeks at a time. I want an internal investigation." she said.

"Oh, do you feel that's necessary? A PDP investigation. Okay." he said.

"Let's do it right now." Channah said.

"Okay. You'll need to see Mrs. Harrison fill out a form and answer a few questions."

He ushered Channah into an ugly old office with wood furniture which was dark from use. Mrs. Harrison, the assistant Postmaster, a young slim Black woman, rose from her chair. She was attired in a kelly green pant suit and looked all business. Shaking hands, she offered Channah a chair to be seated. They began.

"I know for a fact I have not received Court Hearing notices, nor other important documents from lawyers and government agencies." Channah said.

"We will start the investigation. You won't have to pay for it. If someone is riffling or stealing your mail we will find some answers." She said. She accepted the filled out forms.

"Will I have to pay for it?" Channah asked.

"No, it's part of the Postal Service organization. Don't you worry any more." Mrs. Harrison said, showing her to the door. Channah felt a little less fearful now.

No result ever came of it, but her mail was collected until she was released from jail in July, 2006. She had to carry a huge amount in a box on the bus.

Expose: The Reckoning by Channah Gambit

No thoughts of suicide crossed her mind. On January $5^{th,}$, she had a deep experience or vision of a *Sanctuary of Dan Society*. It came in great detail, and was quite inspiring. She was considering the building of a place to help maltreated, missing and damaged children using her teaching credentials. It was the reward of years of waiting, after months of fasting, starving and sincere prayer. It was a way to continue using her professional teacher's training in service to the community, in harmony with those new Christian religious belief. Better yet, it was a way to appease Dad for in her concept, the sanctuaries would be non-sectarian, and named after him It would be a place of safety, where the lions of hostility would be pacified, and kids would be healed by the power of the Holy Spirit. Charity would support it. Doctors would donate medicines, plastic surgery, and their talents. The effect of suffering led to this sublimation. Channah was punch-drunk with divinity with a strong feeling that the Lord was looking down and witnessing her, and would make a job for her.

A psychiatrist would have stated that she was a meglomaniac. She was justified in her avocation for her conversion, and began to build on it.

Duvey sat her computer one late afternoon when she walked in.

"What are you doing? You have one of your own." she said.

"It blew up." he said glumly.

"Why Duvey, that's the kid you got from the man out Midwest and you built it up. A computer doesn't just blow up!"

"Mine did. I came home from school and found it that way! So, I'm using yours until dad can get me a new one." he said. He had a salami sandwich on the steel computer side arm, and was munching it while drinking cream soda from a bottle.

Channah thought *it must have been damaged by the same person who hit my plants pets and clothing. The masked marauder definitely can't be my son!*

"You've been running around a lot mom and staying at motels, I hear." Duvey said.

"Well, that's because Daddy Gambit scares me with arguments." she said.

"I wish you would find a new job and take some medication." Duvey said. "Then I would feel like staying with you. What are you going to do, Mom?" He looked at her with his soft gray eyes. She thought *he looks so handsome today in that black sweatshirt. He's turning into a man very rapidly now.* Her heart filled with emotion. *He's not a man in the way of helping me survive. He still is dependent. Grandpa Gambit was a street peddler at 13. Out on the street pushing a cart and selling screws for a nickel to support HIS mother.* She sat down.

"I've been thinking of taking a train up to Canada. There, I might be able to find a job." she said. She noticed his pained expression as he screw up his mouth into a shape of dislike.

"Now listen, getting away from grandpa Gambit is a good idea."

"He loves you, Mom." Duvey said.

"You think so? With the way he's been shouting at me, and threatening to evict us, and not feeding me, I don't think he cares one bit." she said.

"I might visit Israel too. Maybe living there might be a new start."

"Jamo and I will disaprove of the whole thing." He said. He shut the computer off, picked up the dishes and took them to the sink where he started washing them up. At the galley with his back to her, he toyed with a large plastic *Dawn* bottle.

"Look, honey, I don't know what to tell you. I am really suffering here."

"Then check yourself into a hospital for a while if you're having a breakdown!" he yelled. He turned toward her, looked at her with pained eyes, then took his car keys out of his left pocket.

"I'm going back to Dad's," he said.

"Don't you have to go to school?" she said.

"I haven't gone to school in two days. I can't keep up with my classes, Mom. I've been too upset about things. I need to talk to dad about it." He waved at her halfheartedly in the front foyer.

"I'll be back late tonight, Mom. Try to find a doctor. Get some rest. I still love you. There's a twenty on the kitchen table to help." Duvey said, and went out.

During a visit at the deli two days later, Duvey sat with her in the booth and listened politely. Channah spoke once more of moving far away to find work better. Israel could be an exciting new home. She talked on and on, unable to stop. Her voice sounded like the chatter of a scared creature of some kind, a low breathless monotone of empty words, without substance or power to change others.

"You'll be killed there." he said.

"It's at war, a violent place, a place to far away to help you. Please, please, Mom, get yourself some help."

He was feeding her at the deli where he was a waiter—free meals on his meager salary. She felt guilty. He was also deeply troubled. His studies at college were not going well because he was not concentrating. When she was arrested in March, he had dropped out of school.

Channah was frantic by December to find any job at all. She felt a deep conversion and sidelined her anxiety with pipe dreams of opening a sanctuary for children in the Holy Land.

At the library, running into her cousin's wife Fay, she begged enough money to make thirty copies of her resume.

"I know times are hard. For us to. I wish we could help." Fay said. She was an agile attractive blond with perfect teeth who worked at reception part time. She patted Channah on the back.

"Need to copy one thing more." Channah said. Fay gave her another dollar, and she made ten copies of her fundraising letter for the Society of Dan sanctuary. *If I can't be given sanctuary myself, well then, I'll stop being selfish and build a sanctuary myself in some foreclosed place, and live there with lost and damaged kids!*

"There's my addled cousin." Fay whispered to the fat Hispanic clerk beside her as she waved goodbye to Channah.

Channah had the local Yellow book House of Worship page in her mittened hand. Walking rapidly around town in December all bundled up was invigorating.

She found Father John the Pastor of the Methodist Church on Riverside walking along. He received the letter gladly. "By the way, Father, do you know anyone who might have a spare room. I've got a domestic conflict at home." she said.

Expose: The Reckoning by Channah Gambit

Father John's smile faded. "Place to stay? I'm sorry. We don't do that." His steel gray hair blew in poufs around his hat. "Why not try the government! Surely they can help you! I promise I'll read this later." He stuck his hands into his pockets and picked up pace, leaving her behind. *That was rude!* she thought.

Down in Atlantic Bluffs, the western tip of Long Ditch Island, she found a small temple Beth Adam, and the rabbi a man with a long white beard and black yarmulke at the door to let her in. He too received a letter and allowed her to come in for a moment to warm up.

"I'm really sorry to bother you. Here I am trying to build a sanctuary for children, and I need one for myself." Channah said, giggling nervously. She sat in a brown leather tufted chair in Rabbi Eli's study.

"I'm so sorry to hear you are a war." he said gravely, his eyes encouraging.

"I need to get away from my Dad and brother, really. I can't find a job."

"I hope you will consider joining our congregation. We Jews do try to be charitable. I think maybe you should put this sanctuary idea aside for a while and find a job, young woman." Rabbi Eli said gently.

Channah stood up as if she had been stung and buttoned her coat. Picking up her gloves, she let herself out.

As she walked back through Atlantic Bluffs village, she let the cold wind at her back blow her down the sidewalk. There were a few businesses. She switched the papers in her knapsack. Now she handed out resumes instead. She took Rabbi Eli's advice to heart, but was sore.

In a Century 21 Real Estate store she ran into Sammi Chiliwich, Class of '69.

"Hi, what a nice surpise! How are you, Channah." Sami said. She was an attractive blond matron now with two kids. She gestured to a chair in front of her desk.

"I can't stay." Channah said. "Can you help me find work? Something part time? I can clerk or type. I'm a great typist, Sam." she said. She looked around the warm inviting realtor's office, interior decorated in French Provinicial, pastel colors and fake rubber plants. There were several nice women there at desks. They all looked well dressed and pampered. Channah sighed.

"I don't know if we have anything right now. " Sammy said slowly, lowering her eyes.

"I understand. But perhaps you might know someone who could rent me a room week to week. It's an emergency, a domestic misunderstanding." Channah said.

"I'm sorry you are not getting along with Stephen." Sammy said.

"Oh, no. It's not Stephen Randall. We've been divorced for years!" Channah laughed a little and Sammy followed along.

"I'm sorry, I don't have anything like that. But I'll see what I can do for you." she said.

Channah chatted a little longer about shared good times long ago, then showed herself the door. Sammy would never phone.

As she did so, she grew weaker and more drawn. Channah was sustained on this rocket fuel, the inspiration from this vision of a children's sanctuary network to work on. Around town she went, a slightly bedraggled, cheaply dressed vision with a reddened

Expose: The Reckoning by Channah Gambit

nose, wild hazel eyes, and big ideas

For the first time in her life, Channah had synthesized her Catholic believes, Jewish heritage, and family feelings. The Lord had shown her a good straight path to serve him, to work, to be good and noble. She would thus appease Dad and the children. She firmly believed this would be a path of peace, of health.

The vision had been real. Under privation, she would have another, more vivid one on March 5th, which would be a vision of the Nativity, just prior to her arrest. It would sustain her in jail, throughout that ordeal. These spiritual experiences have a place in a life of faith. They are not aberrations, she attested to others. She shared them, at least the first, on paper. A grand eloquent concept of her own self-importance filled her as she suffered repeated humiliations in town. No one responded with shelter or support, predictably. Channah seemed mad.

Channah lay in the cot and pondered.

What is it about conversion that people should be warned? For starters, that it is an invisible line which can build up powerful animosities. You should be prepared for that rejection by your family and, strangely enough, if you are Jewish, from the equal or greater hostility of the Catholic Church, its clergy, and parishioners. They don't like Jews, and, in fact, many would appreciate it if there were none at all.

When Channah was in isolation at the Nassau County Correctional Center, she needed to use a rosary to pray. That's not allowed, the use of outside worship objects, according to the rules. She had a Gideon micro-bible from a friend Denise, who ended up in F Block, the home of more violent people, for a year. It was quite a gift.

In there, during those first weeks, she asked to speak to the Chaplain. Repeatedly. That was denied. It was about 4 weeks before she was allowed to attend weekend services. As far as the jail was concerned, you could only practice 1 religion. You could not confess. Confession was offered only in the prison guide, since the chaplain was only a deacon.

The nun who did rounds, Sister Evian, seemed to be about 5'11", spindle-thin, and vinegary. Her wintry face would shine like a beacon in the weeks ahead. Her hooded eyes, very rarely, lit up with a smile. Deacon. Mason, resembling the character Ralph Cramden from *The Honeymooners*, spoke his sermons on Saturdays like James Mason. Rotund, eloquent, inapproachable and stern, he moralized well, urging them to repent and mend their ways. His comments on the New Testament were sometimes on the mark. Each week, the sister would hand out little booklets, daily homilies, blank telephone directories, and Reader's Digest –type books with a Christian message.

As Channah discovered, even if you asked for a rosary in writing, it would not do anything. If you handed the note to Sister Evian or Father. Mason, it would get lost or they would deny having received it in the first place.

After five weeks, she finally was given a rosary. It was black plastic, prison issue. Along with it, Sister. Evian gave her a book of prayer for saying rosary, "My Rosary to Our Blessed Mother Mary", by the Xaverian Missionaries. It was Lent. No meat was easy. She started to learn the rosary, and to pray it each day before bedtime.

Sister would not give her a means to confess. She wouldn't sit and listen. Sometimes the Catholic inmates would sit, she'd hold Channah's hands, and say a prayer for her and the children, as requested. That was about all the religious solace the prison furnished.

Channah had been rebuffed by a basically irreligious man who had snapped her makeshift crucifixes in half and rejected her right to worship a different faith. The Church had rejected her as some kind of wild misfit, and denied her sanctuary. In between the two, she had experienced a revelation of the Nativity, after a prior one regarding an avocation.

Channah felt she was walking along with a personal Lord, in the spirit, and that was all she ever would have.

Prior to her arrest, she had prayed daily at home, and lost a lot of emotional baggage as well as weight. Her professional ambitions had been blunted, and she knew she had been accused of crimes. Channah couldn't really feel she had done wrong.

She could recall how one night, just 3 days prior to her arrest, she lay on the futon coach in the den, with a silver brushed steel lamp casting the only light in the room. She was dozing, lost in remembrance of a prior year well spent teaching in a public school in Brooklyn, happy teaching disabled kids surrounding her, enjoying a lesson.

Now, the quiet wind blew in a subdued empty place. The lamp glowed, a type of halo on the ceiling. And then, She was there, and her Son and Channah was just flabbergasted. This visitation was very real at the time.

Channah had blinked, waiting for it to leave, shifting position, expecting it to be a trick of perception. It remained. Slowly, she meditated on the meaning it revealed to her. As she did so, it became clearer to her what the Immaculate Conception was about, and had always been, from the First Day.

She had risen afterward. Two hours had passed and she was elated. She found a marker and traced an outline of the vision on the ceiling. Then she let the lamp burn all night and fell into a tranquil sleep.

The next day she even made an altar under the spot and collected weeds wildflowers and moss to adorn there. She took to praying at home there every day after that.

Thinking back, Channah could admit she had been driven to the edge of despair at the time. But, she was forced to admit as well that there are ways the Lord works on us to lead us up. She supposed visions such as that were part of it. It was more than movie special effects, and nothing delusive or like delirium from drugs was related to this paranormal experience. It was supra-real, and, she now supposed, a means of strength for what needed to be endured ahead.

Now in her cell, she marveled. *My faith was sustained and my strength is intact. The ordeal began to end as soon as I was jailed in March. I fully expected to die but became a believer. I shouldn't record it but know it happened for posterity.*

She recalled once more how she had headed up to Boston the next day, to seek support from a distant cousin. Once there, she couldn't find the house.

That was very bad. The sheriffs had not phoned or stopped by for weeks. Much later her attorney told her that is customary in Nassau County.

The house had been repeatedly entered and vandalized. Her stuff was packed in closets or bins, sealed with makeshift eyebolts and cheap padlocks, or just duck tape.

Expose: The Reckoning by Channah Gambit

The Sheriff's office had no provision for sealing tenant's possessions in rooms for 6 months. It only evicted tenants, throwing their possessions by the curbside. She wondered why this was. A county employee at the Courthouse in the Hall of Records in Mineola had told her to use tape, to print her name, the date,and a signature to legally seal off her property. As if owning property mattered! There were things more important to her, like loving feelings, that had been stolen already.

She mused about all the petty larcenies and breakages in the apartment. Was it remotely possible that Duvey had done it? Her Duvey! She refuse to believe he had anything to do with the destruction of her expensive computer. The software had been degraded. It was as if someone with considerable expertise, in a rage, had torn it apart in a fit of temper while she was away in Boston. Then there were signs that someone had tried to conceal that by rebuilding her computer as well. Concealment had only been partially successful. Her hair had stood on end! So many imponderables to work out. They were a strain, even for a highly credentialed, educated college graduate.

Channah's faith sustained her only partially as she was vilified, ignored by relatives, starved, denied a phone replacement by Sprint, and left out in the cold by local parishes.

It hadn't been easy to convert, or to experience this ordeal, while empathizing with the ordeal of Jesus at the end of his life. This Lent in prison, she thrashed out her feelings for three months in a filthy desolate cell in Medical Observation block, without consolation of family, or the clergy.

She'd be doing the stations, early morning prayer and meditation on the Passion for the first time in her life full-heartedly. Dirt poor, ruined, humiliated, degraded by the treatment she had received while on the wrong side of the law, she'd relate more and more to the Savior. Channah realized that she had been saved from herself, her self-complacency, and self-destructive tendencies. She thought quietly to herself in the gloom of the cell: *I've paid a terrible price in the loss of familiar relationships. My family's actions do not totally bewilder me. This is not a quiet Lenten observance. I have done some wrong acts, but I cannot, as yet, admit it to myself, or hold myself responsible.*

She was deeply angry. It came out with a long diatribe against the poor chaplain. There was an impassioned plea in writing to Father Tom of *The God Squad* at Telecare to come bail her out, which never resulted in any reply. *It was probably lost in the front office.* By this time, with a flat commissary account, she was constructing toothpaste glued envelopes from paper and borrowing stamp money from friends.

Channah also wrote a huge letter to Pope Benedict, filled with the entire history of her conversion, mentioning the vision she had of the Nativity in March. The address came from a Christian Science Monitor borrowed at the law library, and it was addressed to the Curia in Rome. She sent a copy to Deacon. Mason for his comment, but typically he never replied. Channah was expecting either criticism or censure from him. A silent wall surrounded her, and she never heard from Rome. Odds were that her mail was not getting delivered at all.

As week after week extended her jail stay, she grew to find new ways to deal with the relentless negativity. Channah prayed. She did Rosary, learning how. She centered myself in a new faith in the Lord. Girls grew to respect her piety and donated icon cards as they bailed out and left making her happier.

Easter came, and Palm Sunday. They returned from chapel to their cells carrying palm strands. Officer Breeland taught Channah the traditional way to weave it into a crucifix. The prisoner did a splendid job and others noticed. She ended up with a job, making one for almost every inmate in block A. Some girls had begun copying her, getting into decorating their cells with icons and crucifixes or asking for Bibles, which they also read each day. The *Alpha* table even began saying grace before meals.

At times Channah felt deep unrest. Her expectations were unmet by loved ones so she meditated on what real love must be. She thought about loyalty, fidelity, and attachment of the heart strings. The pierced heart of Christ and his Mother became a felt reality to her as her own ached for her children. She understood for the first time, the mystery of God's love for us, shown in his willingness to suffer and die for humanity. They were maturing lessons. Channah read the bible with fervor and prayed with humility. Sometimes she reflected on her egotism and the way she had come to end up there. She had trusted in the wrong people who had failed her utterly.

By the time Easter ended, she was prepared to admit that she had, very likely, scared someone badly by behaving erratically. It just did not justify her being abandoned by family. Channah understood in a more mature fashion what crime was, and what criminals were like as well as the brand of law enforcement American society provided. She did not like the way the guards behaved, their attitudes, or the way she was being manhandled by the legal system.

The greater truth which came to her in prayer was to turn to a talent she had stifled for 20 years. Her artistic talent was still alive! Channah began to sketch religious subjects on scrap paper and on the backs of toilet roll wrappers, every chance she could get. She couldn't stop!

Her hands were guided by a lot of inspiration. Some things she had struggled to express in her youth did not trouble her anymore, like anatomy. Art was delightful. She took pleasure in showing these sketches to other prisoners in the day room.

They liked them very much, and asked her favors. *Will you make a copy of this photograph of my kids? Will you draw my boyfriend?* they would say. She began to use the talent to barter for what she wanted Channah earned peanut butter and some turquoise hair goop shampoo. She did more portraits of her new friends, and they paid in envelopes oranges or milk. What a business! She was quite busy.

Once a day, she also did a picture in my cell of a religious subject. These were little cartoons for stained glass windows, of scenes from the life of Christ. She was reading her way through the gospels, a chapter a day. She kept these drawings in date order, and began to dream living the rest of her life enjoyably, not teaching, but doing art as a stained glass artisan. At law library, she gathered addresses to local glass studios.

The Lord knew she had had a period of instability and that she was being robbed of her profession and freedom. Perhaps He would approve her finding a way to serve others using her talents. These were ideas she reflected on, seeking compensation as she prayed each day. The art provided an enjoyment which reduced and outweighed the pains of abandonment, violation, accusation, and humiliation. Though stifled in her need to communicate, she expressed herself..

Expose: The Reckoning by Channah Gambit

Channah realized that she had a firm resolve to teach disabled children and to earn a fine salary, but that might now be taken away forever by the State. They had charged her with a felony. Even so, she did not feel hatred toward the woman in Westbury who had complained about her. Thoughts of Big's activities incensed her, however.

In Medical Observation block, the ice was broken, and there was a lot of cheer found in being sought out for a drawing. Channah had friends in the other blocks who wanted religious drawings. As respect grew, word spread. They'd meet her in the yard, pay in paper, and hide her art under shirts with big smiles.

Bad things were still routine. Kelly was in lockdown due to aggressive behavior, in cell 7. She smacked away at the shatterproof glass hour after hour, and trashed her cell in efforts to get out. They played cards at nights under the crack of her door, sitting on the cold cement. Her boyfriend, a dealer, had gotten her into it, and then abandoned her with a habit. She looked beautiful, a young Bette Midler. A hostile mother would not give her the legal right to represent herself, so she was held for a month, *for observation*. Also, when she called mom rare times free, she was reduced to tears by a rejection. Mommy would not transfer her to a hospital for care. She needed to be sedated, but nothing was being done. Week after week, she spent 22 hours in her cell. When she was allowed into the day room, the others were forced to be celled in. Kelly had a plastic jar filled with small colored pencils which she lent Channah.

"I've found the gift of a rainbow here." Channah told Kelly.

In April, Kelly had some suicidal moments where she tried to rake cuts in her arms and escape through the slot in her door, frantic and claustrophobic from confinement there.

Channah had had it. As a trained professional, she wrote up a grievance in the form of a letter to Sheriff Rooney, asking him to intervene and remove Kelly to the Medical Center, before she succeeded in another suicide attempt. A few weeks passed, then Channah was called down to a visitor's booth to be confronted by two hardball types dressed in suits and flamboyant ties. They refused to tell her their names but seemed like F.B.I.. They told her they were from *internal security*. By then, Kelly had been moved upstate to do a long sentence at another facility, as inmates believed. They grilled Channah for over an hour, berating her. How did she dare to write to Sheriff Rooney, her—a felon? Where did she come off thinking officers were not doing their jobs there? How did she get off suggesting that Kelly had been sexually attacked by a guard? Channah had a hard job defending myself. Finally, she told the black honcho she thought he was practicing a reverse bias in attacking her for being educated, intelligent, and credible. He left. Channah now had the reputation among the guards for being a troublemaker.

The requests for new underwear and sox came through with a gift from commissary of the needed panties, a bra, and an extra shirt. She was absurdly grateful, and wrote them a thank you note. It was true that, week after week, on Tuesdays, a tough hard female guard would pass over her allotment of 2 free envelopes. She would just skip Channah, or remember her last. The name was Reynolds.

There wasn't as much animosity now. Channah was being redirected, through being prayerful and by circumstances, to a more beneficial perspective on her own life.

Expose: The Reckoning by Channah Gambit

The miracle of the return of her artistic talent increased her faith in the Lord. She was effortlessly drawing anything she wanted. After years of *artist's block*, feelings and emotions were flowing into images. It was a miracle!

The right side of her brain was stupefied and had sustained a shock. She could not connect with memories of the life she had led in previous years. Waves of sentiment concerning the children came over her at times. She fought fears they had left her forever, or had been harmed by the same crazy person who had ransacked her apartment for years. Channah was badly frightened at times for no palpable reason and stayed in her cell.

Even though the Chaplain visited, her condition was not considered *under control*. She was forced to see the prison doctor, Dr. Bridge, who wanted to put her on medication. The stalemate was getting serious, and she was threatened with permanent solitary confinement, like Kelly's, if Channah did not comply. She was referred to the social worker. Only art and prayer sustained her soul.

Expose: The Reckoning by Channah Gambit

Chapter 18: A Visitor & Attorney Come

It is bad enough that a felon is denied liberty and forced to dwell in the company of criminals and vermin. The inhospitable public jailhouse is a far cry from accustomed comforts. Why then, did the government subject them to repeated abuse of freedoms implied in the Bill of Rights? They did not receive enough wholesome food to survive. The poorest inmates like Channah could not communicate with the outside world, by either mail or telephone, nor own a pencil. Telephone service had to be arranged with a specific collect account, set up for some number of the outside and paid for in advance. Mail supplies had to be purchased through the commissary store, and paid for with a commissary account.

She had to scheme, and manipulate social workers or other inmates to gain these services. The guards tormented her with insulting gestures and remarks. Without a willing sympathetic family member or friend, the situation could not be altered. It was a "cruel twist of fate". She was certain that there were many like herself that were there at present, subject to misfortunes, who clearly deserved a chance to be bailed out and stand on their own feet. She was in the process of discovery. She could not be informed, could not obtain correct or reliable addresses or phone numbers, from any printed material or posters at hand. It was enervating.

As far as mail, it was very often coming back stamped *incorrect address*. Grievances were constantly coming back stamped **Nixxie—unclear language**. *Denied. Resubmit.* Censorship was clearly happening. Meanwhile, more fortunate inmates, accustomed to how the system worked, were making phone calls every day to loved ones, or receiving visitors. They were getting daily letters from boy friends or mothers.

It would be infuriating to look back when all was behind her and to think of the days spent fighting a blackout of information regarding her son and daughter. Social worker procedures were the last straw. Though accessible to inmates, and although they seemed capable of making third-party calls to either lawyers, doctors, or family members, they were both corrupt and manipulative from experience.

For example, Carol Muck, long after Channah had one visit from a hostile daughter, would spend weeks in possession, she claimed, of that daughter's cell phone number, denying Channah direct access, on the pretext that "your daughter will not speak to you or visit you until you take medication." She would use intake sessions to obtain an abusive ex-spouse's name. She would call him, extracting a long list of supposed previous hospitalizations regarding Channah's history. Then she would shock her with this, assuring her that she could gain all records without the signing of a release form, because "You are a criminal". She would trick her into signing a release form so that she could try to get her attorney at the Legal Aid Society to visit her after a gap of 27 days, then use it to obtain any medical records she could clandestinely from the facilities.

Carol Muck was a villain. After Channah finally cracked in June, complying with medication due to her leverage, she conveyed the message that

"I lost your daughter's cell phone number." And vacated the building. That was her style. For weeks prior she had dangled the means to communicate with that child in front of the inmate, causing her mounting anxiety, nervousness, and near hysteria. Her sadistic tactics and savagery in denying Channah any lifeline at all reduced her to misery.

Jamo finally decided to come for a visit around March 21st. She arrived, dressed in a hooded sweater. At frisking, she was told to leave, and return with different clothing. Channah's first visitor call ended in an impasse. An hour later, she was called again and went down by elevator. Other inmates, initially incredulous, cheered for her. It had been about a month.

The daughter had anger to display, little else. She fully swallowed the medical model that Mommy was sick. She believed Channah had caused her own problems and let her know just that. And that nothing unusual had happened at the apartment.

Channah cried at seeing a familiar face, nevertheless. She had mailed Jamo a letter granting her power of attorney for a month, she stated.

"You must visit my accountant, and see that he does my taxes, signing for me."

"Alright, Mom. You know coming here was a pain the ass. They searched me because I had on a hooded sweater. I had to take it out to the car to get in!" Jamo said.

"My bail is $1500. Can't you raise it?" Channah said.

"I admit that Duvey and I have no money to spare for that." Jamo said.

"Please try to borrow it, honey, and get me out. Send me a package of *outside clothes* suitable for the court hearing. I'll make a good impression."

"Sure." Jamo said.

She left, never to return. About a week, after that visit, the L.A.S. attorney introduced himself to Channah as Matt Silverwitch. They spoke of the charges, but she bristled with anxiety.

"I'm innocent. I really did not do any of that."

"I'm sorry.You have to take a 730 competence exam, requested by Judge Messe. He thinks you are too sick to understand those charges. And frankly, I'm forced to agree with him. Lady, I think you are psychotic." he said.

She stared at him, incredulously. He omitted detailing the charges, did not read her the affidavit of the chief complainant, Hilda Sandstorm, and did not inform her of the penalties. He just left.

What did he base that on, never having met her before? Why was he willing to represent her, if he was prejudiced before even hearing her side of it? It would be over 29 days before Channah saw him again, due to a *heavy caseload.* He had not, as was his job, explained the charges or maximum penalties to her. He had not sought to have bail reduced for her to win her release although that was within his power. He did, however, decide to send a social worker to her from the Legal Aid, to discuss shelters she might later stay at since the apartment was off limits due to the protection order.

One day in April, the loudspeaker blared during breakfast. "Channah Gambit, visitor." Scrubbing the shower stalls was interrupted, and she threw the rag and gloves on a shelf in the closet.

Taken into glass booth 3, she regarded Karen waiting for her. She was a pert attractive brunette in her early twenties dressed in a neat black tailored pants suit and pink blouse. On the table was a legal pad and pen.

"Hi, Channah. I'm the social worker from the Legal Aid Society. How do you do." she said.

Expose: The Reckoning by Channah Gambit

"Hi." Channah said seating herself.

"Matthew Silverwitch feels you need to plan for when you get out. The Protection Order will not permit you to return to any apartment near your father." Karen said.

"I know. Let me tell you something. I don't feel Mr. Silverwitch fully explained the charges to me. He set me up for a 7.30 competency exam. Also I feel I need to present my defense to someone."

"I understand. First please tell me your history." Karen said. She picked up her pen.

"I'm someone who was sickly during her childhood. It was an abusive situation for myself and my sister for many years. After college I married a man and raised two children. Together we rose a business. Then I divorced and decided to make something out of myself. With a great amount of difficulty I returned to college to finish my degree. Whew. This takes a lot of talking!" Channah said.

"Right. So you have had a long history of domestic conflict there. Very interesting." Karen said writing for sometime on the pad. She folded her hands in front of her. "Please continue."

"Well there's not much more. I succeeded in getting a bachelor's degree in psychology. I worked after that for a few years for an investigative firm out in Suffolk. Got fed up with that and decided to take a shot at becoming a teacher. A professor inspired me." Channah said and grinned.

"So you are an educated lady. Nuts with a psychology degree. That doesn't add up. Someone has to have their act together to graduate from college." Karen commented smiling back at her. Channah felt relaxed and leaned back in the plastic chair.

"I'm almost done. I was taken in by Daddy and permitted to live rent free. I passed the GRE and was accepted into a teaching masters program. While there I went through a period where I was working three part time jobs at once to pay for incidentals. I became a certified teacher by 2003 and spent about a year looking for work. It was very hard to break into my field." Channah said, her brow crinkling in concentration.

"Now we are ready to discuss how you got into trouble." Karen said.

"And my defense. I hope you convey it to the head of your Legal Aid Society." Channah said. There was a paper cup with water on the desk. Karen caught her glance and gestured that she should help herself. She took a swallow.

"Basically I resigned from a job after a head injury. Many other reasons. I tried out at a job in Far Meadows which didn't work out. The kids were way too violent. The woman was not protecting the kids enough and I complained to the Department of Education of New York State. That was a risky thing to do.

"Meanwhile, I could not find a new job. My credit went and the car payments fell behind. Incidents of malicious mischief and theft kept happening at home without forced entry. I was a very educated lady without the ability to earn.

"I went a bit mad. I was malnourished. It was criminal the way my own family would not even give me groceries. My father began to be a problem and took out his frustrations on me.

"Now why was that? You mean he hit you when you were down?" Karen asked. The page was full of scribbles, and she turned it over.

Expose: The Reckoning by Channah Gambit

"Right. Bizarre the whole thing! It got worse and worse. Regarding my mental state, I had a second head injury from a car accident upstate in January. I was scared because I thought I witnessed someone planning a crime next door. I panicked." Channah said.

"That could be used as a defense. You should be hopeful." Karen said.

"I'm not, Karen. I really feel horrible. Besides all that happening, my vault box was tampered with at my bank and mail was being riffled or misplaced for weeks. Everywhere I turned bad things happened. Then I lost my cellphone. That is the one reputed to have made the false 911 phone call. They say they taped it but it couldn't be me as I did not have the phone to make a call. I am trying to get paper records from the Sanyo company showing that service stopped the prior November. I did it to protect my mailbox."

"Hmmm. Very interesting. Tell me more about that." Karen said.

"The truth is, some party unknown actually reactivated my phone after I had suspended service. Sanyo has a record of that. Someone with a voice very much like mine impersonated me and had access to my private family phone directory on that cell." Channah took a deep breath.

"Amazing. Unbelievable. It should have been brought up at the arraignment hearing. That charge would have been dropped. You must be brave now." Karen said. She stood up briefly, rummaged in her valise and sat again.

"What next?" Channah asked.

"Now we discuss shelters and types of arrangements we might make for you if you make bail." Karen said. She had changed the topic so quickly that Channah found it odd.

"Okay. My needs are simple. I need a room with a bed." she said.

"You can get that from the Department of Social Services. Now here's what I think we can do for you…" Karen began.

The conference lasted over an hour more. Channah felt great after Karen shook hands and said goodbye. The two women regarded each other.

"You will help me and convey my defense strategy to Mr. Silverwitch's director?" Channah asked.

"I'll try to help. Let me see what I can do. Good bye, Channah." Karen said. Channah walked down to the guard desk and was put into a holding cell in preparation for returning back upstairs. She waved as Karen walked past heading for the front door.

For over a month afterward, she went back and forth to the basement holding cell in Hempstead for conferences in District Court. Her attorney would see her for only a couple of minutes through the bars to inform her. Karen did not do anything for her and seemed to have vanished into the woodwork. No phone messages to her produced any results. Channah was discouraged. She would eventually seek to obtain new counsel by filing a motion on her own, with the help of the law library's Officer Pulgrid.

"God bless him!" Channah told a guard later.

Her family was non-existent for her. Although she was held in holding for over two hours hopefully, for posted bail, no one showed at the first hearing after arraignment on March 21st. The Carol Muck creature began tormenting with her creative blackmails and leverages. Other social workers, alternates and weekend subs, were visiting their block. They would listen, take down phone numbers, promise to make calls for Channah and never return or simply fail to carry out what they promised.

Irene Burl, one of the kinder ones, finally leveled with her one Sunday.

"Your situation is very unfair. My calls for inmates are being blocked by the Central Communication station. They won't allow it. We're going to lose our jobs if we continue to do so." she said. Channah believed her.

Carol Muck's behavior was reprehensible. Channah felt the brunt of her dislike and noticed that she was not liked by inmates on the block. Powers, after all, drew a wedge between her and a loved one. She worsened Channah's condition both emotionally and situationally. Channah could not say enough about the damage she did to her. She did not doubt that Mucks could drive other inmates to suicide.

"I finally have a caseload. I don't really care about what you do." Mucks was overheard once to chortle to another social worker.

In early May Channah became frantic at the failure of Jamo to return to see her. She was forced to go down to visit Dr. Bridge.

"I've done some inquiries. Been in touch with your family too. Seems you were taking Zyprexa which was prescribed by your physician in Island Tree." Bridge said.

"So? That's surprising that you'd go through the bother." Channah said.

Bridge was deadpan and looked up from her chart at her. "You need a higher dosage than you were getting, Ms. Gambit." he said.

"After being here for six weeks, I feel pretty bad most of the time." Channah said.

"It would be to your benefit if you cooperated with me." Bridge said.

"Okay. Look. I think something is really out of kilter. There must be some reason my kids haven't come to visit me." she said.

"It must be very painful for you. Yes. Your children have abandoned you. There's a lot of pain in facing reality. Frankly I don't think you are doing that. You can't grasp the charges and I'm supposed to probe and advise whether I think you need a 7.30 competency hearing. Well guess what, Lady. I think you do and I'm going to say so."

"Look. I have decided to go along with it. I was told by Muck that if I comply and take meds I can receive a phone call from my daughter." Channah said.

"That might be true. You will begin taking Sequil 20 milligram tonight when the nurse comes around. Let's see how you do." Bridge said. The session was over. He looked pale and drawn. He seemed to blend in with the garish gray and light green walls of his cubicle. His desk was loaded with folders and papers. Bridge had his own problems. Hansom picked her up and escorted her into the waiting stall for return upstairs. She sat and chatted with a doped up inmate.

All the inmates of M.O. were subject to prescriptions, which came around twice daily. Many of them were zombies. These were the strongest psychotropics. Girls would complain to Channah about how they felt tense, or couldn't sleep, or couldn't think.

Ouiji, with a strong freckled Irish beauty, paced the block for hours, wearing a CD player, trying to wear off the meds. Channah tried to console, and told her to ask for a new medication. Dr. Bridge was only too happy to experiment on them. When Channah started to develop severe headaches, she stopped taking the dose prescribed. The doctor acceded in reducing the dosage by half.

"Now, I fit the medical model. They'll come." she thought. But, still, her kids did not return for a visit. She began to fantasize that something had happened to her kids.

Channah asked at times to speak to the Corporal and solicited information regarding procedures should something amiss occur to her offspring at home.

"Yes, they will inform you." Zizzer said, reassuring her. "If there is a death in your family, you'll be informed, and permitted to go to the funeral. It's the law!" He strode out.

Channah also explored the possibility of becoming a candidate for something called *Weekend jail*, where she would work in the community and return each Friday night to lockup. Officer Pulgrid assured her it was an impossibility one Tuesday during law library hour.

"We don't do that here." he said.

The following Thursday, she was taken down to the basement to see Bridges again. He was waiting at his desk dressed in chinos and a brown brushed mohair sweater. It was chilly in the room and the fluorescents downstairs cast an artificial yellow light over everything.

"You have been taking the medication. Nurse Black told me. How do you feel." he asked, pen poised about her chart.

"I'm beginning to feel as if I have been buried alive here and that someone has thrown away the key. I'm going to remain here forever. Worse yet, my children are gone now." he nodded his head, all the while taking notes. Then he upped the dosage on her medications.

The family members who had cooperatively catapulted her into a fearful state, vandalized her apartment, scared her with third key access to her vault box and delayed mail, were out there free and clear. Now, cousins, second cousins, aunts, uncles, siblings, all were hanging up on any third party calls she made with the help of other inmates. Channah wasn't mystified, because she had really done some stupid things out there in prior months. But at the same time it was simply inconceivable to her that they would leave her in jail like this.

Chapter 19: The Architecture of the Trojan Horse

Carmen Road: A prison farm facility was turned one day into something odd: a turret-shaped double tower sunk deep into a hill with an extensive *catacomb* underneath. It was located relatively close to a major private medical facility operating under the umbrella of the Federal government.

The D Block at Carman Road was an unusual facility. Inmates claim was built over 10 years ago. It was supposed to be for drug crimes, but, due to overpopulation, all other types of criminals were housed there, both men and women.

The D block was a split level, with two parallel halves, only joined by elevator. Certain floors were accessible to the north elevator, others to the south. The layout of this structure purposely confounded the minds of inmates. It was supposed this was intentional to discourage planned escapes.

There were 5 floors including two basement levels below. A large tunnel connected D block to E Building, which Channah dubbed the *Heartbreak Hotel*. She saw that was sometimes referred to on magazines brought in to law library as The Law Library run by one James Mason, inviting speculation. Was that Father Mason? Could she gain access to all those law reference books? No, they didn't exist!

E Building had nothing to do with regular female inmate traffic. It may be assumed that it contained barracks for guards on a tour or perhaps a cemetery of ashes. Only glimpses of its interior could be seen from the outside recreation yard through filthy slitted windows high up on the sides. These showed torn and dirty air conditioner ducts, or constantly burning fluorescent lights.

D Building was maintained like a little Pentagon. It was the opposite plan, however, in that, as you went *up*, security increased. The top 3rd floor was therefore like Siberia, permanent lockup, and some inmates never seemed to go down again, for weeks or months. The third floor was remote from the real world, had tighter security, stranger guards, and was more insular. The grapevine stated during Channah's visit that once you went up there, you would never come down again. You'd simply vanish.

The shape of the D block halves was like an octagonal honeycomb, with the guard posts in the center in a glass, bulletproof "beehive", filled with switches and monitors. Around these were narrow catwalks leading to quartered, identical blocks, two-tiered, each one in a different steel paint enamel. "A, B, C, D". Up in the penthouse, level 4, there was 1 more block **F**, for violent prisoners.

The parallel wings, one for men, one for women, were not interconnected on any floor other than floor 2. The intake zone below was coed, and so were the medical suites at different times of day. Male inmates had their own outdoor recreation yard adjacent to Building E and the basement chapel. On the long trip to the chapel each Saturday, passing tunnel catacomb entry to E Building and the special elevator up to officer's quarters on either side, the female inmates would pass the *shrink's wing*, property, and labyrinthine corridors filled with strange musty rooms, behind ancient scarred wooden doors, with comforters or quilts thrown as curtains blocking their view through windows. These were rumored to be *maid's* or *officer's lounges*, with coke machines.

On the way they'd often passed silent male inmates, watching them with curiosity out of total boredom. Then they'd come to the chaplain's tower, with four floors of private living quarters for Brother Mason, Sister Evian, or guests. It sported it's own private elevator.

The block cells, twenty-four to each quad, made Channah think of *Skinner boxes*. She had learned about these baby bassinets developed by a famous psychiatrist. Made of plastic and metal, they featured knobs, valves and buttons which controlled heat, humidity, sound, light, and all else. The infant's environment could be totally programmed and controlled, changing its habits for the better.

.Just like these, the individual block cells contained outside environmental controls, to isolate each inmate, or someone contagious. Prominently featured were black buttons. That really started her pondering, as day passed after day.

Each cell had it's own individual water pump for the sink, and an individual pipe drain for the toilet, which she believed could be filtered or checked. These entered through a turquoise control box in the wall next to each cell, about three feet by one foot.

Who had dreamt up such a strange setup? Did it have a *cold war* functionality?

Individual cells could be totally contained, through venting, water, and the intercom in the wall. Sometimes, moist mist blew in through a vent during the morning or night. One night, after a particularly odious windy period, Channah developed labored breathing and had to request an infirmary visit.

In the middle of each block, cemented and welded to the floor, was a huge, nine foot high black steel apparatus. You could stand up on it and do leg lifts. You'd have to be a basketball player male, however. This seemed a great place to chain an inmate and administer 40 lashes. No discernible use existed otherwise. The menacing nature of this apparatus was unnerving.

Another scary piece of apparatus was a chair, adjacent to the visitor's center in a search area, built out of steel and wood, painted black. It resembled a classic electric chair. While Channah was strip searched there in May, she was tongue-lashed by a female guard who showed it to her with glee.

"Is it necessary to so frequently strip search inmates jailed for misdemeanors?" you may ask. A class action suit against Nassau County for this practice dating back to the 1990's has been permitted by a Judge at last.

Channah felt that D block must have been dreamt up by an architect frustrated by the loss of a bid for designing a medical/Intelligence facility. It had been funded by someone high up in the military hierarchy back in the 1970's. That was fairly obvious.

The imperviousness of the building, the way it was built around a central core with controllable access, the fact that there was an attached building large enough to house an entire battalion; the close proximity to a hospital; the fact that it had a highly sophisticated communication center with programmable trunk lines, all made an alternate government purpose palpable. The local government could be maintained here during a time of surprise attack by a foreign power. Any enemy insurgents could be thrown into the Medical Observation block and incapacitated or *broken down*, one at a time, in individual cells. This D block was an ideal central command post for more than just penal enforcement. But actually it was the Sheriff's personal preserve and that was a large part of the problem.

Expose: The Reckoning by Channah Gambit

Channah decided, after research, that Collin Powell was the bright rising star who must have given his approval to funding, or some crony below him, to have it built to completion sometime around 1990.

The central communication center monitored all incoming and outgoing calls. Some fairly sophisticated programming was in use. She found that her outgoing calls were being routed through the 2nd floor medical wing. Channah actually heard the calls being screened there one day when she visited the podiatrist, Dr. Golub.

The facility was paramilitary in bearing; not just a jail. It was built originally for the purpose of containment of those hostile to the state, to break them down psychologically to interrogate them or to contain a medical epidemic.

The protocal for handling prisoners with lies, false identity tags and erroneous facts addressed in signs, telephone books and governmental phone listings pointed to that also.

"I wonder if anyone will ever reveal these truths about *The Trojan Horse*." Channah thought.

It is written clearly in the stones and designs of the D Building there on Carmen Road for anyone who knows what to look for. It was not just being used as a correctional facility to hold those awaiting trial or doing sentences up to a year. The men and women manning the place had an alternate agenda, and had been recruited for cross-training for other purposes, best known to Sheriff Rooney and the County of Nassau, New York.

For one, they had invented their own new national anthem. Female inmates heard it one afternoon in late May while at outdoor recreation. It wafted in the wind, sounding like a cross between a patriotic song and a beer drinking tune. At least 50 voices of sheriff's officers, of both sexes, in unison, practiced the song, strong and loud. Not quite the Star Spangled Banner, it sounded vaguely threatening. Had Ed Rooney, up in his plexiglass control tower, finally flipped his wig? Was this Benedict Arnold developing an independent taskforce, for something not unlike a new duchy of Luxenborg?

Expose: The Reckoning by Channah Gambit

Chapter 20: The Pillsbury Doughboy

Channah had hopes, long after Jamo's first visit, that she would be bailed out of this inner rung of hell.

As day passed into night and back to day, she lost anything resembling her old identity, as her personality suffered a total collapse. What sustained her at times were memories of "One Day In the Life of Ivan Denisovich" by Alexander Solzhanitzen.

There was a hearing coming up in late March, around the 25th, and she was brought down with a bunch of black foul mouthed witches to the second floor cell prior to travel down to District Court. She was hand-cuffed to a crack head mother out of wedlock. She was singing a Janice Joplin song about a Mercedes Benz as she stood in the doorway.

Along the corridor came a chain gang made up of male ornery male inmates, and in there was a young man, about 6'6", 220 pounds, curly brown hair, the Pillsbury Doughboy. He was cute, and plump and pudgy. She saw him pass for a split-second. And that was her son Duvey, stammering, cheeks blushed red with anger, right after some kind of arraignment, being brought in. Her mouth fell open at this apparition.

Thoughts flooded her mind? Had he been arrested for gambling? He dearly loved playing poker. Had he been caught with a joint in his car? He had experimented with it once when he was 17. Did he seem slightly older? He did. Wasn't he her boy, couldn't be! But was this a continuation of the kind of contrivance and strong-arming that she had experienced from her own family? Was this a reprisal of sorts directed at her immediate family, to dishonor them all. If it *was* her son, she doubted he'd survive the ordeal. He was an idealistic boy, home-grown, soft, without any skill at defending himself other than intelligence. This cherub that had flown by seemed some sacrificial lamb. He was, in more ways than one, as it turned out.

Ace, dubbed *Hoppy* in her head, was a skinny Nigra crackhead there on a dope charge, hanging out, listening to her hum. She was like a black tintype of Wondra, Channah's cousin, and looked like an Egyptian queen in dreadlocks. She was Channah's comfort now. In the merry-go-round ride of that day and others in the future, she'd be at her side, protecting her knees from the blows of a club, witnessing things. There was a hazing to be endured, going in and out of District Court. They'd take them down after about 2 hours in holding, for a ride in a crowded van through the Hempstead streets to the court. One gal, Shelly from Albany, a soft winsome blond baby lost in drugs, had done the merry-go-round 12 times, she claimed. Channah believed she was some kind of stooge or probe, put in by the bulls, to find out things. She would travel in with them. They'd then endure about 7 hours in a basement group cell, cold, without comforts other than a crap stall. She'd lead them on, to confide all their evidence, hopes or fears, and then travel back with them, after they'd met for a second with the lawyer going upstairs, to meet "in conference". Sometimes, girls like Shelly would not meet a lawyer at all. The day's peak moment was the spicy bologna sandwich and pint of whole milk they'd drink. Ace slept on the hard cold floor. Others just rapped away non-stop in prison slang.

She waited around for Silverwitch to show. He waved through the bars.

Expose: The Reckoning by Channah Gambit

"Well, you'll have to expect that 7.30 test. The contempt charge for missing your Family Court hearing has been dropped. That puts the bail down by $500." he said in a flat tone of voice. His deadpan face barely looked at her. Channah thought she might as well be a heifer standing at the fence around a paddock then a grown woman fighting for her dignity.

"I'm glad to hear all that." she managed to say.

"Oh, you might like to know that one of the charges about stalking was mislabeled in the system a felony. It's actually just a misdemeanor." Silverwitch said.

Her face lit up. He noticed it. "Right. Wow." Channah said.

"But it's still a Class A Misdemeanor. That's more serious." he said.

Her spirits drooped back to where they had been before. Tears started pouring from her eyes. "Mr. Silverwitch, will you please call some of my friends to help me borrow to make bail?" she said.

"Okay. I'll do that." she was surprised to hear him say. He jotted down some names and the telephone number for Richard her therapist then left.

When several hours had passed, one girl made bail and was released, but Channah's cavalry never arrived. Dazed, confused, she was brought back to jail, thinking about the *Pillsbury Doughboy.*

What exactly did I see? she thought as she sat in the cold room, hunched over to keep warm on the bench. Her face had gone pale. *Was that some kind of twin to him? It was such a similar build. The hair and everything were his! Is his absence or my need making me see him everywhere? Or did he run away, and is he in trouble?* All the ride back, she rolled it over in her mind like a big rubber band ball.

They were readmitted with a strip search, a change in the wardrobe room under Aero's watchful gaze, and an elevator ride up to the second floor. Checking in with the Lieutenant, they were permitted to help themselves to the Styrofoam trays left for them on the guard's side table.

One spy made out best. After all her good work probing and questioning on the sly, Shelly was rewarded, *out of the blue,* with two extra suppers when she came in to the strip search area. That's what she worked for. She now knew all Channah's wishes concerning her professional career. They had been expressed and wormed out of her during the long boring hours sitting and yacking in the holding cell. Like a dust magnet, she'd known enough at the start of their meeting to state she was trying to become a teacher. Steering the conversation she'd broached the subject of Channah's losing her credentials. She had an enemy inside. She was certain someone there had a personal ax to grind. The way the family at home had rigged all the incidents and called the police, time after time in a contrivance to paint her black and humiliate her, was a similar tactic. Perhaps dragging the boy in was just another way to ruin her by an enemy.

The next day which was Thursday proved to be more interesting. Goul was the guard on sentry duty. A ghoulish gray skin covered him from head to toe. He looked Teutonic and he admitted to someone that Germany was his first love. Hispanic-German, he fixated on her early on, and took great pains to boss her around. Ace and Channah returned after recreation having missed lunch and were locked in their cells. Channah lay on her back, on the lower bunk, crowded thoughts in her head. Officer Goul strutted past

Expose: The Reckoning by Channah Gambit
the door

"Hey, Hey, Hey" he hissed at her, then he laughed.

The newspapers recently had been dated later, and now were only a couple of days behind in the share bin under the serving table out front. A few days later, she read a strange story of a hit in the City. A young man, a Barton John Heyman, had been up in Harlem, and came up from a subway platform. The photograph showed a white, Semitic looking black-haired young man. Emerging onto the streets, he had appeared somewhat *flablongered*, that's Yiddish for confused, disoriented. A net of teen gang members, traveling in a cadre, had come up in a v around him and driving him forward with catcalls and jeers, caused him to lurch into the street, directly into the path of a speeding Mercedes Benz. Barton had deflected off the hood, and the cadre had dissolved into the crowd which formed. He had spent 4 days with a severe head injury at St. Luke's Hospital in a coma and then, without regaining consciousness, died.

Channah's imagination played with the story for several days, the boy melding into the night dreams she had. She was certain Goul would have loved the story, with his

"Hey, Hey, Heyman" playing in her head. At mass on Saturday, she stated her intentions for B.J. Heyman's soul as they stood at attention. Then her thoughts turned to the Pillsbury Doughboy and she said her intentions for her beloved son Duvey as well.

Like E.L. Doctorow, she imagined as a writer, a corrupt ex-Nazi officer, there at the prison, calling hits on the outside with a racist agenda. A contact came in, like Ace, and received his instructions from the John Giotti inside. He went out and his gang did what was ordered, and were paid off with early release, bail, or money. What an easy thing it would be here at the Correctional Center, with full access to vulnerable criminals, to set up some kind of hit system and keep your hands clean. Her imagination, fed on an acrid, criminal diet, worked overtime. She kept cool doing art, reading the Book of Isaiah in her Gideon. Sometimes she prayed that the Lord would be merciful to her and her offspring.

On April 25th, as she passed down through the second floor medical area, she glimpsed a young man struggling with two guards, Hubby and another, seemingly having some kind of anxiety attack, partially collapsed in their arms. He looked like a former chiropractor of her's, and also like a character from Doonsbury. She saw there also, a young man in a wheelchair closely resembling her ex-husband. Speaking to Wont, the guard on patrol outside, she asked for permission to say hello.

"That's not permitted. Why do you want to know who they are?" he said.

"I haven't seen him in years. I suppose the boy—might be my ex-husbands'." she said.

"You'll have to wait until you're out." Wont said.

Shortly after, as she lay tanning in the sun, he marched by, stomping on her outstretched hand. Status quo for Wont.

There were two little lambs being mistreated in the medical wing, she thought. Then, there was the Doughboy, perhaps someone very much like her beloved son. Nostalgia, sentiment, and heartache robbed her of peace day to day. When they returned upstairs, desperate to verify whom she had seen, she wrote up an infirmary request form, asking her social worker to make a call to someone concerning her son, whom she believed she had seen there. When Muck queried her on the request a day or two later, denying contact privileges to anyone, Channah stated

"I'm just leaving a paper trail." To her, it was obvious that innocents could be brought into the place and simply *disappeared.* Kids without ties, runaways, or those acting as informants for pay—might be betrayed and be left in, for days.

A friend in the holding bay, on another merry-go-round day, told her that she and her friend worked as informants at various jails. They received about $50 an hour to do so, and wherever they stayed they were kept in cells with shag carpets and perks, the works! They mixed in with inmates, informed on what they heard on the grapevine, and worked off a sentence by service to the State. Both men and women did this, traveling back and forth to the outside, well known by the arraignment guards, an extraordinarily difficult deception to maintain, not without risks. Young, stupid, and malleable, they aided law enforcement in framing a suspect, or building a case. Shelly was one. Denise was another. They were well known and heartily disliked when their cover was blown.

The Pillsbury Doughboy had been another.

On April 25th, a young man at the D Block, held for hours in a basement room, found a canister of what he thought was water, and took a shot of acid. He suffered for hours, his alimentary tract singed, and died on May 8th. His body was removed and seen by a pathologist at the Nassau County Medical Center. Burial was in a potters field, in a plain pine box, without ceremony. This was an invention of Channah's, one afternoon on her cot.

Coincidentally, on April 25th, she suffered a severe attack of *acid reflux,* from what she thought was chocolate pudding in the M.O. Block. She suffered a *burn* for over a day. Then, slowly, the burn faded away. Channah dreamt of her body, lying in a dusty moldy room somewhere, on the floor in a corner. Flan and Wont were there. Officer Gasp kicked her body, and it did not move.

"It's too late. He's gone." Wont said, and left. The vision faded.

Channah never saw the Doughboy again, although she saw Shelly. She knew she had shared something with someone else at the prison, in her delirium. She desperately tried to see her own boy Duvey to dissipate the fear inside. Why didn't he come or her daughter with Big? Because of the glimpses she had had of police brutality, she believed there were some concealed mortalities at that facility. But, she also knew that her sanity was now hanging by a thread, and resolved to turn to medication, to dull her senses and psyche until she was released. Channah decided to put herself into suspended animation, to numb herself, until she was back in *the real world* again.

Carol Muck was told of her intention. She would get to call her daughter, and obtain parity with her own private life. She immediately conveyed her acquiescence to Dr. Bridge.

Channah was prescribed Pepcid AC and a psychotropic drug sometime around May 9th, which coincided with her deceased mother's birthday.

Did the boy die there on May 8th and disappear without a trace?

She would often think in months ahead as she tried to sleep after the whole ordeal, whether a visit from the forensic scientist Dr. Shoken at the Visitor's Hub was for something more than just a 7.30 competency exam. It came weeks after Silverwitch had disappeared, and relentless pressures from the Legal Aid Society made her see the doctors prior to going to one of a long series of endless conferences in April and May. Forensics? She should have asked him about the Doughboy, or the familiar figure she had seen being worked over by Hubby and friends in a room in the Red Door Medical Suite.

Channah had pursued one lead, through the nurse who wheeled her cart through at night. Nurse Francis Black was nice, and she had observed her passing notes back and forth with Page. Channah figured she did favors for bribes. She showed Black a little news clipping about a young man, a 21 year old victim, who had been shot in the stomach somewhere in Freeport sometime around April 25th. Anonymous in the papers due to a police investigation, he had been taken to Nassau County Medical Center. Her anxiety over that young man, generalized fear from the lack of a visit from Duvey who had gotten her incarcerated in the first place, led her to ask Ms. Muck to inquire about the status of the boy's condition at the hospital. Channah wanted to do a *novena* for him. She was sincerely interested and took the clipping when she left.

A few days later, at evening medication time, Miller beckoned to Channah. "There was no sign that such a young man has ever been admitted there." she said.

"Thanks." Channah took the clipping back, shaken. Another *desaparado*?

Dr. Shoken came in on Friday and asked Channah one night to tell him her story.

It took a long time. "I was a highly regarded teacher with a Masters degree helping six children in Brooklyn two years ago. Prior to that I was a divorcee who lost custody of her children three times in the courts." He shook his head sympathetically.

"Go on. Take your time. This is just to get acquainted so that I can help you prepare for the 7.30." he said.

"I never had the charges or penalties clearly explained to her. I wasn't refusing to cooperate, but needed to see my attorney first. It had been, by this point, over 27 days without contact with legal counsel. I am heartily fed up with Silverwitch. Pulgrid has provided me with a form 67, an application for change of counsel."

"Sounds like a plan." Shoken said. He stood up from the long table, brushed down his slacks, then left.

Channah was nervous because of interactions with other doctors besides Shoken. Dr. Bridge in the catacombs had changed his name badge from Medini the first visit to Bridge in the second. In grey suits most of the time, he really seemed to listen.

That is, until he opens his mouth. she thought

"I assume from your actions that you are delusional. I have no sympathy for your plight as a victim of domestic violence." he stated after their first thirty minute talk therapy session in March.

"If you want me on your side you'll have to take medication. I'm pro-meds." Bridge said.

"I think not." she said firmly.

"I think you are going to have to cooperate to get out of here sooner." he said. Then he took some notes in his book with a burgundy *Mont Blanc* pen. She was dismayed all the walk back under escort to her cell. Channah grasped for another doctor, someone to relieve the torments. Goldshine, the psychiatrist who popped in and out of the 3rd floor hub area most often, only related to certain ingénues and promising protages among the inmates who were his particularly studies.

One night soon after that, she approached him near the bubble. "I'm sorry. I'll listen to you, but I refuse to evaluate you for the 7.30." Goldshine said.

I'm not young and pretty enough to sway him. she thought, deeply disappointed as she went into her cell.

Dr. Shoken, a forensic scientist there for a 7.30 exam at the Visitor's Center shortly afterward, did not take a liking to Channah.

"I really don't know what to say. I need to speak to my attorney to get the charges explained to me. He never did that." she said.

Dr. Shoken seemed to agree to that willing.

"I promise to see you in two days." Channah said.

Dr. Shoken was actually insulted. He fired off a letter to Judge Messe stating that she had cursed and used foul words in a reaction to his visit. This was patently untrue, but it did her a lot of harm in gaining credence with the court and reduction of bail.

What about the *Little Lost Boys*, as she had come to call the victims of mishap she read about in the paper or observed on the nightly news. *I'll assume they survived. There must be some explanation why Newsday got the hospital name wrong. Perhaps the boy was not shot at all. And that Pillsbury Doughboy was certainly not my Duvey. But where is my son now? He most certainly would do nothing wrong to get himself admitted to the Carmen Road facility. He never could act that young or confused.* She doubted herself and her own intelligence at every moment. She didn't trust an educated hunch as she suffered from foggy head and blurry vision and problems hearing people speak. *I'm falling apart in many ways. Twelve years going through college and gaining a profession. I've been toppled from a glass mountain.* She thought as she lay on her cot. Seeking privacy, she started sleeping on the top bunk feeling like an eagle on a crevice looking down at everybody. After three weeks guards made her move back down to watch her better at night. She almost got written up for doing it.

During these weeks, she had thinly suppressed fear, even while medicated. The architecture of a maximum security medical block featured, as the topper of toppers, several large gas jets prominently placed in the day room. These were undoubtedly remote controlled, designed to suppress an inmate uprising if necessary.

The gas which blew in from the vents in her cell #1 was silver or white—more than condensation. Channah liked to think now it was due to filthy, uncleaned fixtures and filters, rather than directed with intent to harm her lungs or sedate her. The effluvia smelled sweet sometimes, like ether or sweet air. It made her drowsy and sometimes headachy with fits of labored breathing afterward. Vents could be closed off individually, and she heard one compressor shut down around midnight.

Inmates looked for fresh air in the recreation yards. These were access by stairs directed downward from the second floor to below ground level. Identical approaches to the yard, from different directions confused Channah for weeks. One was below ground north. The other was east. The inmates, not unlike *eggs* were permanently sorted into Norths or Easts, never the twain to meet.

Adjacent to these was intake and processing, for new arrivals of both sexes. It was quite a maze of an entry, with large holding rooms of glass and steel, rough waffle steel benches and steel *crappers*, rooms for intake, fingerprinting, photographing, and administration.

D Block was like a fortress, a miniature city, humming with activity late into the night. The guards came and went in a flooded stream. During her stay, she saw at least 300 different faces, and name badges were swapped not unlike baseball cards.

The block *Medical Observation* was turquoise, in the West Wing. Channah thought it was just the color of Cesium 60. During April, she read a book about world poverty, written by some Christian Socialist from the 1950's. It stated that in the 1960's, on Long Island, naïve scientists had conducted research on hydroponic fruit and vegetable mutations, for the benefit of Mankind's food supply, but using slugs of Cesium 60 in close proximity. These slugs were described as being the same size as the strange oblong metal panel doors adjacent to each glassed cell. They were highly radioactive and turquoise, just like the paint in there. The book mentioned *Bethpage* as the site of the research project. It said that these slugs had been quite dangerous, mass-produced, and discarded in ignorance at the end of the study. Her mind played with these facts.

As she walked aimless laps around Block A each morning, she eyed these slug panels warily. Were there isotopic slugs or radium discards behind them adjacent to her water pipes? Was it possible there were freezers behind these doors? Was this block designed for biological warfare experiments funded by the military? Her fertile imagination, bored to tears, hatched some pretty fantastic stories regarding her new cage. Shades of *Andromeda Strain* by Crichton. The things she was witnessing there, and the brutality of the guards was really shaking her up and changing her attitude.

For example, there was a stairway up to floor 4, at the top labeled "Program Room". It was only accessed by officers. What programs were they running? Over their block, near the fire door, was a room sign labeled *Machine Room*, rarely used. What was in there? After about 2 months, while coming up from the visitor's area with guards on the elevator, she solved the puzzle. There was a floor marked "PH" above the 3 button. It was a fact that the Machine Room was only accessible by elevator. Perhaps it contained armaments. Channah did experience one weird incident there involving some inmate before she left. It seemed as if someone had been kept up there for a time, and upon release, collapsed on the rug. She saw the guards standing around, looking down at someone. Heading down for recreation on the stairs, the inmates knew enough to look away.

"What the heck is going on?" someone said. No one replied. Channah had a conference to go to. As she left the building, she observed a plumber's truck and ambulance there.

"A female inmate has locked herself in the bathroom." an escort outside said to another officer.

On the way back from recreation that day, all inmates were "pressure" searched for concealed pencils or notes in their clothing. It was not a relaxed day for either guards or prisoners.

Chapter 21: More Seances

INCIDENT RETELL (Incident with Other Biased Inmates)

Duration: 1 hour

Location: D3 A Block

Time: 5/15/06 at 2 p.m.

<u>SUMMARY:</u> Three women attacked me verbally, after the trio was instructed to go to Sick Call, with someone in the Triage Room on the third floor. They shout about a "grievance I wrote about them" as soon as they return. Retaliation, possibly for my complaint to a guard, which I had requested be kept confidential, of a curling iron, a potential weapon, kept by Deborah Page and used at the entry to my cell (#1). (No confiscate, no lockdown occurred to her for the rule infraction and she found out it was me, by inference). No guard assists me. The actual offense is a minor one-placement of some dirty laundry on the floor, in with my own wash. Mine was placed on the orange chair before. Babs Cooper's wash is "missing or stolen". Officer Robertson states "you made a mistake". And offers me "protective custody, a removal to solitary in F block". This is where the more violent prisoners are isolated together. He admits I will be in lockdown 22

hours a day there, to "protect me from those prisoners". After the confrontation, which nobody wins, the entire block is placed in lockdown for several hours.

Involved Parties: Purge, Jen, Cooper, Wondra, and Myself.

Action: I put my wash in and add three items in from the floor. Cooper looks for her wash and harangues me. Jen comes over and states "Don't do that." She gets loud. Wondra comes over and spews hateful remarks. Deborah joins and yells, "you're paranoid; a lunatic; sick! I am writing a letter to your judge. I'm telling the D.A. You're mentally ill. You wrote a goddamn grievance against me!" I wait for Officer Robertson to react. He calls me over. He tells me "You made a mistake (with wash)." I apologize profusely. I experience 15 minutes more of posturing and a tirade from Babs. Jen's remarks, as she climbs up to room 13, is more offensive and filled with hurled expletives. I advise her to "yell into her toilet bowl, and flush." She returns downstairs. Robertson comes over, near cell #1, between the four and me. He is passive. They work themselves up for 5 minutes more. Babs sorts her wash out. Robertson speaks to the Corporal. He then says to me "We'll put you alone, in protective custody." I remark about how they are like a gang, how I fear they'll irrationally chase and hurt my kids and me after I get out. He says, "Nonsense."

Robertson is a strange duck. He resembles Joe Camel, he's about 6'6", and that week there is photograph in Newsday that closely resembles him. It's an intelligence officer named Mendez, killed in Iraq, a man with wife and several kids from Long Island. Almost a body double—how odd. I tell him t hat no, I won't go into "protective custody". I'll just stay in my cell most of the time, and ask him to shut me in. This attack on me happens right after a "speak to" for the four women by an officer in the bubble control room, Goul, I think.

****

INCIDENT RETELL (Incident with Other Biased Inmates)

Duration: ¾ hours

Location: D3 A Block

Time: 5/16/06, from 6:45-7:15 a.m.

Summary: Officer Cannagh (a female, sans badge), is here

watching us from the desk during breakfast. My hearing date has been postponed. I advise her about the incident on the prior day. I state that Jen and Purge are meddling in my case. Jen is called to the Bubble, and tries to say something about a conference. I state, "You contrived something to cause trouble. Get the f–k out of my cell!" She sarcastically notes that I actually cursed. I retort about her epithets yesterday, such as "paranoid" and "lunatic".

Cannagh is witnessing all this with disinterest. Jen comes over to my cell now, and begains to harangue me, pointed finger in my face. "You're psychotic!" I retort, "You are! Find another target!" I find my gate closed. Cannagh writes some entry in the guard journal at the desk. They return to their cells. During the day, they constantly mutter epithets as they exercise or speak to Wondra or other inmates. I hear it referring to me distinctly. After a particularly viscious verbal attack near the phones that night, I ask to speak to Corporal Zizzer about it. He calls Denny Purge out afterward, and after that, they pretty much desist.

My comment is that these drug addicts, <u>undermedicated</u> and consistently exhibiting violent, aggressive and attacking behaviors, are directing it at one target—a scapegoat, me.

This attack occurred after all were spoken to, once again, on a "medical visit" downstairs, just prior. Whose yanking their chains? Carol Muck? Who is the master puppeteer?

Denny Purge is in cell #4, Jen Blank is in cell #13, and Wondra Roberts is in cell #12, and they have all been in the block for months longer than I have. They are all career criminals.

If anything happens to me or my kids when I get out, I will use this statement to go after them legally, and prosecute them to the full extent of criminal law. That's my right.

Channah Gambit

x__________________

Notary Public

****

Expose: The Reckoning by Channah Gambit

"Seances at night" were excursions by prisoners in cahoots with guards after curfew, to indulge in hanky panky or other nefarious activities. One young attractive brunette in pony tail in cell number 10, dressed in borrowed surgical scrubs, left with a female African American guard one night, at 2 a.m., heading past the empty bubble, down toward the Triage Room. Perhaps there were liaisons in medical, with male inmates. Maybe they were pigging out on stolen food in the basement.

"M. Dot. How are you?" she asked the thin sleepy blond one morning before breakfast.

"I'm alive. But I don't feel like it. When am I getting out?" M.Dot said. She wrapped a curl of the blond hair around and around in her fingers.

"I saw cell number 10 leave last night. What do you think it is about?" Channah said. She told her the whole story.

"It happens here from time to time. Yeah. There's a guard I know, Todson who is a boyfriend of mine. I'm seeing him sometime soon. He promised to come see me."

"What's it for?"

"Sex, stupid. She probably met an intern at the Infirmary wing." M.Dot said.

"I guess life must go on." Channah said. M.Dot snorted, then rubbed a bony hand over a cobalt blue eyes. She stared at her plate of food, uneaten. Then she stood up and took the tray to the garbage to dump. Slowly and carefully, she treaded up the stairs to cell 24 and went in.

At night, the bubble television monitors were filled with movies. Inmates were not permitted to watch the Bubble through glass windows for any length of time. However, on one occasion, Channah was asked to go down to Sick Call rather late at night. Amazed, she observed two burly guards watching a surgery show, broadcast, she supposed, over cable.

Other night antics included "babysitting" by guards of new or difficult lockdown prisoners. When someone first came on M.O., they were put in lockdown for about a week until they acclimated. This had not been done in her case. Babs Kilo, in cell number 7, endured it for weeks with one female guard after another posted next to her slotted door in a soft black leather office chair, with clipboard. Inmates were forbidden to socialize with these prisoners, on penalty of being in lockdown themselves.

Special Brown was sick and tired of being in solitary and made no bones about it one day in early April. "Let me out of here." she screamed through the slot in her door.

"Now you stop that, Special. You know it's for your own good!" Officer Quickson, a young male Black in his twenties said. He was seated in front of her cell in a black leather easy chair reading a newspaper. He was relieved by Officer Deedle.

"You stop all that shit, Special Brown." Deedle said.

"You let me out or I'll go crazy." Special retorted. She moved restlessly back and forth in the cell, from side to side. Wrapped in a green shift of plastic, she clutched the sides to her.

"You get back down on the bed. Don't you give me sass. You deserve what you get for messing and arguing with other prisoners. I'm going to lock you in and throw away the key."

"I'm cooperating." Special said. She could be heard sniffling by other inmates.

Expose: The Reckoning by Channah Gambit

They were used to this give and take.

"You earned your cell when you refused to testify about that robbery you saw." Deedle said. She was surley.

"I don't want my brother and mother to get whacked, Officer. Someone will snitch on me." Special said.

"Now you know you should do the right thing. You just reconsider, and maybe we'll let you back out." Deedle said sternly. Then she picked up her clipboard and jotted something down. Special started to sob at her desk.

Meanwhile, Gibbons, another officer, was sweet talking Babs Kilo nearby in cell 10.

"You be so much trouble. Why you go and throw your milk under the door." Gibbons said. Also seated in a black leather office chair, she was a large round matron, a copper skinned Polynesian with a mean temper.

"You're just outrageous. You won't get dressed. You threw toilet paper wads all over the wall. How you going to get well doing that?" Gibbons said.

"I'm getting out! I want to be taken to the hospital." Babs said.

The inmates were all fed up with these standoffs which had been going on for quite some time. They ran on into that night, with harangues and cajoling administered over and over.

It went on into lights out time. Inmates tried to sleep, but were unable to, due to the noise in the block.

"If you don't stop banging that wall, Babs, I'm going to take you down to medical to get you sedated." Gibbons yelled.

BANG. BANG. BANG. Babs wasn't talking to anyone anymore. She was feeling better hitting the steel door with a cup.

"Shut up. Let us sleep." Someone in the upper tier yelled down.

"Special, shut the f--k up." Suzette yelled down. Special was crying loudly.

Deedle was fed up after sitting there for hours. She rose up.

"Okay now. Get dressed. I'm taking you down to get sedated." she said.

"What did I do? What am I doing?" Special's voice rose an octave, plaintive and loud.

"You know you're supposed to go to sleep." Deedle said. Special started to scream and yell. Deedle walked over to the desk and spoke into the intercom. Shortly after, Robertson entered. Special's cell was opened from the front entry switchplate. As they approached next door, Channah could hear the terrified woman shuffling around, moving.

"Why, I didn't do anything. I been good." Special said.

"Get out." Robertson said, brandishing a night stick.

"And you up there! Go to sleep. It's light's out." Deedle yelled to the upper tier. There was heavy silence except for Hawaii the new one who liked to sing to herself all the time. The sing-song echoed through the large room.

The two guards escorted Special, walking all slumped over heavily toward the front glass door.

The others were thankful for the silence after, because now they could fall into a fitful doze. Special didn't return until the wee hours of the morning. Hearing the neighbor cell clank open at about 3 a.m., Channah rolled over on her other side. *Damn, it's cold. This goddamn blanket.* she thought, returning to sleep.

The cruelest, most unusual practice Channah witnessed there was that of disrobing troublesome lockdowns, and dressing them in weird, bright green *teenage mutant ninja* turtle shells. These were made of plastic, three inch thick waffled foam sheets, wrapped around with Velcro and held up by suspenders. Inmates looked like hobos in barrels. Wearing the suits made prisoners feel extremely vulnerable and frightened. They were actually half-naked, without permitted underwear. Channah knew, from her special education Masters studies, that they were good for *proprioceptive disorders*. That is, for kids with sensory overload, or nervous system confusion in the brain. Wearing such heavy tactile stuff was pleasant, and made a kid feel safer and more secure. He would feel as if he was being hugged or touched all over, and calm down. That was the textbook theory. It seemed like centuries ago since she had been in that professional atmosphere.

In M.O. block, however, it was another kind of hazing, and degrading. One night, Special's plaintive demands for her prisoner uniform back drew catcalls and yells from annoyed inmates for over an hour. She could not stop, after spending at least 3 weeks dressed in nothing more than a rubber blanket bag with suspenders, forced to remain lying down on the bed for warmth.

There was a big commotion on a Wednesday with Babs again. It started without a babysitter guard. Her arms began to appear sticking through the slot in the steel cell door, clawing and forcing out as far as they should go. Inmates watched with moderate interest. Some Blacks were preening at the east trestle table, corn rowing each other's hair with grease. Babs was crying, cursing and yelling. Officer Goul seated at the desk looked up from his newspaper for a moment, then returned to it.

Channah walked near the cell. Babs had begun raking her arms with her nails, drawing blood. Today her hair was in pigtails and she was wearing only a brasserie underpants and a flat white sheet tied around her body. Channah walked over to the other area of the day room, feeling rotten.

Goul looked up and phoned someone. He gave an audible sigh. His handlebar moustache bristled greyly, he adjusted his holster belt and saundered over t cell 10. He looked in.

"You stop that, sweetheart, all right?" he said to Babs.

"No. Let me call my mother." She came over to the slot, sticking her arms through repeatedly, almost to the point of spraining them.

Goul shrugged. Deedle came in, and took up a leather chair, wheeling it over to the now screaming inmate. She sat down and began to croon to the prisoner, soothing her with promises. Goul sighed again. He looked around impassively, his gray eyes under their brows glowering somewhat a the card player table. He returned to the desk.

Later that day, Babs got her wish to call mommy. They first took her down to the Infirmary to bandage her arms. While she was away, all the women were urged into their cells for temporary lockdown.

"What'd we do wrong?" they yelled. There was complaining and bitching from a lot of slots there.

Two guards came in and emptied out Babs' cell, throwing everything into a bag. A janitor came in and mopped it out after a few minutes. He soused the water into the sink inside the utility closet and left the mop there. They all left. The women's doors were opened. They poured out for lunch.

A subdued Babs showed up escorted in just before time for recess. She was subdued. The guards escorted her to the pay phones immediately where she sat down in a chair and dialed.

"Mom, I'm sick and tired of being here in solitary." there was a pause. "It's 22 hours a day, Mom. Transfer me into a hospital, please." She listened for sometime on the phone. As she did, she began to weep and fret, pulling on a pigtail.

"You've got to let me out. Sign me out. You have to come visit. Don't hang up! Don't hang up!" she yelled. Then she hung up the receiver with a bang.

Wailing and weeping, she sat in the chair for sometime. Gibbons came in for a shift, and walked over to Babs. Her attitude was sympathetic. She took her back to her cell, closing the door. Babs started to yell.

Gibbons pulled up a chair there sat down and began to read a paper. Babs would most likely cry for hours.

The previous week, Channah had spoken with her as they played *Spades* under the cell door. "I'm sick and tired of being here. I know I did wrong. Ted, my boyfriend was a cocaine dealer. I helped him." she said.

"Drugs are dumb. I don't judge." Channah answered. She was winning.

"I've been in here for 14 months." Babs said, biting her lower lip. She was still pretty even dressed in inmate fatigues.

"That's impossible." Channah told her.

"No it's not. They're getting even with me because I slept with one of them." Babs said.

Channah said. "This is a short term place. They don't hold people here that long." but she was uncertain.

The next day, Babs spent hours crying and complaining while banging on her steel door. Nervous with her hysterics and tears, Channah grew increasingly concerned. She had training in school to avoid suicide, and saw clear signs there. Therefore, she wrote a letter to Sheriff Edward Rooney through internal mail. She advised him that Babs was suicidal, and that a scandal would result if she succeeded in harming herself while at his jail. Channah urged him to send her to the N.C.M.C. for treatment and sedation.

The last week of May, the "Goon Squad" better known as N.A.S. sent for Channah to come down to a booth at the Visitor's Center. She hurried there, expecting to see Jamo with Duvey in tow, visiting for a second time. Since her first visit weeks before there was no sign that she had used Channah's letter granting her power of attorney to see the accountant and sign the prepared tax forms. She obviously had not kept a promise to raise bail.

Channah met the "goons" inside Room 6 of Visitor's Block, to her chagrin. They were dressed in suits with flamboyant ties, and looked like detectives. Refusing to give any names, they told her they were from N.A.S., and that they had to speak to her about my *very presumptuous letter*.

For over an hour and a half, they grilled her. The Afro insulted her regarding her intelligence.

"Who are you to tell us officers how to do our jobs? How dare you write a letter to a Sheriff, you, a felon!" The purple paisley tie jeered at her. The other, a white dude, stared at her silently, with cold eyes.

One Friday after that, Deedle called Channah over to the guard table. He gestured to the bubble, indicated Zizzer wanted to chat with her, and opened the huge steel door for her. Zizzer, his grizzled gray hair shiny with Vitalis, opened the door and regarded her cooly. "I know you have been trying to help Babs Kilo out. They say she had an affair with a guard. That's nonsense, Gambit. I do hope you are not listening to gossip. She'll say anything to get attention." he said.

"Yes, sir." Channah said.

"You better worry about yourself." he said. "No more being a do gooder. If you think you're so smart, let me ask you a question: If you have a college degree, what are you doing here?" he laughed at her.

"My family screwed me over. Can you please find out about my daughter? Maybe she had a car accident." Channah said.

"All right. I'll check the police website." he told her.

Gibbons, also standing watch at the control consoles, gave her a big look. "Gambit, stay out of trouble." he said. When they both failed to intimate her, they rose in accord and allowed her to leave.

Babs finally was moved several days later. She emptied out her cell, giving Channah several cardboard icon cards and a container of colored pencils as a gift.

"She's been shipped upstate to serve her sentence." Ace told Channah the next afternoon in recess. They were standing in bright sunshine, watching the walkers and hard ball teams work out.

"Probably New Bedford, that women's prison upstate." Ace said and strolled away.

Well, she finally made it out of solitary confinement. Channah thought, moving into a shaded place. It was hot for April. *But I think she'll soon be dead by her own hand.*

Because she meddled in the treatment of another prisoner, the guards began to eye her warily. Even though Channah was a model prisoner, gentle and cooperative, she was being targeted by the German *Alphas.* For about 4 weeks, she only came out of her cell if she had to to avoid confrontations. If she was written up, they could slap 90 days more onto her sentence. Unsentenced as she was, she had already served over 75 days.

Channah was cool to other prisoners now. Most of them were not worth knowing. *I don't fit in. They hate me because I have some college and use big words.* she told herself. She sat and read the same two magazines over and over. Either that or she sketched what was around her. There were some she could pity and tolerate knowing.

Loza was a little monkey-like girl, more like a boy than anything, who had moved into cell #10. She had a short crew cut, tough words, and came out about her being a lesbian. Channah talked with her, and discovered that she had crummy grammar, lack of ability to express her needs, and a total disregard for femininity.

Expose: The Reckoning by Channah Gambit

The passion of the block to pass time was playing cards. There was a game unique to the jail called *Spades*, which was something like *Crazy Eights*. It required a shrewd alert mind to win, and it was an honor to be invited to be someone's partner. Everyone was an expert, but it took time and practice.

Loza was seated one Friday night at the table, playing with Ann against Joan and Sally. As the block watched, she stood up suddenly, throwing the deck in Sally's face.

"What happened?" Sally said, rising to her feet, putting her hands on her hips and glowering at her.

Loza was a wiry petite Filopino with curly dark hair and black eyes. She looked like a boy. The plastic rosary around her neck had been given to her by Channah. Now it whipped around her flat chest, as she started to pace. "You cheated!" she said, gesturing furiously.

"Now you calm down." Robertson demanded from his desk. He took his booted feet down and sat back Loza went into a rage for about an hour while Joan and Ann watched in disbelief, nervously chatting with others about it in the day room. Finally, Robertson had enough. Rising and pocketing his key ring. He walked over to Loza, roughly grabbing her by the shoulder.

"In you go." he said. He pushed her into cell 11 and closed the door with his override key.

Loza peered out angrily, hotly watching Sally.

All was forgiven the next day and Loza was allowed out with the others. Still angry, she refused to talk to others.In the outside recreation yard, she played basketball alone, or tandem handball with deadly intensity. She would no longer play *Spades*.

One night, Loza disappeared from Block D3, after being removed by a couple of guards.

"Leave me alone. Let go of my arm." she said. Then there was the sound of kicking and slaps against the wall. Channah's and everybody's ears pricked up. Some came to their doors to peer out. The voices receded, rose and fell far away, just on the edge of hearing.

"You goddamn wacko. You dykester! When you going to start wearing a skirt?" a baritone said.

"None of you business." Loza said.

"Put her in here. Close the door." A higher voice said. They heard the door slam and it was silence once more.

About fifteen minutes later, the door opened, and they heard the voices again.

"You goddamn son of a bitch. I'll get you for this!" Loza yelled, the sound of sobbing in her voice.

"Shut up, you filthy slut." the baritone said. A steel door slammed once more.

Perhaps they had tempted her to run downstairs by leaving a door open. Channah, lying on her cot, dreamed lightly about the second week in M.O. block, when she had had the opportunity to escape. It was a moment when most inmates were snoozing or quietly reading in their cells before dinner. There was no guard at the sentry desk. The door to the hub was slid open. Peering out through the glass, she had noticed that the far door, leading to the stairs was invitingly open as well. She had actually thought for a moment of tip-toeing down.

"Ah, Ah, Ah!" Jen said, eyeing her with a twinkle in her eye. "I wouldn't do that if I was you!"

"What?"

"You will get three years for trying to escape added on." Jen said primly, waggling a finger in Channah's face.

"That's so? I'm not going to." Channah said.

"It's a trap, I think. They do it on purpose." Jen said. She was wearing her gift white sweatshirt brought from home to keep warm. March air blew through the block, even though no windows were seen to be open.

"Why do they do it?" Channah asked. She was annoyed that someone had read her mind.

"They're bored!" They both broke out in laughter. Jen patted her on the back, then started to walk around the day room to get some exercise.

The morning after *the sexual brutality in the closet* as Channah called it, Loza had her situation resolved in a permanent way. After that, the next morning, she was quiet and glum, slouching around, more and more on the edges by choice, her face pinched and sad. Then, a few days after Babs left, Loza disappeared from cell #11, without saying goodbye to everyone. When asked, the guard stated that she had been released.

It was prison practice to shuffle prisoners in and out, processing them, while the entire block was outside for recreation, or left in by choice, locked inside cells individually. There was never a transition for arrivals and departures. Relationships were never cemented, or in tidy bundles for future use. Promises to send gifts or candy in to a friend were never kept. Phone calls to be made for you once out were not. Neither were offers to pull strings and find you a job out there through a relative, once out. Carmen Road was the Phantom Zone, from start to finish. You'd pinch yourself day to day, to feel relationships there were real. All the sensory deprivation, the cold, unpleasantness, sank into you viscerally. You couldn't avoid feeling as if you were living forgotten on a real rung of Dante's Inferno. Tormented, your crushed identity was some stuffed green shirt, or a turtle suit, hung on a hanger by Officer Aero in Wardrobe, inside some velvet burgundy bag for the duration and to be restored upon release.

You couldn't establish a relationship which would last with others, or gain a foothold with career criminals. You wouldn't want to. They would all suddenly go, or transfer. So would you.

Channah hunkered down in survival mood and vowed she'd survive no matter what.

Expose: The Reckoning by Channah Gambit

Chapter 22: Legal Tangles, Part Two

There was such a thing as a bail reduction, Pulgrid reassured Channah. The petition for Change of Counsel (Form 67), had been suggested to her after three weeks of phone calls, all unanswered, to the Legal Aid Society. That man had disappeared from her life after the first month, leaving her marooned high and dry in the Court.

Silverwitch knew she was displeased and so did his superior Ken Belsen, the Social Worker from the L.A.S. Karen, had spoken with her superior, Ms. Dean, saying something about Channah's mental state. Channah had spent a cheerful hour with Karen, right after Silverwitch's visit, defending herself against the charges through circumstantial evidence and incontrovertible reasons. She had been almost hopeful after that. Dean went to bat for Silverwitch, and decided to request the Court to do a 7.30 Competency Exam, because she seemed rather lost and befuddled.

Pulgrid gave her all the procedures and loopholes in print from a big blue book. She studied them for hours. If she failed the 7.30, she could be placed into involuntary hospitalization for 90 days, for "observation", forced to take medications, and become a Ward of the State of New York. She could very likely cycle through court hearing dates for months, never being released. The future looked grim.

About that same time, Flavia transferred into Block A. She was in her sixties, a career criminal in her own words, and fresh in from the Nassau County Medical Center, where she had spent weeks in a back building, a *psycho ward.* She quickly filled Channah in regarding both politics, the chain of administrative command, and conditions in the locked ward she had inhabited. Flavia had once worked at that same Medical Center for a doctor. She was inclined to believe what she said, comparing it to comments made by the Social Workers. Channah grew concerned.

There was a place there, run by a doctor Dorman, where she could be locked up and watched constantly by 7 orderlies and matrons. The hospital itself, operating in the red for years, wasn't Federal or public as people in the County assumed. To avoid malpractice suits, according to Flavia, it operated under a Federal umbrella. Dan Boggs at the top, was a surgeon who liked to perform elective operations in his spare time, sometimes accepting charity cases. Channah grew uneasy. She hadn't enjoyed Shoken, the *forensic physician's* visit very much for the first 7.30 interview. At all costs, she could not bear the thought she might go there.

Matthew Silverwitch came to see her in early June, about 43 days after his last visit. He finally told her, clearly, her charges and their maximum penalties. He read her the affidavit from a woman whom she did not know, a Hilda Sandstorm. He admitted that the phone number of the *false report* charge was not mine on record and that the State had a flimsy case full of holes.

"But, you have to go through the 7.30. Judge Messe can't retract his Court Order." He said.

"I don't need to. I'm fine." she said. They were seated in glass booth number 3.

"Either you do it with a doctor from the court-appointee list, Channah or you will be forced to do it in front of a judge. If you refuse, you'll get in a system merry go round." Silverwitch said, peering at her from behind his horn rimmed glasses.

Expose: The Reckoning by Channah Gambit

"I don't understand what you mean." she said. She was sweating profusely in her thin green v neck shirt.

"You'll be asked to come back a few times, to answer in public any questions to test competence. They will delay the process of the Court for weeks or maybe months. I don't think you would like that to happen. If you flat out refuse to answer questions before the Judge at well, then, you'd be indefinitely hospitalized until you appealed, or complied, or were deemed competent to stand trial and answer charges."

"It's absurd," Channah said. She held her arms with her hands, and shook slightly.

"You're nuts, I think, not me." Silverwitch implied, by every remark he made, that she was psychotic.

"Can you get me a bail reduction this week? Let's get me *ROR-able* and released in my own recognizance at least." she said to him, while he looked noncommittal.

"You know, you're biased against me. Where's your integrity? You should resign from the appointment by the Judge." she said. He looked away, uneasy. She handed the Change of Counsel form to him. As he left the visitor's booth, he tried to make her take it back and it fell to the floor.

"No, that's your's now! You are going to lose your job." she said. After that, she had to submit to a strip search in the *electric chair room*.

After another conference day at the District Court held in the pen for hours, she was told by her attorney that no motions could be made until she had the 7.30.

She had decided, temporarily, not to *change horses midstream* and told him to represent her. After all, he had actually come, after 7 weeks, and explained her charges to her. Her expectations had been lowered by the jail time she had done.

The doctors came a week or so later, and she had a new lawyer by then, named Casey. The change of counsel form, although not notarized and mailed to all parties, had been followed by Silverwitch's supervisor appearing at a hearing, suggesting that the L.A.S. no longer wished to defend her because she was "difficult". An 18-B attorney had been appointed, a much more qualified counsel, and she had reason to believe she'd get some action at last instead of a round robin. Silverwitch had claimed he had delayed helping her win release, *due to a heavy caseload.*

The day for the 7.30 came. In the presence of doctors, with the new attorney there, she told her life story in minute detail, while they took notes. They asked her to explain the charges and penalties. She was now able to. They questioned why she had been offensive to the Court in her reply to Doctor Shoken by using expletives when referring to the Judge. She denied this.

Shortly after that, Casey told her she passed the 7.30. In mid-June, after over 90 days of imprisonment, she had some defender to talk to. Channah begged her new attorney to contact her daughter.

"I complied with medication. Now Carol Muck claims she lost my daughter's cell phone number." she said.

"I'm incredulous." Casey the Social Worker said.

"You've got to help me." Channah said. They were seated at one of the long trestle day room tables.

Expose: The Reckoning by Channah Gambit

"I'll agree to make a few outside phone calls for you." Casey said. She was a tired matronly blond woman who looked a bit tired and bedraggled all the time. Channah thought her heart was in the right place but she was ineffectual.

"Thank you." she said sweetly.

"I'll even mail a few bail request letters for you and pay the postage." Casey said, standing up and clutching her clip board

"That's great." Channah said. She felt like she was floating on Cloud 9. She returned to her Cell A-1. Maybe, just maybe, she'd be *ROR*, and someone outside would pay a reduced bail.

As days passed, however, little change occurred. No one phoned, came to visit her, or wrote letters. Her attorney could not recover correspondence she had sent out, which had been given earlier to Silverwitch. It was missing. Regarding a letter to the editor asking openly for donations from charitable people to create a *bail fund*, as far as she knew, it was never published. There was no way to check that. Letters she had mailed to colleagues in the teaching profession, acquaintances, and distant relatives went unanswered. She was at the full mercy of the District Court.

Would her bail of $2,000 be reduced or removed? If so, she'd end up in some battered women's shelter, without even bus fare. Channah was able to send some rather complicated legal letters to the Court secretary at Family Court, Rozzie Scribes. She felt strongly that the contempt charge, for not appearing at a hearing for an order of protection brought against her by Daddy Gambit, was unfounded for the April 14th date, as she had conflicting hearings scheduled. Sure enough, one Monday, while having Pulgrid check the County Sheriff's database of inmates, she discovered that that charge had vanished, and her bail was now back down to $1,500.

What stood between a rock and a hard place for her was the new attorney: square, strong, Irish Catholic, and relatively sympathetic.

One day at breakfast, Wondra sat down beside her. Channah was surprised as she had no friendship there. "I've been listening to your story." Wondra said, munching on some toast.

"What?"

"Well a lot of inmates here like Special and Jen don't think you belong in. It's terrible what your family is doing. I really liked that portrait of my boyfriend you did for me last week. I mailed it to him." Wondra reached into her shirt, pulled out a few envelopes and handed them to her.

"That's payment. Thank you." Channah said.

"I know some rules and such, and you know, with your bail reduction to the minimum amount of $500, an inmate would be considered *released on their own recognizance*. The rule is that you must be released after 90 days by the Sheriff, due to a rule on the books regarding misdemeanors. So you should get out next week." Wondra said.

"That's silly. Can't be." Channah said. Wondra immediately rose to her feet.

"No, I'm telling you for your own good. They shouldn't be holding you next week." she said.

Silly hope filled Channah's heart. Wondra patted Channah on the back and left her.

"You're out of here!" Channah told herself. The following Tuesday was library visit day. She'd be able to ask Pulgrid his opinion.

Next, she spent several hours trying to get some verification of that rule from the American Civil Liberties Union. They were at an 800 number and a toll free call on the pay phone. What luck!

"Hello. This is Margret. How may I help you." the representative said.

"I've got a low bail, only $500. I've got a few misdemeanors. My family has refused to pay the bail. According to the letter of the law, since I've never done anything wrong before, I must be released on my own recognizance in 90 days." Channah said.

There was a long pause on the line. "Actually I'm sorry to tell you that with your case that is an impossibility." Margret said.

Channah went into a depression that same day. Still hopeful, she pestered the guards she saw daily, even Flan. Days 91, 92, and 93 came and went. She called Silverwitch about it. For a rare moment, he was in. He listened to her for a time.

"No, sorry, you're wrong." He said. He hung up without saying good bye.

Walking slowly around and around the day room, Channah's feelings grew ugly. *Wondra played me. Out of sheer mischief and malice she made that all up. I am no match for con artists.* she told herself

.

Expose: The Reckoning by Channah Gambit

Chapter 23: The Gates of Tarturus

During June, there was a heavy turnover in occupants of Block A. Sometimes Channah tried to fit in. That was easy if she drew or sketched inmates. She did several portraits of children. Word spread in the recreation yard, and inmates from other blocks handed her photographs to copy and paid her in paper and envelopes.

EXPAND

Channah's alarm grew as her children did not return to either bail her out or visit. With too much idle time on her hands, she speculated and had anxious dreams of being harmed by neighbors or others. Her dreams were filled with memories of the theft of small objects. It had really traumatized her.

She'd be out shopping at Key Food, and return to find that the tropical fish, all colors sizes and types in a happy community, were floating on the top of the water. Again, she'd run to fetch the PH kit. Shaking, she'd test the water and the acidity would be off the scale. An aloe plant plump and juicy in the den corner that morning would be all gray and oozing, for some mysterious assailant had dosed it in vinegar or chlorox. She'd see mirrors and windows everywhere covered in frost and smelling of mold and decay. Looking down at the pink warm tiles of the Florida room floor, she'd relive the moment when she found a small dead baby sparrow, just hatched from an egg lying their like a talisman of evil. In another dream, she'd walk to the closet where she kept her coats and approach the leather jacket she picked up at a thrift shop, warm and fashionable. Picking up a sleeve, she'd register once more the lozenge of leather neatly cut off the elbow. Her eyes would travel feverishly to the buttons which were also leather to discover one missing and not to be replaced. Another moment of delirium and dread would come late in the night. She'd dream of walking to the hall closet opening it to survey her linens and once again discover that several strange towels with purple yellow and pink stripes would be folded there along with the others. So many times in Cell 1 she would wake up all in a sweat and fever shivering under the thin gray flannel.. Eight people, including neighbors, had keys to the front door. Now she dreamed of the incidents, magnified. She thought to herself, *I'm so intelligent, educated and I didn't have a clue!*

Her health deteriorated. She visited the sick call room at least once a week. Sometimes, they gave her something. Usually, they could do nothing. Once, the "Pepcid AC", received from Nurse Fran Black, gave her a terrible headache and she vomited it up, along with supper. She felt crummy for a day.

Sometimes Channah felt as if she was on a microdose of Mescaline, very sluggish and delusional. She thought, *How ironic! I'm in the D building, normally a place to incarcerate drug addicts and dealers. I'm not, at all. I'm experiencing strange things here.* Many girls there were addicts, going through withdrawal with some medical assistance. In June, she was told that, due to overcrowding in other buildings, the County Sheriff was housing ALL types of woman criminals in the D building. Channah guessed there was therefore no addiction stigma attached in being there.

One time, she had a strong fantasy that people were dying inside, never having been allowed to leave the prison system. Like Lauren, Babs Kilo, and Joan Grillo, a chronic detainee of the State for decades, she was isolated. Behind the left wall of her cell was a fire staircase going down. It was only accessible through a red door in Block A, kept locked at all times, and descended three stories. She dreamt it was a phantom hiding place. Souls of the damned went up and down to the Nether regions, the "root cellar". Sometimes, they stood behind her wall, and spoke to her, or told her their stories as she dozed.

"Hi, I'm Chucky." the maniac doll from cinema would say. He'd tell her that he needed to be found since he had been living on the staircase for weeks. He'd been in the root cellar and was very unhappy.

The other night visitor was a blond little girl, in a pinafore from the 1800's. She claimed she too lived on a ledge on the staircase. She was actually Herman Melville's daughter who had watched her daddy go to sea.

"I'm upset. He abandoned me. I'll scribble a book while he's away. Then she'd begin to write down *Moby Dick* when he was away. He returned in the dream, to reunite with his best girl. Picking her up in his arms, he took the journal and read it by candlelight, adding his own chapters describing whaling and life on the sea.

There would be very amusing reveries to fill the wee hours of the morning. She had fitful, twisted nightmares. In the gray hours near dawn, she would awaken, and listen to the scary sounds of the guards walking down the halls, laughing, shouting, or yelling, somewhere in the distance. Steel doors to rooms would slam loudly. Sometimes movies would run all night in the *bubble* loud and echoing.

Sentries would change shifts and make rounds, aiming high-intensity flashlights at her head.

"You have to sleep with your head to the door, or be locked down for 3 days in your cell." one would say through the slot window. That happened to Channah in March and she did not risk it again. She moved, instead, upstairs, to the top bunk, where a steel frame kept the light from hitting her eyes as she slept.

One night, around April 28th, a guard resembling Duvey in age and appearance climbed down from the third floor and did his rounds, a flashlight on top of his head, as if he was a locomotive.

In the morning, Robertson was on duty at the desk in the day room. "Robertson what did I see last night?" she said.

"I don't know. What did you see." he asked.

She described the strange figure with a mining lamp on its head.

"I dunno, I'm very puzzled." he said. He started writing something down in the roster book about their conversation and Channah backed off.

"Whoops!" she said.

On another night, a little man arrived whom she dubbed *Jack the Ripper*. He carried a plastic doctor's bag, heavy and clanking as he put it down on the desk at about 5 a.m.

Ace might need oxygen, she assumed, so the medical apparatus made sense. Sometimes Ace be removed late at night in a wheelchair, only to return later with a tank of air connected to her nostrils with a plastic tube. Jack was a Deutchlander, knock-kneed, in his late 50's, balding, just a little unassuming man doing strange things. He never did anything with the doctor's bag.

After that, the same week, Robertson wheeled in a huge barbecue and left it in the day room. It looked like a George Foreman grill. It stayed there for a few hours, until he was told to trundle it out of A block. That was tucked away somewhere, and the whole pantomime struck Channah as very odd.

Finally, one day in May, she was called to from the desk.

"Hey, Gambit, you gotta go down to the Infirmary." said big fat Officer Smythe. An emaciated young mustached guard, led her down to Doctor Zettie, the Podiatrist. It was treatment for bunions and inflammations on her big toes. They had developed from walking miles habitually that past winter in search of a job in tight boots, in the freezing cold, while enduring hardship conditions.

He made her stand on some yellow footprints painted on the floor, so she could not read the paperwork on his desk.

"Oh—I'm a yellow person—I must be Asiatic!" she thought to herself, as he pared away the skin with a scalpel. Channah recalled standing on bright blue painted footprints at the outhouse on 1499 Franklin to have her *mug shots* taken twice.

"Wow—not a *Blue Man Group* member." she thought.

"I'm not ever going to win those white footprints now." Maybe she was going to graduate up to red footprints, when she returned to the real world as a liberated American citizen. Channah couldn't ask Doctor Zettie when and if that would be. He just gave her some salve for a few weeks, and she wound up bartering it for shampoo or postage.

Officer Smythe eyed her like some tasty morsel he'd like to eat. Or date. Was the only way to break out of this unjust imprisonment to cohabitate with guards or marry in?

One guard's wife, Sara Cannon, had attended a recent Saturday Catholic mass and sat with her. During the invocations for shared concerns, she offered up a prayer for someone close to her. They shook hands, as she noticed a strong resemblance to another young woman she knew, *on the outside*. Rumor had it that she was an officer's wife.

The next week, Sister Evian offered up the Mass for an officer's wife who had died suddenly." Two inmates whom she had observed silently the weekend prior chatting with Sara Cannon sobbed, holding each other for comfort. Was Sara Cannon the one mentioned? She never reappeared. Rumors on the grapevine pointed to someone else and said that she had not been an active officer anyway for some time. She was a very beautiful woman. It appeared to be some tragedy and Sister Evian was unusually sober for a week or two.

Now, as Channah stood bemused in the medical room on the second floor, she was called in to see a brunette lady with brown long hair. They spoke of the asthma and headaches she had developed, and she offered Channah some Tylenol. The room they were in had only one entrance: the African-American female officer who had brought three patients down stood by the wall cart, talking on the telephone, a revolver strapped to her hip. The doctor's paramedic, *Linda*, sat at a desk with a PC on it, looking at Channah's chart. She left the room briefly, to stand in the adjoining wait area, in preparation to returning upstairs. But, she had to ask a new question. Nurse had been talking about some doctor's son *Duvey*, and how he had had to have his head examined. Was she trying to make Channah paranoid by using her son's name? Was she referring to the mysterious *Pillsbury Doughboy*? Channah reentered to ask her for a change of medication, and the Nurse had vanished! Poof! Linda was not there. She must have walked through a wall. About 8 minutes later, the Nurse walked in from the hallway, passing through the waiting room, by Channah, and taking her seat once more at the desk. How could this be? Identical clothing and appearance, it was apparently Linda. But the medical exam room had only one door in and out and no one had seen her leave. A phantom! A Casper-the-friendly ghost! Channah felt her grip on sanity shake a little. They were at the Gates of Tarturus, she assumed. There were, behind these walls, other corridors and rooms unreachable to normal mortals. These were places where many of the guards, nurses, and inmates could pass. There were spirits in the prison block, disguised as people. Absurd but there was this event to deal with and explain.

Channah tested her perception of reality with the dull old Mulatto lady, Gertie, who had accompanied her downstairs. Holding her cane, Gertie was too sleepy and inattentive to have noticed anything. The guard, on the other hand, watched her intently, eyes glistening. The other inmate exchanged a long glance with the nurse. Shortly afterward, Gertie and Channah were led upstairs. Such a thing did not reoccur during her 112 days in the Carmen Road facility.

Channah was quite dismayed and lay immediately down on her cot. Several weeks before that, in May, Louboy, a Black prisoner in cell #10 had pulled another mystical event. They had been locked in for the night, but, while Channah dozed, someone had come up to her cell and started to flick the black button on the wall causing the overhead fluorescents to strobe and annoy Channah. She had raised up on one elbow, to glimpse Louboy outside her cell, staring in through the glass with hungry black eyes. A moment later, Channah stood up and ran to the door to look out. A guard was doing her rounds, sticking a key on her chain into the locks in the walls. Loubie was nowhere but could not possibly have been outside her cell. *Were my eyes playing tricks on me? Has my head injury really damaged my sense of time?* Someone had strobed those lights. Louboy was a phantom, on the astral plane. She avoided Louboy after that.

A few weeks after that, she decided that what she had seen must be in error. There had to be a logical explanation for everything. At any rate, Channah would soon go insane, either here or in the hospital ward. Perhaps it would be best if volunteered to dose herself into somnambulence with some real sedatives.

Go ahead! Ruin that fine brain! her conscience answered her.

NO. I want to see my daughter now! her heart chided it back. She knew she would defend herself more poorly if she was a dulled zombie like Dinah, M. Dot, and other women there. Channah just couldn't deal with the place the way it was! With those *Gates of Tarturus*, it was a portal into the Netherworld. It was worse than that! It was much more like *Stargate SG9* the cable television show. There was a crack between parallel worlds here. Through the Sheriff's facility, strange things came and went: ghosts, phantoms, elementals, vampires, human snakes, and disembodied spirits roamed freely. They formed and mingled with disenfranchised people, criminals, and corrupt guards, taking on their characteristics and roles. Changing badges or names, faking out observers who might suddenly disappear into a sub-floor basement room forever, entities played around.

It was a chilling experience to witness a woman leave a room without any other

Expose: The Reckoning by Channah Gambit

entry than the door she was blocking. Ever since she had been 21, she had studied paranormal and psychic phenomena, and knew many eyewitness accounts of stranger events. Here in Block D, there was some bridge between two different subcultures, worlds, and dimensions. If you took a wrong turn, you might wind up permanently in Goul's parallel universe, and never see a familiar soul again. It was best therefore, as she resolved, to do exactly what was expected of you and stick to familiar routines and places.

The crossing point or gate had been opened by design, to scare Channah. Perhaps criminal acts were being committed at the jail, out of the eyes of the general public. Coercive techniques, foul food, contrived charges, interminable delays in the judicial process, confused identity tags were breaking the inmates down; victimizing them all.

Soon, they'd be eaten! There were *rats* in the kitchen! She reminisced one night about her favorite ballet *The Nutcracker Suite* and recalled one time when Stephen and herself had visited Tully Hall around Christmas to see it. That was many years ago but such a happier place.

Channah did rosary. Memorizing the prayer to St. Michael the Archangel, she recited it morning and night, seeking to protect herself and loved ones from inexplicable happenings. She began to feel less like signing up to visit the Infirmary.

Channah was sure she had seen what she had seen. She was now, somewhere in the deepest recesses of her psyche, deeply terrified. But her face remained deadpan.

Expose: The Reckoning by Channah Gambit

Chapter 24: The Factory & Shower Slams

During Channah's stay at D Block jail, there was a dead-end location within the complex of the N.C.C.C., where the paddy wagons, returning from the District Court, would sometimes unload prisoners, usually male. It was a long building, at the opposite end to their's, and connected directly with the Men's section. This *Factory*, she was told, was a work area where inmates sewed and patched garments, and performed other menial occupations. These did not include rhythmic whistling or basket weaving.

As far as *shower slams* as she heard on the grapevine at recess, it referred to the 30 or so female inmates, many of them young, who walked around with canes. These injuries were the after-effects of "falling accidents", in the shower or elsewhere. Channah's scientific and faltering mind found the percentages non-random, and slightly more than accidental . She had noted that inmates on the upper tier, should they be attacked by a neighbor, would have no other escape to avoid physical injury than to jump down a story. How often that happened, she believed, was seldom.

Once, where Channah was taking a shower upstairs, a male officer, doing his "key" tour, passed her shower briskly. Behind that plastic sheet, she was totally disrobed.

He stopped at one of the closets which were always kept locked, putting his key into the register keyhole in the wall. He started whistling. "Hey, you all right in there?" he said in a whisper. He waited for an answer. She didn't. After about thirty seconds, Mendel the alternate for the weekend walked his patrol downstairs. He had stopped whistling.

It was disquieting to this middle-class prude, and she never took a shower anywhere afterward without bringing a stout broom pole inside with her. That was a technical infraction to rules in itself.

The incessant pressure to find an older female to call *Mama* offended her. *Here we are in the Isle of Lesbos!* she told herself gaily. Some of these tough bull ladies she had no wish to get close to let alone chat with for obvious reasons..

"Hey, honey, let me guard your bootie while you shower tonight!" Suzette told her. Her nine inch nails, chipped and peeling, raked the air as she sat watching Terminator with the others.

"Nope. Just me tonight." Channah said, taking a look into eyes that had seen much too much in forty years. Suzette wore her hair cropped short like an African Ameican, but she was white.

"What are you anyway?" Channah said.

"What you mean? Am I gay. Hell yeah!" Suzette said.

"No, I mean where did your people come from?" Channah asked. Her cheeks reddened, and she played with the towel and soap she carried. Carrie, Suzette's best buddy, sitting at her side, stopped playing solitaire to look at Channah closely.

"Hell, from Russia and Ireland, I guess." Suzette said. She then lost interest, and turned back to the screen.

"I'm afraid you're not her type." Jen said, beckoning to Channah to join her at the Suduko table. She walked over and plopped down, tired.

"Can you avoid them? And you know what I mean by *them.* Well, if they don't behave, they'll end up in the factory. I'll talk to Zizzer." Jen said.

"I don't understand." Channah said.

"Oh, you will, Sweetie. You will before long." Jen said. She stopped herself from adding to that, and began to play Sudoko with full intensity, forgetting about Channah. After five minutes, Channah returned to her walk upstairs to shower.

But, what was that *Factory*? She wished she knew.. Inmates did not like the idea of going there.

When Channah had visited the District Court building for about the seventh time in early June, the paddy wagon visited the Factory. She was certain they'd be unloaded there and her curiosity would be rewarded.

Ace, who was traveling back and forth with her that day, got nervous and rigid at her side, muttering an anxious prayer. Ace then did something strange. She protected Channah's left knee cap with her hand until the truck started moving again, delivering them instead, as they had originally anticipated, to the other place, our parking lot at the D Block building.

"Whew, that was real close." Ace said.

"Weird!" Channah said.

"Honey, you don't know the half of it. People go in there and never come back out. They get turned into canned dog food."

"Yeah, right." Channah said. They were eating double dinners, courtesy of some kind inmates who had saved some extra for their return. At the long table, during the final relaxed portion of free time, both were hungrily chewing on breaded chicken fillet.

"Listen, it's true that you can get hurt around here. They have a closet all full of canes. Permanent damage for no reason other than they don't like your face. Of course, your face is okay now. But, if there's a shower slam that's not going to be easy to forget."

"What in the world is a shower slam?" Channah asked.

"I can see you never been in jail before." Ace said. She was starting her dessert, peeling her orange with a plastic spoon. "It's when you shower on the left side, see. You don't ever use the stall on the right. That's for girls who are old and tired and have to sit down while they get wet. On the left side, even then, be careful."

"Why's that?" Channah had stopped chewing on her chicken.

"Well, they come along, you see, and they just open it up and throw you against the wall and walk away."

"Oh." Channah stood up stretching. She didn't think she had anything to worry about.

"Night." Ace said then walked over to the can to throw away her tray. She absentmindedly ruffled up her 'fro, looking at the Bubble where the guards were sitting around looking bored. Her eyes narrowed with dislike.

"Night." Channah said, scratching her nose and walking obediently to her cell. It was time for count down. Then they'd be locked in with about five minutes to read or brush their teeth.

"You look out for me and I'll look out for you." Ace called out from the other side of the general area.

Expose: The Reckoning by Channah Gambit

"Right." Channah said. She thought it amusing that she now had a friend.

After supper that night, Channah mused in her cell if prisoners returned from the Factory at all, or whether THEY were the prison garments being patched there. They were recycled and rearranged there. Who wanted to learn the truth?

She'd see something in the last month she was in. A woman in the adjacent C block would slip and fall in the shower, causing pandemonium to break out. It happened very quickly. Then the orderly from the medical ward came wheeling a wheel chair and she left all pink-cheeked and purple, saying "Owww. OOOOOOO."

The next day in the courtyard, the gossip offered by the handball court was that she had not kept her promise to another buddy to have her mother bring in some candies and snacks during visitor's hours. She had been paid back plenty.

Expose: The Reckoning by Channah Gambit

Chapter 25: Release

. Channah's new brown hiking boots with the steel toes, estimated value $45, were not written up on inventory by Officer Aero. She would notice it a few weeks later, and would have to complain in writing someday.

Description of contents returned.

A brown paper bag was handed over the counter. There was an empty wallet, contents 13 plastic cards without monetary power; a key chain, a sweater, a pair of sweat tights, a pair of socks, a bright green winter jacket and hood.

Her wrists crossed in front of her chest, she was uncuffed at last. Led into the Discharge Office, she regarded Sheriff's Officer Gruber, who stalled for several moments, then handed her some paper to sign.

Patty, a svelte young pony tailed officer in her twenties, entered the room, carrying a paper pad, and spoke silently to Gruber.

"You wait in the hall, please." He said to Channah roughly.

Patty walked over and put hand cuffs on her once more. "You're being taken over to the hospital first, before release."

"Why's that?" Channah spluttered, turning red in the face.

"We don't think you're competent to leave." Officer Gruber said, turning to pick up some chains. He walked cooly over to her, and put her legs into ankle shackles, to her amazement.

"What's this? I'm not a violent person." she said.

"Oh that? It's just in case you get any ideas." Patty said. They walked beside her as she hobbled down the hall, then into a waiting van. It took several long minutes for the car to drive down to the locked section of Admissions for the Nassau County Medical Center.

"Wow. I simply can't believe this. I'm fine. This is insulting, to say the least." Channah said.

Patty escorted her through doors which swung in and out. She was seated in a chair in the waiting area on a long hallway with some patients sitting alongside. Patty signed her over to Reception, and then left after removing the shackles. The wait was about an hour, until Channah got to see a doctor, an Asian woman named Chang.

"They recommended you stay a day for observation." she said.

"There's nothing wrong with me." Channah retorted.

"I understand. But they say you are unstable, and might be suicidal," Chang said.

"Look. You don't have to do this. I can't be driven into debt. I'm penniless. Why don't you listen to me? I've got a Masters degree, I'm a teacher, and a good person. Just give me a prescription and I'll be fine." Channah said.

"Okay. I understand. I'll let you go on the condition that you take your medication." she said.

"God bless you, lady. I will say a prayer for you. I am so grateful." Channah stammered.

"You get yourself into some therapy as soon as possible. I'll give you my phone number if you want me to find someone here." Chang said, busy with writing the prescription.

Expose: The Reckoning by Channah Gambit

Channah grabbed it and put it into her wallet. Holding her breath, she started walking silently toward the locked swinging doors.

"Miss Gambit, wait a moment." the Reception guard said. Her blood froze, her blood pressure shot up, and she began to breath rapidly. Turning smoothly she looked his way. He gestured her back to the Doctor's office.

"I know you have no money. Maybe a Metro card might help for a bus." Chang said, self consciously.

"Oh thank you." Channah said. She gratefully accepted the card, and added it her wallet.

"Goodbye now. Be careful out there. And be good." Chang said.

Channah did not have a problem in walking through the doors this time. As she took larger strides, her face lit up with happiness. She gulped down air at the bus stop and waited for sometime. It was now after four, and dusk was setting in. Pretty cold and windy, with no prospect of a haven for the night.

In an hour there she was in downtown Hempstead. Channah could not tolerate her getup. Those sweat pants were indecent. She walked down Fulton Street to the large Salvation Army store there. It was closing in fifteen minutes.

"I don't have any money, but I can barter for some summer clothes." she said.

The black cashier looked her up and down, chewing gum and smacking her lips. "You need to see Miss Fanny." She pointed toward the back of the store.

Miss Fanny, a large buxom middle-aged lady was counting bills in the rear office. She was very pleasant and kind. "No dear, I can't lend you money for that top or those tights." she said.

"I really need to look decent enough to be on the street. I promise I'll pay you back sometime soon." Channah said uneasily.

"Dear, just pick out a few things and give this note to the cashier. That will be fine." Fanny said. Channah resisted the impulse to hug her.

She was attired in dignified jeans and a proper sleeveless blouse within ten minutes, and heading up toward the vicinity of the bus depot. Some vague idea of spending the night under the stars on the beach at Long Ditch was in her mind.

Special had told her about an apartment building she used to live in, near Jackson Street. She walked there now, as the sun went down and the light rapidly dimmed.

Watching some of the tough Hispanic types hanging around corners, she started to recall how nasty Hempstead was at night. In another hour, she would not be safe outdoors.

At the apartment house, she spoke to the lobby window man. "Can I please be let in. Do you know Special Smith?"

"No." he said, looking through his records. "What you want, lady?"

"I just want to spend the night, maybe sleeping on someone's floor. Maybe I can sleep in the lobby, or the rear of a hall. Please?" Channah stood there trying to look her best.

His dark hairy forehead crinkled in concern lines. His beady black eyes looked at her for a moment or two. "No, Lady. Not here. There's a lot of crack here. Not a good place for that. If you don't know anybody, you can't stay."

Expose: The Reckoning by Channah Gambit

Back on the front steps, she spent a minute or two asking a lady munching a candy bar if she might give her some shelter. "No." the woman said, rising and going in. The street was silent, in the hush of drawing night. Channah didn't have any idea what to do. It was great to be free, to feel rushing air on her arms. She put the green coat on. Walking past the *Angel Deli* on Franklin, she felt her stomach tighten into a knot of hunger. Walking in, she watched the Cuban owner making a sandwich, his cigar resting comfortably on the wooden server. The place was deserted. He noticed her after ten minutes.

"What can I get you, Miss?" he asked, his voice in gently lilting tones.

"Please, Sir. I have no money at all. Can you spare a candy bar?" she asked.

"You mean a sandwich, don't you? I'll make you any one you want. What would you like to have?" he said.

Channah couldn't believe her ears. "Well, turkey and tomato." she said.

"Turkey and tomato it is." he said, smiling, and starting to slice the roll.

"You know, I am just so grateful. Thank you." she said, gulping with tears coming into her eyes.

"Get yourself a can of soda to go with it. I do this all the time for people." he said, brandishing the knife.

"Thank you." she said later receiving it. Embarrassed, she waved goodbye and walked outside. It was dark and lights had come on in the bus depot. People were milling around everywhere, having a normal day. You could still see through the dusky indigo of the street. Channah found the stoop to a store for sale and sat quickly beginning to eat.

What would she do now? There was no where to stay or be. Walking aimlessly down the street with a full stomach, she passed the Jackson Baptist Church, enjoying the warm gold and red tones of the stained glass windows. Organ music emanated from the half open doors, and she looked in, enjoying the warmth. On a whim, she entered.

A gospel sing-along was in full swing. A young black gentlemen saw her, took her by the hand, and placed in it a tattered torn Bible. He gestured to the side pews and opened to a page for her. She sang and sang, enjoying the safety and personality of the people around her. They were animated joyful and well dressed, belting it out for all they were worth. Her worry and anxiety receded for a little while.

They returned at the end, when everyone finished and started to leave. The gentleman spoke to her. "I'm sorry to bother you, but is there a possibility at all that I might stay here tonight, and sleep on one of these pews?" she asked.

There was a large woman in a brightly colored floral print dress with a wide brimmed bonnet. Her kind brown eyes regarded Channah with understanding. "Hi, I'm Sister Edith. I'll help you." she said warmly.

"Oh, I couldn't ask." Channah said. Suddenly realizing that she had been saved for the moment, she started breathing deeply.

"My daughter and I can put you up in a motel. Why don't you come out to the car and we'll drive you there. You don't have to explain anything." she said. Her daughter, a beautiful young woman in her twenties also with warm brown eyes came over and smiled at Channah.

They helped her into a large white SUV and with her direction drove to the

Expose: The Reckoning by Channah Gambit
Courtesy, the cheapest motel in Hempstead.

Once inside, Sister Edith wrote up a room reserve. As Channah watched her face incredulously, she calmly paid the $90 for one night with a personal check.

"Now you're all set." Edith said.

"You are a life saver." Channah said.

"Well dear we do the Lord's will, and charity doesn't have to repaid. It is our pleasure to give charity and help those who are unfortunate."

"I know." Channah said humbly.

"And if you do want to repay me, make a donation to our church." Edith said, preparing to leave.

Channah watched them go out, received a key from the attendant, marched down the hallway opened her door and went in. The munificence of a cleanly sheeted king size bed faced her. The hot shower seduced her into a sudsy experience. Enthralled, she placed her Gideon bible and a rosary into the drawer.

After a good night's sleep, there would be a few quiet hours to make a game plan and pick up the pieces of her life.

The next morning, she begged enough change for another bus drive and took it to the Department of Social Services on Charles Lindbergh Avenue. She had enough nerve to ask for a free overnight stay at a public shelter.

Several hours later, that gift was hers and she was spirited away to a long line of shelters and empty nights with strangers.

It was survival and a start nevertheless. Wasn't enough for her to recover from her damaged state of mind and body, nor enough stability to get poised for the job market. But she would survive. Somehow she knew that.

Enough was recovered from the belongings at the house, with her son's car, to allow her to camp out at a local park in Beeritz. Being in town made her shake and shiver, but it was the cheapest night in town for $7. Duvey very quickly came to her defense. He couldn't abide her suffering. One night after she tented he picked her up and drove her to a fine motel in a nearby city, putting her up at personal expense. Duvey felt extremely guilty, and sided with her against her brother and sister.

"I still feel that you brought it all on yourself, Mom." he said.

"Where's Jamo?" she asked.

"I don't know Mom. You really freaked her out. She doesn't want to see you for a while." he said solemnly.

"But I've still got you." she said.

"Yes you still have me. I love you Mom and don't you forget it."

Somehow this made it all worthwhile.

Chapter 26: Epilogue

Ten Months Later...

Time has passed since Channah was sprung from the cage on June 12, 2006. She has not progressed very far in the local courts, nor has she recovered enough to stand alone on her feet economically, due to domestic conflicts. With her 18-B court-appointed attorney Phil Casey, a careful series of motions he has filed have led to the County backing down on one misdemeanor, the stalking charge and reducing it to an aggravated harassment charge.

The District Attorney's actions, or lack of actions, has been simply incredible, to both herself and her attorney, who is an advocate and mentor. For one thing, the District Attorney Kathleen Rosenby has approached her family and talked them into reducing the misdemeanor regarding contempt of an Order of Protection to just a violation. The District Attorney, however, has failed to make a plea bargain offer regarding the damaging A Misdemeanor, and that is exceedingly disturbing. Several attorneys she has spoken to for new perspective have told her that the District Attorney must have some additional information causing her to take a hard line on a citizen with a prior clean record. Her Counsel reasons that the District Attorney would like to make a plea bargain, however, cannot, because she cannot contradict the wishes of the complainant. The logical question then is, why is Sandstorm out to get Channah?. Does it matter at this point, or should they discover if there are patrolmen in the family?

Channah has long felt something is wrong with her own attorney's lax defense, but has no other option but to accept his help. To have a new, aggressive attorney defend her in a trial to reduce the charges further would cost about $10,000. Imagine—to keep her professional employability: $10,000! She had spent close to twelve years and over $76,000 earning her first precarious teaching job.

Outside attorneys Channah has consulted agree that it is highly unusual that the Nassau County District Attorney has not offered a plea bargain to reduced charges. It is either that, or it is the fact that her counsel, a former Assistant District Attorney, is a *bumbler*. She liked him from the start. She has no economic support from family to launch an expensive defense.

Channah is lucky enough to be able to pay an attorney to go into bankruptcy court. Also, some help has come in the form of monetary gifts and food from a local church pantry. She now has a tiny room in a quiet neighborhood and a job for a pittance wage which allows her to mimic some of the skills she honed and crafted over two years in a Brooklyn Middle School. Even that is a problem, since teaching is not quickly approved by New York State. She can teach on the fringe without approval by inspectors. Still, Channah is grateful that she need not descend into prostitution to support herself at age 55. Besides, she is now much uglier than she used to be, so that is a moot choice.

No, Channah can't resume her teaching legitimately until the State of New York gives her routine fingerprint clearances. She is therefore a slave, available at bargain basement prices and is caught up in a type-of *Simon Legrie* system. Her case languishes postponement and postponement and month after month in Court.

After an exhaustive examination of her *emotional disorder*, the State of New

Expose: The Reckoning by Channah Gambit

York has denied her Social Security Disability application.

"You seem to have stabilized yourself—you have 16 years of education, so go back to work, and do some "simple" task job!" Mrs. Thomas her caseworker says.

Stephen Randall's family, in several instances, has provided negative feedback on her. Channah suspects they have leveraged to increase the bias of the local District Attorney It's a curious amount of rancor and bad timing since it is now over 12 years since her divorce. Channah thinks losing custody of Duvey and Jamo was enough punishment for marrying him.

Actually, much of her present torment and hand-wringing over the years is directly attributable to those terms of the divorce decree like the removal of her children, and a turning of the kids' attitudes from love to something like distrust.

Still Channah tries to look towards a good future. She may soon consider finding a new spouse or resettling in a new country. With good therapy she may put all this behind her.

As far as her naïve idealism, middle-class sentiments, and blunders, these are all a thing of the past, as she now considers the government of her own country, and how it impacts on her life. Something inestimable has been lost. There is much damage to her heart.

Here's something she wrote in her diary recently:

The paternalistic notion that it is government's official duty to go after the unstable, destroy their professional standing, hard-won, and ruin them economically to fit some pre-determined profile, adversely impacts the rights and civil liberties they are supposed to enjoy as citizens under the American Bill of Rights—including the right to a speedy trial.

America, this home to her for over 54 years, now appears to be a wasteland. She wants to emigrate elsewhere, and voluntarily give up her precious citizenship. That is her initial reaction.

Two years later...

Daddy Gambit died in August, 2007 and left his estate behind. Channah, Ben and Mellow each inherited a third. With her share, Channah was able to pay off virtually all her debts and move from a woman's shelter into a small studio apartment. She began to recover from the nightmare, through visiting a talk therapist and medication to relieve anxiety.

For all purposes, she was left alone by her family. In fact, several relatives left New York State, relocating to get away from the *tsimis* which means trouble in Yiddish. Jamo rejected her mom permanently, and did not share an explanation for the desertion at the jail. Duvey, to the contrary, picked her up at a tent park, paid for her to stay at a local motel, and provided enough monetary support prior to August, 2007 to restore the loving tie between the two of them. He then departed for another state, to live with a girlfriend's family.

Channah spent over a year and a half looking for work. Discouraged by the lack of a hire after a year, she took her therapist Dr. Kluck's advice and became an instructor of handicrafts at local continuing education programs. This was a balm to her wounds. Attempts to win friends through the internet were unsuccessful.

Over the course of ten months, from 2007 to 2008, she continued to seek work in her chosen profession. Altogether she was hired thrice and then disqualified due to the misdemeanors on her record. Employers were rude, evasive and told lies after learning the truth.

She went through over two years of continued illegal entry into apartments and rooms she rented, with the theft of family photographs, sentimental objects and valuables. Local law enforcement did nothing, as there was not enough evidence to provide suspects. Channah went to great lengths to discover the culprit, writing letters to the landlord, hiring private investigators, and asking law enforcement detectives to launch an investigator. She became certain that the fireman neighbor next door back in Beeritz was a sick man and the instigator.

Regarding her social life, Channah finally approached some dating websites to find a new partner, and dated once or twice. She did not find it easy to mix, but is still optimistic as we speak.

Her life is solitary. She spent two weeks visiting Israel and tried to become a citizen there. She was refused due to her instability.

After four years of suffering, she lost her faith in Jesus Christ. To make less conflict in life and have a feeling of belonging, she has joined a local synagogue.

Her best therapy by far has become writing this memoir. Channah has launched a new promising career as a professional writer. If the first book sells at a Book Convention in 2008, she has some children's books to illustrate and publish as well. She is also working on an anthology of poems from her teenage years.

Perhaps most disturbing is the effect of the foods and medications she has taken after leaving jail. In July, 2007 she finally collapsed into a depression while homeless which led to a voluntary hospitalization. Channah was heavily medicated, and put herself through a partial program as an outpatient, gradually developing new poise. Unfortunately, there are perceptual problems, new and chronic since the jailing. She frequently has blurred vision and cannot read for a long time. She cannot concentrate, and no longer reads books for enjoyment to any extent. Channah has had bouts of asthma, which was in remission for over 25 years. She also has new troubles with spellling, remembering names, and a tendency to be vague. Relearning crochet tasks or teaching practices she once knew by rote are the norm. She has a lot less stamina now, tired easily, and often takes naps during the day.

Psychologically she is a basket case. She frequently has nightmares. There are delusions of a fearful nature regarding her family. Bouts of anxiety or panic incapacitate her once or twice a week on average. She sometimes has hearing discimination problems.

Practitioners tell her it's a natural sign of the aging process. Channah is dubious, and has resolved that sometime in Summer, 2008, she will visit a psychologist who will evaluate her cognitively and neurologically. He will determine whether damage or deterioration has occurred. Dr. Borrelli will make a report which will stand in Court. Perhaps Channah will sue the County of Nassau for the poisoning she feels she sustained.

Perhaps she will simply try to live her life as best she can and let bygones be bygones. In the interests of peace sometimes that is best.

If the memoir sells, she might make a leap into fame prosperity and security for her retirement years. That along with living in another country are long term goals she carries.

Expose: The Reckoning by Channah Gambit